W Yale

SPODE-COPELAND-SPODE

THE WORKS AND ITS PEOPLE

1770 - 1970

SPODE-COPELAND-SPODE

THE WORKS AND ITS PEOPLE

—— 1770 - 1970 ——

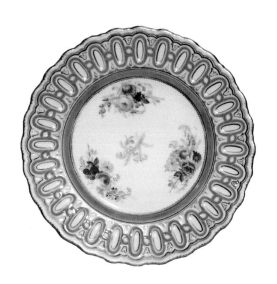

Vega Wilkinson

Antique Collectors' Club

This book is dedicated to
Harold Holdway, Designer and Art Director
who served the Spode Works from 1934-1978,
without whom there would be no book

British Library Cataloguing-in-Publication Data
A catalogue record for this book is available from the British Library

Frontispiece: Pair of fine earthenware vases, both sides of each vase painted and signed by W. Yale,
c.1880s. Rare pieces. Copeland China Collection

Title-page: Copeland bone china dessert plate, c.1860, pattern no.D1718, Windsor shape,
painted by Swan. Mark 235. 9in. (22.9cm)

Printed in Italy
Published in England by the Antique Collectors' Club Limited
Woodbridge, Suffolk IP12 4SD

ANTIQUE COLLECTORS' CLUB

The Antique Collectors' Club was formed in 1966 and quickly grew to a five figure membership spread throughout the world. It publishes the only independently run monthly antiques magazine, *Antique Collecting*, which caters for those collectors who are interested in widening their knowledge of antiques, both by greater awareness of quality and by discussion of the factors which influence the price that is likely to be asked. The Antique Collectors' Club pioneered the provision of information on prices for collectors and the magazine still leads in the provision of detailed articles on a variety of subjects.

It was in response to the enormous demand for information on 'what to pay' that the price guide series was introduced in 1968 with the first edition of *The Price Guide to Antique Furniture* (completely revised 1978 and 1989), a book which broke new ground by illustrating the more common types of antique furniture, the sort that collectors could buy in shops and at auctions rather than the rare museum pieces which had previously been used (and still to a large extent are used) to make up the limited amount of illustrations in books published by commercial publishers. Many other price guides have followed, all copiously illustrated, and greatly appreciated by collectors for the valuable information they contain, quite apart from prices. The Price Guide Series heralded the publication of many standard works of reference on art and antiques. *The Dictionary of British Art* (now in six volumes), *The Pictorial Dictionary of British 19th Century Furniture Design, Oak Furniture* and *Early English Clocks* were followed by many deeply researched reference works such as *The Directory of Gold and Silversmiths,* providing new information. Many of these books are now accepted as the standard work of reference on their subject.

The Antique Collectors' Club has widened its list to include books on gardens and architecture. All the Club's publications are available through bookshops world wide and a full catalogue of all these titles is available free of charge from the addresses below.

Club membership, open to all collectors, costs little. Members receive free of charge *Antique Collecting*, the Club's magazine (published ten times a year), which contains well-illustrated articles dealing with the practical aspects of collecting not normally dealt with by magazines. Prices, features of value, investment potential, fakes and forgeries are all given prominence in the magazine.

Among other facilities available to members are private buying and selling facilities and the opportunity to meet other collectors at their local antique collectors' clubs. There are over eighty in Britain and more than a dozen overseas. Members may also buy the Club's publications at special pre-publication prices.

As its motto implies, the Club is an organisation designed to help collectors get the most out of their hobby: it is informal and friendly and gives enormous enjoyment to all concerned.

For Collectors — By Collectors — About Collecting

ANTIQUE COLLECTORS' CLUB
Sandy Lane, Old Martlesham,
Woodbridge, Suffolk, IP12 4SD, UK
Tel: 01394 389950   Fax: 01394 389999
Email: sales@antique-acc.com Website: www.antique-acc.com
or
Market Street Industrial Park, Wappingers' Falls, NY 12590, USA
Tel: (845) 297 0003   Fax: (845) 297 0068
ORDERS: (800) 252 5231
Email: info@antiquecc.com   Website: www.antiquecc.com

CONTENTS

ACKNOWLEDGEMENTS

I gratefully acknowledge the help and support given to me over the last ten years by my many friends who have contributed to this book. Spencer and Jean Copeland invited me to explore the archives at Trelissick where so many treasures were unearthed, including Alfred James Copeland's diary, and they encouraged research into the many pieces in their ever-growing collection.

Robert Copeland taught me how to research and has had infinite patience over the years with the never-ending stream of questions. My special thanks go to Harold Holdway, whose vast intimate knowledge of Spode and the workings of the Spode works have been invaluable. His composite pen and ink drawings of the factory buildings and detailed work on all the plans will give future readers a picture of a great factory.

Photographs are the main requisite of any book on ceramics and I thank most sincerely Spencer Copeland for allowing J. Mathews of H. & B. Graeme, Fowey, Cornwall to photograph the Copeland China Collection, Harold Holdway, Bill Coles, Mark Diamond, Jack Shaw, George Worlock, Tom Gadsby and Douglas Chadbone for providing so many interesting and excellent photographs.

My thanks go also to Rodney Hampson, for his invaluable help with the manuscript, and for providing more research material; Peter Roden, whose new research on Josiah Spode I has clarified so many hitherto mysteries; Gordon Hewitt for his help on Chapter 5 and for making available the Hewitt archives; William Fowler Mountford Copeland's son-in-law, the Rev. Gregory-Smith, whose research into the Copeland family history has been invaluable; Judy Spours, Ann Roberts, and Joan Jones, who gave sound and helpful advice from the beginning, and to Olwen Grant, especially for her help with the appendices, Marguerite Coles, Ann Stamper, Eileen Hampson, John and Celia Smith and Penny Franklin. Thank you to Peter and Margaret Dunn and to their family past and Mark and Sandra Diamond.

This book would not have been possible without the help and cooperation of all at the Spode Works, under the guidance of Paul Wood who gave me permission to explore the factory, talk to the many long-serving employees and research the Spode archives.

FOREWORD

In this world of change the pottery industry has not escaped, nor would it expect to. The entire history of the area has been one of responding quickly and effectively to changes in taste and competition over the centuries and this willingness to adapt must be one of the major underlying causes behind the survival of most of the major brand names in this industry, when so much of the original flowering of the Industrial Revolution has succumbed to global market forces. Most of the responsiveness in the industry has been brought about by the flexibility of its workers rather than radical restructuring of the factories.

Even in this area, however, Spode is unique. Driven by people who believed that there would always be a profitable market for the very best, little attempt was made to introduce 'efficiency' for its own sake. Since the business has never moved from the site, it kept all its historical assets in dusty old chambers hidden behind the walls of the ten acre site. However, one of its greatest assets was, of course, the people.

In this book Vega Wilkinson has undertaken a professional, diligent, academic pursuit of the facts surrounding the physical history of Spode and the processes involved in the centuries of potting on the site at Stoke and combined this with her fascination with the lives and stories of the unsung heroes, the potters.

Slip is, as most readers will know, ceramic clay in its liquid form, and if one is regarded well by the potters in the area the ultimate accolade is to be described as 'having slip in your veins'.

Vega's interest in the oral traditions of the people of Spode has allowed her to create a wonderful mix from the ceramic clay and the true lifeblood of the company, its work-force past and present, who definitely have slip in their veins.

The author has created a warm and intricately detailed pot from this old clay which I am sure you will enjoy.

Paul Wood
Managing Director
Spode

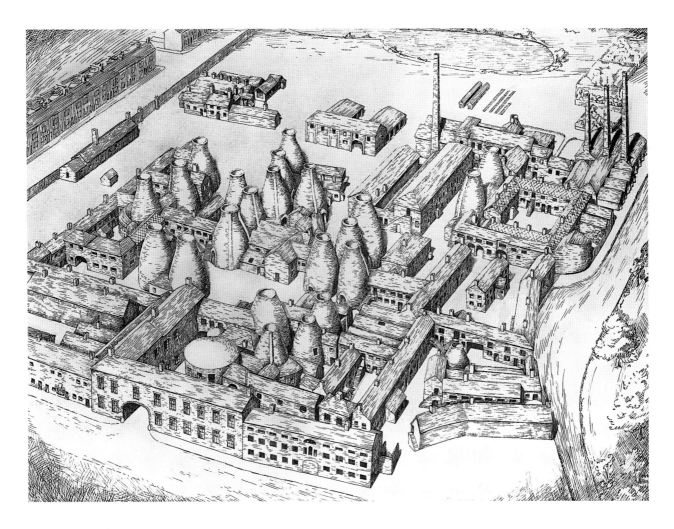

Chapter 1

SPODE I – 1770-1797

Plate 1. The Spode Pottery in Stoke based on the 1833 plan. Drawn by Harold Holdway.

In the middle of Stoke-on-Trent is the pottery of Spode, makers of fine earthenware and fine bone china for over two hundred years, and the oldest working pottery still to be standing on its original site. The Spode works was to become an area covering between nine and eleven acres, employing as many as eleven hundred workers at one time, although exact numbers varied throughout its history, and eight hundred seems to have been the average number.

Old plans show that some parts of the works were called 'squares' – there was the Printers' square and the Dishmakers' square. Larger areas were called 'Banks' like the Black Bank, where black basalt was made, and the China Bank, where the china clay makers shaped the ware which was later placed and fired in the bottle ovens. The word square implies a tidy, orderly scheme of buildings and production, but this was far from being so. As the manufactory grew more bottle ovens were built and more workshops were added, all with apparently little thought of industrial design or efficiency.

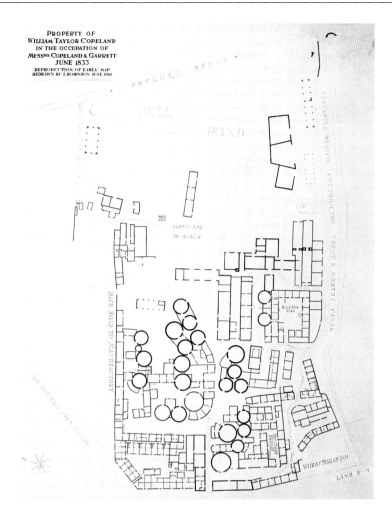

Plate 2. The Spode Pottery c.1833. Redrawn by J. Robinson in 1964 from the old plan on the site. Spode Archives

The layout was haphazard; there was no knowledge of assembly line planning. Labour was cheap and accustomed to hard work, poor conditions and long hours. The whole area was a huge, rambling assemblage of buildings, with piles of broken pitchers and shards around the ovens and boxes of clay scraps outside the making shops. Narrow, treacherous wooden or stone stairways ran up outside the old buildings, rooms were ill-lit, clay dust lay everywhere. The ware was carried backwards and forwards across the yards in all weathers. As new processes were invented ovens were demolished and buildings changed their function almost at a whim. The more we learn of the way in which the pottery operated, the more of a miracle it seems that not only has it survived and prospered for two hundred years but that it has produced such remarkable wares.

In 1949 Harold Holdway, the chief designer, found small glazed earthenware pieces of miniature model factory buildings in one of the old disused rooms at the Spode works. He realised that they had been potted exactly to match the 1833 plan of the factory and, using this as his guide, he painstakingly reassembled them. The model of the works is now displayed in the Visitors Centre at the Spode factory (Plate 1) and shows the site as it would have been in the days of the Spode family. When William Taylor Copeland bought Spode in 1833 he had the plan in Plate 2 drawn up for insurance purposes, and the

Plate 3. The Clay Bank, Stoke, 13 July 1899.
William Fowler Mountford Copeland

model could have been made to show to his London customers, a sales promotion of that time. It shows clearly the large number of ovens and kilns on the site. At the left of the gate entrance was a fine two-storeyed building while the one on the right was three-storeyed. The use of these buildings has changed constantly over the years, although their usual function was to house the artists, painters, paintresses and engravers on the top floors, with the turners and throwers on the lower floors. At the northern corner of the model one can see the large mill pond and heaps of raw materials weathering (Plate 3). On the eastern side are the three slip house chimneys and the buildings housing the slip kilns. The north side of the plan shows all the maintenance buildings, the blacksmith's shop, his forge, the joiners' shops and the crate makers' workshop.

The Spode works of 1800 would be very much like this 1833 plan, but perhaps a little smaller. John Thomas[1] summarised the development of the pottery industry in the following statement:

> During the period from the latter half of the seventeenth century to the middle of the eighteenth century a small potworks would be run by a family of craftsmen; from the middle of the eighteenth century to the nineteenth century this establishment would have grown to a much larger potworks now called a Manufactory and run by a Master Potter and skilled families of workers. Lastly, from the nineteenth century to the twentieth century, a capitalist employer would have a large factory.

1. J. Thomas, 'The Economical Development of the North Staffordshire Potteries since 1730' with special reference to the Industrial Revolution (London University, unpublished Ph.D. Thesis, revised abridged transcript). Held in London University Library.

This is exactly how the Spode works evolved over the course of two hundred years. In those early days every master potter had to prepare his own clay and experiment to produce a body which would appeal to the buying public, whereas nowadays ready prepared clay bodies can be bought in. The ingredients were brought to the site by horse-drawn wagons, along a track from the Trent and Mersey canal which had opened in 1777. It was not until 1795 that the Newcastle canal, a branch of the Trent and Mersey Canal, was opened, and they came by narrow boat straight to the Spode works. The ingredients were Cornish stone, flint and bone, and the clays which were left out in the open in large piles to 'weather'. It is possible they were left for twelve months, exposed to all types of weather which turned the clay into a homogeneous mass, and bleached out soluble salts which would be detrimental to the pottery clay.

The recipes for the making of the bodies were kept a closely guarded secret. Industrial espionage is not just a modern conception and potters would go to any lengths both to guard their own secrets and to bribe, steal, and trick their way into the workshops of their rivals in an effort to keep in the forefront of the market.

The production of pottery is a complicated business, but briefly was divided into four main parts:

The preparation of the clay body
The making of the ware
The firing of the ware (see Chapter 2)
The decoration of the ware (see Chapters 2 and 3)

The buildings used in each of these stages are the vital elements of the Spode works. The plans will show the changes which took place throughout the different periods as new methods were invented.

In the 1700s the ingredients for the making of the clay body and glazes came on to the site straight from the clay pits of Dorset, Devon or Cornwall. China stone came direct from the quarries of Cornwall, bone from the slaughter houses and flint pebbles from the seashore of south-east England. The flint pebbles were first 'calcined' (burnt in coal-fired kilns) and were then friable enough to be crushed and ground. The flint and Cornish stone were separately crushed into small pieces by a 'stamper', then ground into powder form in large circular pans. Water was added and slowly the flint or stone was reduced to powder. The resulting 'slip', as it was called, was then run out over sieves into 'settling tanks' in the room below to remove all impurities. The quantities of prepared slop of flint, Cornish stone and clay were carefully measured according to the particular recipe, the correct amount of water added and all mixed together in a trough known as a blunger. When thoroughly mixed, the slip was again run over sieves and magnets to remove the traces of iron. Large horseshoe magnets were laid in rows in a box and the slip passed over them. The removal of all impurities was of great importance as any that escaped detection would affect the finished ware. Some slip was sent straight to the casting shops to be made eventually into holloware and the rest sent to the slip kilns.

The 1833 plan shows six slip kilns with three chimneys and it is possible that three or four were used for the earthenware body, one for the coloured bodies

Colour Plate 1. Spode pearlware dessert plate, willow pattern, c.1790-5.

and, when Spode II produced bone china, one for the china body. Later plans show up to eight slip kilns; perhaps two more were added after the invention of Parian. In the slip kilns the clay was dried by fires lit under each bed evaporating the moisture. The slip was then in a plastic state, ready for transfer to the clay cellars. Large bronze spades, which would not contaminate the clay, were used to cut pieces from the slip kilns and put them in the cellar ready for the process known as wedging, the last stage in clay preparation. It was all done by hand. The clay was cut into wedges, lifted, kneaded and banged down together to ensure that the moisture content was equal throughout the body; it was important no air remained in the clay. The clay was now in workable pieces and was carried by labourers to the potting shops each day where it was made by the workers into cups, saucers, plates, vases and all the many varieties of ware sold by Spode I and II.

All who contributed to the production of Spode's ware were craftsmen of the highest quality. Len Potts, when aged eighty-two, told of how he got his first job (Plate 4). As a boy he had watched the men carrying the ware around the pottery on long boards balanced on their heads and, as his father knew a plate maker at Wedgwood, he persuaded him to take Len as a 'mould runner', whose job was to fetch and carry, known in pottery slang as a 'gofer'. Len recalls the

Colour Plate 2. Spode bone china plate with an imaginary view of the Spode works c.1785 by a Spode artist in c.1810.

times of the great depression and how he stood in the dole queue until in the 1930s he got a job at Copelands, half time plate making and half time labouring. Here he stayed for the next forty-two years. He was one of the finest china plate makers at the Spode works and eventually ran the plate making department. There he met his wife who was a clay counter, checking and recording the output of each worker, and their son also joined the firm, becoming head of the engraving department. This illustrates the fact that Spode and Copeland has always been, in every sense of the word, a family business. From the grinding mill to the boardroom, son followed father and daughter mother, each inheriting a critical affection for the 'Bosses' and a fierce pride in the product, which can be seen in the belief that Mintons or Wedgwood are nowhere near as good as Spode/Copeland.

The throwers were highly skilled men and in Spode's day would be using a string potter's wheel. A large wheel was connected by a 'string' to a smaller potter's wheel and turned by the thrower's apprentice who was told to turn faster or slower as the thrower threw his pots. These small boys or girls were often members of his family or children of a friend. They worked the same hours as the thrower and ate as he did, at the wheel. They may have been taken on as full apprentices and would be paid from the wages negotiated by the throwers.

Plate 4. Len Potts, plate maker, 1930s.
Harold Holdway

Plate 5. Members of the
Burton family making saggars,
September 1900.
William Fowler Mountford
Copeland

When the clay had been made into pieces of ware it was called 'green' (un-fired) ware and after drying was carried to a warehouse called the 'greenhouse'. Here it was dried further to remove the last traces of moisture and then selected for placing in the biscuit oven. First the ware was carefully packed into 'saggars', oval or round fireclay containers made on the site by the Burton family, handing their skill down from father to son (Plate 5). The skill of filling the saggars and placing them in the oven was of the greatest importance and the 'placers' who did this and, after firing, unloaded the oven, could demand and get good wages. When the ware came out of the oven, these 'biscuit' articles were checked for quality before being sent on to be decorated, after which they were glazed and fired again to give them the shiny appearance. They were then checked yet again to make sure that none but perfect items were offered for sale to prospective purchasers. (These final processes will be described fully in Chapter 4.)

The late eighteenth and early nineteenth centuries were exciting times in the history of the Spode works. They were now producing several different bodies from which to make fine quality earthenware. However, the real breakthrough, which was to establish Spode as a master potter of foresight and talent, was when he was able to produce earthenware of good quality decorated with attractive and varied designs, and particularly the underglaze blue printed decorations on the biscuit ware, which was then glazed. The effect on the industry was spectacular. Underglaze blue printing revolutionised the decorating process. Previously all ware had been hand-painted, but this new process of hand-engraving a copper plate from which a transfer could be made and then printed on to the biscuit ware was a great achievement.

This method of underglaze printing was first developed at Worcester in the 1760s, followed closely by other potters until in the 1780s Josiah Spode introduced it into the Spode works where he perfected the art. It was an immediate commercial success, appealing to all sections of the market. Spode I chose patterns copied from the Chinese. 'Mandarin', the first, was followed by the now well-known 'Willow' pattern, of which there were seventeen variations (Colour Plate 1). One of the most famous of Spode's blue and white prints was called 'Blue Italian' and it is still one of Spode's best selling patterns today (Plate 6). In 1846, William Evans reprinted a concise and accurate 1836 description of the process.[2]

Blue printing is the name for the manipulations of taking impressions [in colours, blue, green, pink and brown] from copper plates engraved in a style peculiar to the artists of the pottery districts... The press is placed within four feet of a stove plate, kept constantly heated, that when the copper plate is laid thereon, its engravings may more easily admit the colour as it is rubbed over it... The colour is well mixed on a very hot iron plate, into a fluid, called technically an *oil*... The printer places his plate on the stove, rubs in the colour, with a broad pallet knife scrapes off the excess, and then with his boss [pad] cleans the plain sides, and places it on the bed of his press; he next brushes the sheet of tissue paper over with a solution of soft soap and water, puts it on the plate, rolls it between the rollers, and the instant the return of the press leaves it dry by the hot plate, he carefully takes it off... A *cutter* [a little girl training up for the next manipulation] takes the impression, cuts away all the white paper, then separates the impression into its parts... A transferer with considerable tact and judgment, places on a biscuit vessel the several parts in their proper arrangement; and then, with a rubber of flannel ... she rubs the paper upon the article with much force... The

2. W. Evans, *Art and Pottery of the Potting Business* (Shelton, privately published, 1846), page 37.

Plate 6. *Spode New Stilton cheese pan, 'Blue Italian' pattern, c.1816.*

Plate 7 (left). A worker in the printing shop, c.1900.

Plate 8 (below). The printing shop, c.1900. A journey woman applying the print and an apprentice washing it in.

Plate 9. Spode early ware dish, hand painted, c.1790s. Mark: Spode impressed.

dry and absorbent porosity of the ware aids the adhesion of the colour in the oil … each vessel … is immersed in water, and with soft water and a sponge the paper is washed off… The ware is kept in a heated room to evaporate much of the water imbibed in washing off the paper, which is requisite to prepare it for the fluid glaze; and also is heated to red heat, to *harden* on the colour, and volatilize the *oily* particles, else the glaze would not adhere… (Plates 7 and 8).

Transporting the wares from the pottery to the point of sale, whether country fairs or London shops, had always been fraught with difficulties. The roads were appallingly bad; the ware was carried on horse-drawn wagons, with attendant problems of slowness and weather. But by the end of the eighteenth century these problems were eased by the development of the canal system and the new turnpike (toll) roads.

The canals were a godsend to the potters. Not only could the raw materials be carried right up to the side of Spode's works via the Newcastle Canal, but also the finished articles could be carried to their final destination more gently and safely. There is no evidence that Spode I or II had any financial interest in the canal (which is as well since it was not profitable), but because the canal was to be cut through Spode's land (which meant some of his buildings had to be demolished) he and Thomas Wolfe (who was in the same position) were allowed to have their goods conveyed free of toll for the short distance to the Trent and Mersey canal and reaped full benefit from it.

Both Spodes were turnpike trustees. Part of their duties was to value land which might be needed in the near future for road building and, when the estimates received for the making of the road were not satisfactory, the Spodes joined with other potters to construct the road themselves. Spode I was Clerk

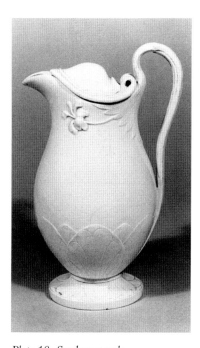

Plate 10. Spode rare early creamware jug with hinged lid. Mark 2a. Private collection

Plate 11. Spode basalt teapot c.1800. Mark 2B. Height 4in. (10cm). Private collection

to the Trustees and George Steedman, Spode's partner in a flint mill, was also a Trustee. John Thomas stated[3]

> Josiah Spode Senior was the most regular attender at the Trustee Meetings, because his factory was the largest pottery in the 1½ miles of the turnpike road. from its junction with the Black Lion Inn.

In the late seventeenth and eighteenth centuries the making of pottery was done entirely by hand, from the making of the clay to the finished article. Then the Industrial Revolution had a profound effect on the pottery industry, changing it from what had been almost a cottage craft and removing a lot of the drudgery, although the skills of the artist and craftsman were not to be superseded until the beginning of the twentieth century.

The first step in mechanisation was the horse-powered gin mill, an adaptation from the local corn and grist mills, then water-driven wheels and windmills. These were not reliable enough for the pottery industry, but help was at hand in the shape of Newcomen's fire engine, an atmospheric steam pumping engine. In 1775 Wedgwood and Turner visited Cornwall, saw these engines in use in the tin mines, and recognised that they would be invaluable in their business. It is thought that Josiah Spode became the first master potter to install a fire engine.

Spode's engine pumped water to a height of 13ft.9in. (4.2m) to flow over a water wheel 12ft. (3.7m) in diameter and 4ft. (1.3m) wide. This wheel drove a pan, 7ft. (2.1m) in diameter, for grinding flint at the rate of three hundred pecks (2,700 litres) per week and some small pans for grinding enamel colours. Water for the dam was obtained from the Fowlea brook.

3. J. Thomas, *The Rise of the Staffordshire Potteries* (Bath, Adams and Dart, 1971), page 78.

Plate 12. Spode redware with basalt decoration – a scent jar, griffin candlesticks and a small oil lamp. Mark 2a.
Copeland China Collection, Cornwall

Plate 13. Spode cane ware teapots with enamel hand tracing. Mark 2a.

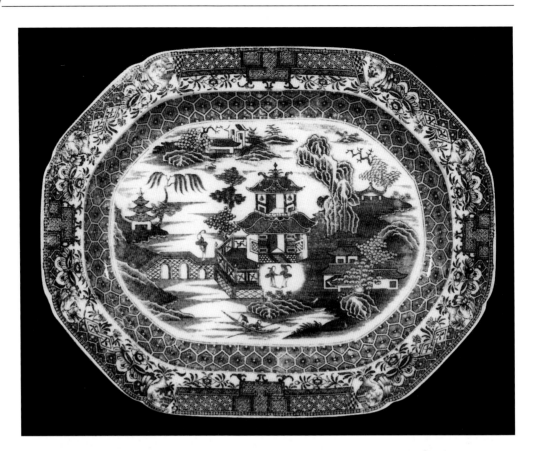

Plate 14. Spode early earthenware dish, pattern 'Two Figures', late 1700s. Mark 1d. 16in. (40.5cm) long.

Plate 15. Spode earthenware dish, Japan pattern, c.1815. Mark 1d impressed.

Plate 16. Spode sprigged designs, c.1800s. Left to right: china beaker, white with dark blue; spill vase, dark blue with white; stoneware beaker, light blue with white and dark blue band.

Plate 17. Spode jasper candlesticks and teapot. Mark 2a. Heights 10in. (25.4cm) and 5in. (12.7cm).

Plate 18 (right). Spode brown glazed earthenware, sometimes called 'Rockingham Ware', c.1800s. Impressed Spode.
Private collection

Plate 19 (below). Spode travellers' samples showing simple hand-painted border patterns, c.1800s.

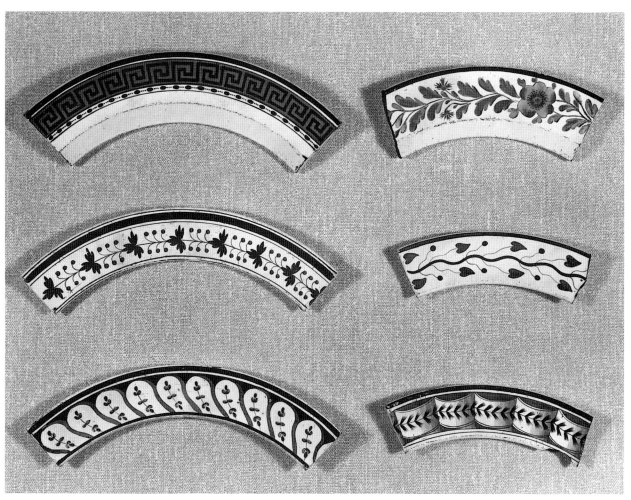

Plate 20. Spode stone china dessert plate c.1820. Ship border pattern with the centre crest of Bristol Corporation. Copeland China Collection, Cornwall

An 1833 indenture[4] reads:

> To make, support and continue a Dam across the Fowlea Brook afore said at the site of the present Dam near the North Eastern corner of the said piece or parcel of land and there to impound the water of the said brook to the height or level of the present dam which has been ascertained to stand exactly seven foot [2.1m] lower than the level of the pavement or floor of the new Parish Church of Stoke-upon-Trent and at all times hereafter to take and carry water from the said brook at such dam or pound as aforesaid into the lands and heriditaments hereinafter described and covenanted to be surrendered for the purpose of the fire engine or fire engines to be employed at the Potworks.

This land was bought by Josiah Spode I originally, and one can assume that the millpond was designed first for the Newcomen engine in 1779 and perhaps extended when Spode bought his first Boulton and Watts 10h.p. rotative steam engine.

In 1810, eight years later, he bought a more powerful 36h.p. engine from Boulton and Watts. Now throwers' and turners' wheels could be steam driven and also the large paddles used in the grinding pans would have far more power to drive them. Spode, however, did not abandon his first engine. It is said to have been still in use forty years after its installation.

4. Keele University Library: Spode MS 520, Jeremiah Smith. The Release of Freehold 1833.

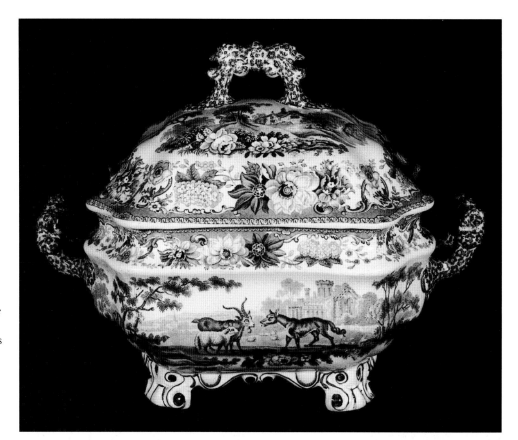

Plate 21 (right). Spode earthenware tureen. A rare example of the Aesop's Fable pattern, blue and white underglaze printing.

Plate 22 (below). Spode earthenware tureen and stand. Indian sporting scene series taken from Oriental Field Sports, Wild Sports of the East *by Captain Thomas Williamson.*

Plate 23. Spode earthenware pattern 'Lugano', c.1819. The scene is taken from the aquaprint of the bridge at Lugano from Merigot's Views of Rome and its Vicinity, *1795.*

Like Wedgwood, Josiah Spode I was a great pioneer in the pottery industry of the eighteenth century; but he was far more than that, namely the first entrepreneur in the history of the Spode works. Recent research shows how he achieved this accolade and how he acquired the site known as the Spode works on which he developed all the processes just described.

Josiah was born in 1733 and at the age of six was fatherless. With few actual facts to support the story, he was next heard of as working for Thomas Whieldon in 1749. This presupposes that he had in fact been learning the potter's art in another pottery and because of his contacts and natural ability was taken on by Whieldon, an established potter of note at the time. By 1754 Spode had left Whieldon, having truly learnt his craft, and the next year married Ellen Finley who is known to have had a haberdashery business and was six years Spode's senior. It is possible that the true facts of the next years in Spode's life will never fully be known. However, his association with Turner and Banks at their pottery in Stoke, and with other Staffordshire potters served him well. Spode lived in a time when he saw many of his contemporaries, although master potters, hit financial problems, the Baddeley family being a prime example. They are known to have been bankrupted twice trusting business associates who were to prove unreliable. This was a salutary lesson for the young potter. No doubt Ellen had a far greater influence in those days than has hitherto been acknowledged, encouraging and advising her husband on all aspects of his business dealings.

However, the most significant facts which are documented are Spode's partnerships with William Tomlinson (1767-74) and Thomas Mountford (1772-79). They probably supplied the cash and Spode the expertise eventually to establish the Spode Pottery in the village of Stoke-upon-Trent, which was to expand and produce some of the finest ware of the whole area. The evidence taken from the Manorial rolls which have been recently painstakingly researched by Peter Roden show how the factory site was expanded. On 15 May 1751 the first known owner of the site was Benjamin Lewis who owned much of the land and access rights in and around what we now know as the Spode works. He transferred a small pot bank to his son Taylor Lewis. It was described as 'All those newly erected workhouses pot oven and warehouse formerly a barn'.

Note the single pot oven, suggesting a small cottage industry. It is not until the Sun Insurance Company recorded a policy taken out by William Banks, Potter, Stoke-on-Trent, 12 November 1763[5] that the site was shown as having four kilns, a marle house (where the marl clay used for making saggars was mixed), workshops and chamber over, one to make dishes. The details reveal that there was a crate making shop on the site, a saggar house and slip kilns with slip houses, a large establishment at this time capable of a vast output – probably one of the largest in the area in 1763.

Over a period of sixteen years, Benjamin Lewis slowly released more land and also access rights across other land to the owners of the site. On 8 May 1756 Mr William Clarke owned the small site and on 7 November 1759 sold it to William Banks and John Turner. It would seem that this partnership developed the site from 1759 to 1764 when it was sold to Jeremiah Smith. Whether Josiah I managed or worked on this site has never truly been proved. The site now included a large piece of land called Madeleys Meadow which was first bought by Banks in 1764 and sold to Smith six months later.

By 1767 Spode, aged thirty-four, was in a position to interest prospective business partners and formed his first partnership with William Tomlinson. His potting expertise had been established; he had the experience of working for Turner and Banks, though just when and where is still not clear. In September 1758 Josiah and Ellen bought land and a house in Stoke near to the Spode works, which was described accurately as late as 1831, after the death of Josiah Spode III in 1829, as 'a dwelling house and shop on the north side and fronting to Church St Stoke upon Trent'. Here Ellen ran her haberdashery business.

Spode's employers and activities from 1758 to 1767 are still open to conjecture. However, he was successful not only as a potter but also as a businessman, as the two partnerships in which he was involved prove. When the pottery owned by Michael Ward just over the road from the Spode works became available at an

5. Guildhall MS. 119361150.

Plate 24 (left). Spode earthenware pierced plate c.1811. Pattern 'Rome', sometimes called 'Tiber'. Taken from the aquaprint of the castle and the bridge of St Angelo from Merigot's Views of Rome and its Vicinity.

Plate 25 (below). Spode earthenwares. Left to right, top to bottom. Gadroon shape teacup and saucer, 'Union Wreath' pattern. London shape cup and saucer, 'Waterloo pattern'. Baby's feeding bottle, 'Tower' pattern. Toast rack, 'Willow' pattern. Trinket tray, early 'Willow' pattern.

economical rent on 27 October 1767, here was his chance to run his own business, probably supported by his new business partner Tomlinson. It is significant that the date for the Spode and Tomlinson partnership is 11 November 1767 – Martinmas – the accepted date when many pottery business agreements are known to have been started. William Tomlinson was no doubt impressed when Spode came to him with a viable pottery site on which to operate. Tomlinson, as far as we know to date, had little or no knowledge of the pottery business.

What Spode produced in this pottery is not known, neither is it known how big it was, but it is reasonable to assume that he was making creamware and redware. On 11 November 1772, five years into his partnership with Tomlinson, Spode, obviously with the agreement of Tomlinson, entered into a new partnership with Thomas Mountford, who was not only interested in the art of making pots, but had money. Perhaps Spode knew him well. Mountford tied up the agreement clearly and concisely stating that no other agreements could be formed. The two partnerships ran together for a period of two years. By 29 February 1776 Spode had achieved his ambition to have his own works by buying the Spode site from Jeremiah Smith on a mortgage. Initially it was probably run by Spode II whilst his father was in Shelton with the Mountfords but Spode I, forty-three years of age, now possessed a potworks of his own.

There are no surviving documents from which we can study the actual size and layout of the pottery in which Josiah Spode I started his business. The only evidence is a plate now in the Spode Museum at Stoke (Colour Plate 2) which depicts a small factory with smoking bottle ovens surrounded by green fields. It shows four bottle ovens and in the background three chimneys which could well have been the chimneys from the slip house and kilns itemised in the Sun insurance policy of 1763. The china dessert plate is marked Spode and c.1810; no doubt the Spode artist, when asked to paint a pottery scene, would choose the view he knew best, perhaps his own place of employment. This scene gives the only known pictorial evidence of what Spode's factory could have looked like in the late 1700s and it gives us a basis on which to trace the development of the Spode works.

From the plate to the 1833 plan we can see how the site had grown under the Spodes. The improvements they made were the result of the expansion of their trade over the three generations. The original four ovens grew to over two dozen ovens for firing earthenware, frit kilns to make the glaze, glost ovens to fire the glaze on to the ware and decorating kilns in which the decorated ware was fired, perhaps even a brick kiln. As the orders flowed in more ovens and kilns would be erected to increase capacity. More potting shops were built in which the cups, saucers, plates and hollow ware were made, as well as buildings in which the paintresses worked. The Spode works was totally self-sufficient; there were even joiners' shops and crate makers – indeed everything that was needed to produce, pack and dispatch the finest Spode ware. Plates 9 to 25 show the range of the ware Spode produced at this time.

Plate 26. Spode I's house at the Spode pottery c.1790, drawn by L. Brammer in 1965. Also shown is the weighbridge.

When Josiah Spode I died in 1797 he left two sons, both trained by him as master potters. In 1778 Josiah II had become a member of the Spectacle Makers Company in London, thus enabling him to run a business which he started at 29 Fore Street, whilst Samuel stayed in Staffordshire and is known to have been running the Foley pottery at Fenton about two miles from the Spode works. Josiah Spode's will was quite clear and fair to all members of the family. His eldest son Josiah was given the opportunity to take over the Stoke-on-Trent Pottery and pay into the family estate a fair valuation of its worth; if he refused the Spode works went to Samuel. However if Josiah II did take the Spode works, Samuel had to be given the opportunity of buying the Foley Pottery which he already occupied, but was owned by Josiah Spode II. It is possible that Samuel had played a significant part in all the experiments of his father, who saw a future for his sons working together and ensuring that they each had a potting business.

But what a decision for Josiah II! Should he return from London where he was not only running a very successful business but had achieved a position of some social importance, or let Samuel take over? The London business had been expanded into larger premises and the Spodes had by 1784 acquired the services of William Copeland, the son of a Staffordshire yeoman farmer. No doubt Josiah Spode II, having assessed the situation, realised that he could leave the London business in William Copeland's capable hands. Copeland was living on the premises, he had just had a son and was therefore unlikely to leave. The relationship between the two men was one of trust.

A highly astute business man, Spode II could forecast market trends. He knew his main task now was to continue the search for a satisfactory porcelain started by his father which would enable the business to compete in the future with the fine porcelain coming from the continental factories of Sèvres and Meissen. Successful as the Spode business was, it could not stand still. It must continue the forward looking innovative style of Spode I, so he took up the challenge and returned to Staffordshire (Plate 26).

Chapter 2

Spode II – Copeland and Garrett

1797-1830s

Plate 27. 'The Mount', Spode II's residence (taken in 1933).

As the demand for Spode ware increased, so the Spode works was expanded, and from 1800-1833 more bottle ovens and workshops were built to accommodate both the increase in orders and to facilitate production. Meanwhile, throughout the country there was great concern about working conditions in the cotton mills, so the first of many Factory Acts was passed, in 1802, making it possible for any factory to be inspected. No doubt any inspector employed by the government after 1833 would have been amazed at the size of Spode's manufactory and the apparent lack of organisation. He would have found it difficult to comprehend the many processes involved in the making of the ware and totally at a loss to know who was in charge. At the same time, he would have noticed the camaraderie which existed between master and men.

After Spode I's death his son continued to expand the business. He was to be given the credit by future generations for perfecting a bone china body. This porcelain was made from approximately 50% bone, 25% china clay and 25% Cornish stone, a body which had the capability of being made into all varieties of ware. The ware was decorated with taste and originality and sold well and profitably. In 1821 Spode II introduced another form of china in which feldspar was used to replace Cornish stone, possibly because feldspar was less expensive. It was mined at Middleton Hill on the border between Shropshire and Montgomeryshire and was bought from Thomas Ryan.

Master and men shared the same roots and the same self-respect and love of the product. The Factory Act was the result of great concern, especially for the children working long hours in appalling conditions in the mills and mines, but although this was investigated as early as 1816, and again in 1833, the resulting acts did not apply to the pottery industry. In comparison with mines and textile mills the conditions for children in the pottery factories were not thought bad enough to warrant legislation. Master potters were thought to have a paternal interest in their workers and to be able to take care of their own work-force.

Around the Spode works Stoke-upon-Trent was growing rapidly. More and more houses were being built, some by the master potters for their own workers. In 1803[1] Spode II built some forty-eight dwellings, the most notable group being called Penkhull Square. Throughout the years he continued to acquire property from which he received a revenue in rents. In 1803 he bought a large piece of land in the village of Penkhull where he built a fine house in parkland which he called 'The Mount' (Plate 27). It had good views over the valley and yet was near to his pottery. Also around this time he extended the Spode works, building a new imposing entrance (Plates 28 and 29).

1. D. Baker, *Potworks – The Industrial Architecture of the Staffordshire Potteries* (London, Royal Commission on the Historical Monuments of England, 1991), page 43.

Plate 28. A composite pen and ink drawing of the original Spode factory entrance c.1800s. Harold Holdway, 1993.

Plate 29. A composite pen and ink drawing of the Spode factory frontage c.1810-1929. Harold Holdway, 1993.

Plate 30. Spode basalt jug with Turner mould and engine-turned decoration. Basalt Cane shape coffee pot with engine-turned decoration. Mark 2a. Height 6in. (15.2cm).

Plate 31. Spode earthenware pierced basket and stand, printed and painted, pattern 3909, c.1815. Spode Museum

Colour Plate 3. Spode felspar porcelain dessert plate marked Spode, pattern 4485.
Photograph Mark Diamond

Colour Plate 4. Spode New Stone soup dish, badge of the 89th Regiment, marked Stone New China impressed.
Photograph George Worlock

Colour Plate 5. Spode felspar 'Bowpot' candlestick, pattern 2584. Marked Spode. Photograph Mark Diamond

Colour Plate 6. Spode bone china candlestick, pattern 2161. Marked Spode. Photograph Mark Diamond

Colour Plate 7. Spode bone china candlestick, pattern 3993. Marked Spode. Photograph Mark Diamond

Colour Plate 8. Spode bone china candlestick, pattern 3644. Marked Spode. Photograph Mark Diamond

Colour Plate 9 (above left). Spode bone china candlestick, pattern 3328. Marked Spode. Photograph Mark Diamond

Colour Plate 10 (above right). Spode bone china candlestick, pattern 967. Marked Spode in red. Photograph Mark Diamond

Colour Plate 11 (right). Spode bone china candlestick c.1820s. Marked Spode. Photograph Mark Diamond

1803 was also the year Spode II began decorating his ware with fine bat prints. A description of this process, by Thomas Battam, is given in Chapter 3. His range of merchandise consisted of stoneware, stone china, blue printed earthenware, printed and hand-coloured earthenware, bone china and in 1821 the new feldspar body. The dinner services, tea and coffee services, vases, menu holders, candlesticks and snuffers, door furniture and garden pots were all of the highest quality and of the finest decoration. They were sold in large quantities to all levels of society from his showroom in London, and throughout the country (Colour Plates 3 to 11 and Plates 30 to 33).

Spode realised that design was of paramount importance if he was to maintain his place at the head of the market, and that he had no training in this area. The business needed what we now call an Art Director, someone who was capable of running the decorating department, a role next in importance to that of the master potter. We have already seen that Spode II was good at finding the right man for a job, and in the search for a designer he

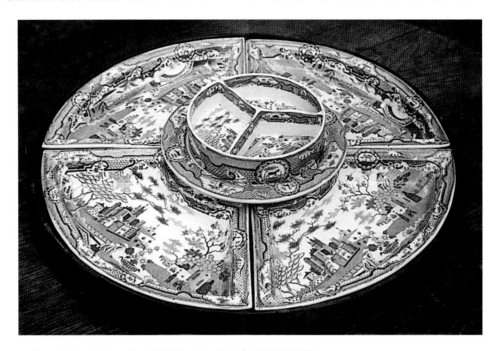

Plate 32 (Above). Spode earthenware supper set, 'Gothic Castle' pattern.
Private collection

Plate 33 (Left). Spode earthenware jar with lid and pierced inside cover, c.1821. 'Cracked Ice and Prunus' pattern. Height 9in. (22.9cm).

found the right man again, on his own doorstep. He was Henry Daniel, at that time operating a decorating business with his partner John Brown in Hanley. By 1806 they were also running a decorating establishment within the Spode works as Daniel and Brown had dissolved their partnership on 7 June 1806 and Henry Daniel was free to develop the art of enamelling on Spode's fine ware.

The 1833 plan (Colour Plate 12) shows three decorating kilns surrounded by decorating shops. The kilns were owned by Daniel until he left in 1822, but he rented the decorating shops. It is possible that when Daniel and Spode

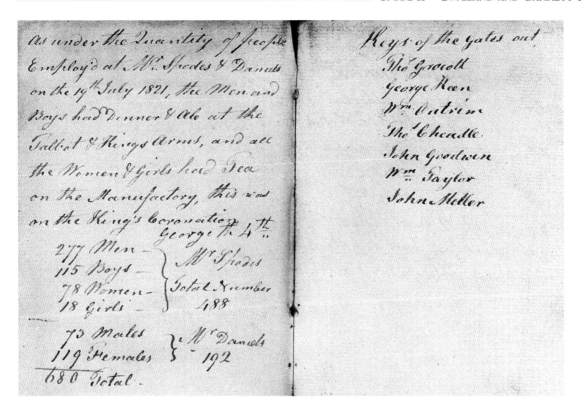

Plate 34. Old document dated 1821 showing the number of employees Messrs. Spode and Daniel had in the decorating department at that time.

met to discuss the enterprise, Daniel actually designed this part of the Spode works, but we have no proof of this.

Len Whiter (author of the book *Spode*) deduced from the 'Ode' by John Daniel,[2] which he found, that the decorating kilns were built to a higher standard than was usual for the time. If Daniel indeed had designed them, his ideas were sound, for this part of the works remained the decorating area until the coal-fired kilns were replaced in the twentieth century. Daniel trained and controlled his own staff and ran his own business as an independent concern (Plate 34). Spode II made the ware and paid Daniel to decorate it. Here were two men, both masters of their own trades, whose combination of talent and enterprise produced exquisite ware.

Henry Daniel left Spode in 1822 to start his own pottery. The parting was amicable; no doubt both men recognized that the time had come for a change. Daniel left Spode a wonderful legacy, a fully equipped, well-designed decorating department with talented artists, hand paintresses, hand painters and gilders.

Decorating the ware was and still is a highly skilled craft. First came the mixing of the colours used in the painting. Colours were ground and mixed on the site, frequently being given numbers or the names of those who had created them. The actual mixing of the colours was a closely guarded secret. Even in the mid-1930s, the then Art Director Thomas Hassall would lock himself into the colour room before beginning to mix the colour, and great would be his wrath if he was disturbed! The secrets of the glowing colours had been handed down since Henry Daniel from one generation to the next.

The process known as ground laying is also thought to have been the invention of Henry Daniel. This is the method of oiling the surface to be

2. L. Whiter, *Spode: A History of the Family, Factory and Wares from 1733-1833* (London, Barrie and Jenkins, 1970), page 48.

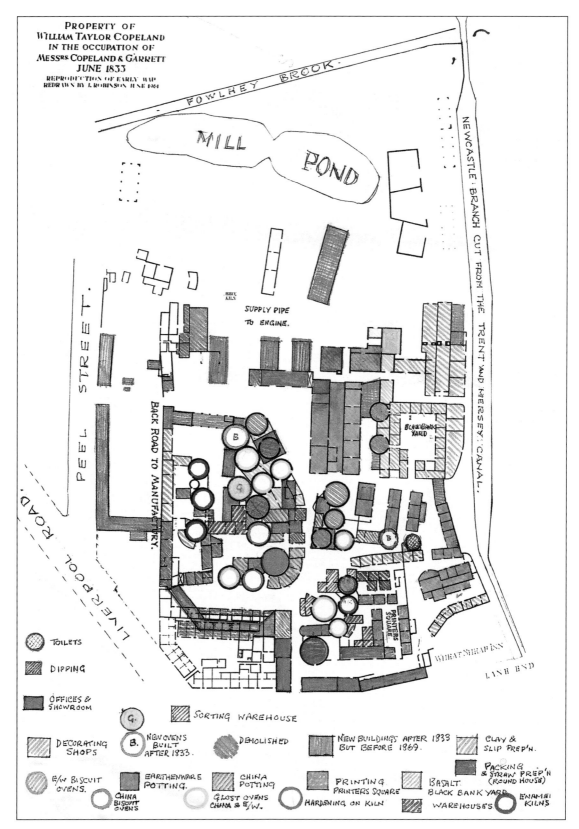

Colour Plate 12. Plan of the Spode works before 1869. All new buildings were superimposed upon the 1833 plan, and colour coded in grey to show the development of the site. This plan also shows where buildings have been demolished.

coloured, then dusting it with colour on a pad of cotton wool instead of a brush. Certainly by 1824 it was a recognised process and attributed to Daniel at that time.

Gilding has always been a specialised art which has never been given the attention it deserves. Spode's pattern 1166, designed in 1806, shows this art to perfection and is one of the decorations most sought after by Spode collectors. The design was used on many different articles, and was extremely costly to produce and very expensive to buy (Colour Plates 14 and 15).

Of this pattern, Harold Holdway, Art Director of Spode from 1956 to1978, wrote in 1992:[3]

> The decoration consists of floral groups set within a royal blue ground-laid colour interspersed with hand gilt medallions. The background was most intricately patterned with gold scaling. The handles on the vases were usually in solid gold and the beading on the edge and foot left white on a gold band.
>
> The first process is the application of the floral spray compositions on each side of the china glazed vase and the outline of the gold medallions. This is lightly sketched in with a water based Chinese black ink. [Colour Plate 13A.] When dry a resist composed of jeweller's rouge and syrup mixed in water is applied to the areas of the decoration which have to remain white. [Colour Plate 13B.]
>
> When the resist is dry to the touch, the groundlay of finely ground Cobalt Blue is applied and after drying the vase is then immersed in water and the resist painted areas are gently cleaned off with cotton wool in a bath of water which then reveals the white areas to be decorated. The vase is then sent to the kiln and fired at a glost temperature of 1100 C. [Colour Plate 13C.] After an interval of days or weeks, the artist who created the floral group arrangement has the vase returned to him with the white area silhouetted ready for painting. So great is his skill that he can re-compose the original design to fit the irregular white space. The floral decoration would probably require several enamel firings to produce the finished painting of the groups. The final stage of decoration is performed by the gilder who paints the scale decoration all over the blue areas of the vase. The gold is dark brown in colour so a water based medium is applied to act as guide lines: this fires away in the subsequent gold firing. Finally the vase is finished with burnished gilding of handles, bands and lines at the foot and edge. [Colour Plate 13D.] A method called Pouncing was used when a motif had to be repeated

Colour Plate 13. The method of decoration of pattern 1166 on a china vase.

3. Harold Holdway's description of the decorating process involved when creating pattern number 1166.

Colour Plate 14 (opposite). Spode covered vase, pattern 1166. Mark 21. Copeland China Collection, Cornwall

Colour Plate 15 (above). Spode two-handled Roman shaped bowl with (left) an inkwell with 'squirrel' stopper and (right) a violet holder. Pattern 1166. Copeland China Collection, Cornwall

round the rim of a plate. This easy method was most often used by gilders. If a design motif had to be repeated eight times on the rim of a plate and had to be joined to create a continuous border, the following method of pouncing was followed: the design motif which covered ⅛ of the border area was traced from the original design, the tracing paper is then laid on to a very fine lead sheet. The sheet and the tracing are next laid on to a felt covered board which is in a fixed position to prevent any movement. The artist or gilder then pricks through the tracing and lead sheet following the lines of the design motif until the whole surface is a pattern of very small holes. The plate, having been marked off into eight sections, receives the perforated lead pounced design in the exact border position required. A small margin of lead is bent round the edge of the plate to ensure that the correct position is maintained while the gilder or artist dusts the perforated design with black stumping chalk which passes through the tiny holes, leaving a perfect impression of the pattern on the border of the plate. The design is now ready for the craftsmen to follow with great accuracy, producing perfect freehand work.

As far as we can tell from the evidence left to us, the Spode site held at this time the following different types of ovens or kilns: earthenware biscuit oven, china biscuit oven, earthenware glost oven, china glost oven, a hardening-on kiln, a frit kiln, and finally an enamel kiln.

When the clay had been made into articles by throwing, turning, pressing or casting into the finished form, they had to be fired in an oven. Before firing, the pieces were 'placed' in saggars and carefully stacked in the oven. Clay ware

Plate 35. Ashton Maskery, earthenware biscuit fireman, 'baiting the oven', i.e. adding coal to the fire every four hours, c.1950s.
Photograph by Harold Holdway

Plate 36 (opposite, above left). Placing pieces of ware in the saggar ready for putting into the glost oven. In the foreground are clay strips which were placed on the rim of each saggar to create a good seal. These strips were thrown away with many other small pieces of clay which were used to separate the ware and then dumped on to heaps called, in the Potteries, 'shardrucks'. Children were often to be seen sorting through the shardruck to find the shards with which they used to play 'shop'.

had to be fired at differing temperatures – china much higher than earthenware. After the firing of the clay pieces – which were now called 'biscuit ware' – they were meticulously selected and stored in the biscuit warehouse until needed to fulfil order requirements, then the pieces had to be 'dipped' in liquid glaze. After drying, they were once again placed in saggars to be fired at a glost temperature which is lower than is needed for the clay firing. Selectors and placers were highly skilled workers. Slowly they filled the oven, taking several days to complete the loading. Every type of ware had its own place in the oven, according to the temperature required. This work was supervised by the oven or kiln fireman, whose word was law. He knew exactly how the ware should be fired and it was his responsibility to make sure that, when the firing had been completed and when the oven was 'drawn', the ware had been correctly fired (Plate 35). Even the master potter would not overrule his judgement. If he was asked to load more ware, his refusal was accepted without question. In the dipping house, the ware was dipped by hand. The hand-painted, highly gilded ware was selected and placed with tremendous care in the smaller enamel kilns. Stories are told of how many a wad of tobacco changed hands from artist to enamel fireman to ensure that the hand decorated special vase was well looked after.

The hardening-on kiln was used solely for underglaze printed and painted wares. When the transfer had been applied to the ware, the oil used to apply the print had to be fired away, so that the subsequent application of water-based glaze was not rejected.

Several writers have cited different numbers of ovens and kilns at the Spode works which, when compared with the plans included here, seem inaccurate. Possibly they were using journalistic licence to illustrate the importance of

Spode trading as Copeland and Garrett from 1833. The plans show how the pattern of ovens and kilns changed. Ovens disappear to be replaced with new potting shops, or new ovens are added. Building a new oven was a simple task, for Spode employed his own bricklayers; indeed, this was so right up to the 1950s. Spode is said to have fired his earthenware and china biscuit wares on a three kiln system, one being filled, another being fired up and cooled and the third being emptied. An early production line, it also accounts for the number of ovens and kilns. An oven when filled was said to have held 500 to 600 dozen different articles. One of the placers still employed at the Spode works remembers the days of the coal-fired bottle ovens, of how hot it was and how many pints of beer and ale he consumed in a working day. He is a very small man and used to tell American visitors how many inches in height he had lost throughout his working life as a result of carrying the saggars on his head, roaring with laughter when they believed him. He also remembers climbing the wooden ladders in the ovens, which were known as the 'Big' and 'Little Oss' (a corruption of horse), and how often the fireman came to check the oven as it was being filled (Plates 36 and 37).

The base of Spode's first china bottle oven can still be seen on the Spode site with a small plaque telling its history. The complete oven structure (hovel and oven) was to have been kept as a memento of the past (Plate 38), but unfortunately the hovel crashed to the ground in 1972, narrowly missing Robert Copeland. The rest of the oven was then dismantled.

Plate 37. A placer standing on the 'Little Oss'. Note the saggars outside the kiln waiting to be placed, c.1930s. Photograph by Harold Holdway

Plate 38. Spode China bottle oven c.1950, opposite The Terrace Spode works. Photograph by Harold Holdway

Colour Plate 16. Spode bone china Antique jug, no pattern number. Marked Spode in red. Photograph Douglas Chadbone

Despite the Napoleonic Wars, with the resulting difficulties in trade, the Spode works were busy and in 1806 the workers were privileged to see the Prince of Wales and his brother, the Duke of Clarence, when they paid a visit to the site.

Shaw[4] described the scene:

Mr Spode had so arranged, that all the persons employed, of both sexes, were in their best attire, to manifest their respectful and loyal attachment to the Heir Apparent, and the Family on the throne: and as the Royal and Noble visitors passed thro the different apartments, the appearance and demeanor of the working classes, drew forth repeated eulogiums. The Large warehouse [117ft. (35.7m) long] was then visited, where were arranged every variety of Pottery and Porcelain in the most elegant and curious productions, manufactured by Mr. S. whose loyalty and respect were so highly appreciated by the Royal visitor, that Mr. S. received the appointment of *"Potter to His Royal Highness the Prince of Wales"*.

4. Simeon Shaw, *History of the Staffordshire Potteries* (Hanley, privately published 1829).

46

Colour Plate 17. Spode earthenware plate, 'Musicians' pattern 4207. Spode Museum

Colour Plate 18. Spode bone china conjuring cup, pattern 2009. Photograph George Worlock

A sequel to this royal visit came in 1817, when Her Majesty Queen Charlotte visited the London showroom. When the Prince of Wales, by then Prince Regent, ascended the throne in 1820, Spode was appointed 'Potter to His Majesty King George IV'.

Still keeping ahead with new innovations, in 1810 Spode used gold for bat printing and, to increase production, he installed a larger steam engine, shown in the 1833 plan to be sited in the engine house. Spode had acquired more Cornish clay rights and a supply of cobalt from the Wheal Sparnon mine with his friend and neighbour, Thomas Wolfe. The Spode works continued to produce quality products, having expanded its capacity to cope with the many orders coming from the London showroom. Colour Plates 16 to 24 show some of the vast variety of the output of the Spode works at that time.

Towards the end of the first quarter of the nineteenth century, industrial unrest was beginning to spread through the pottery industry. The working master potter had largely disappeared, to be replaced by the prosperous businessman and entrepreneur, remote from his workers in every way. The workers began to feel that they needed to band together in order to have an organised voice to speak for them and negotiate pay and conditions. Hitherto the rate for the job depended largely on the ability of the worker to fix his price, thus the system had developed that no worker knew what his neighbour was earning, and this secrecy exists up to the present day. When work was plentiful, the price fixed would be high but, when work was slack, it could become very low indeed. Skilled workers could find themselves doing the work of the labourers, fetching and carrying the ware.

1815 had been a very lucrative year in the trade but by 1824 trade was slack and wages poor, so the climate was ripe for unrest with the growth of unions

Colour Plate 19. Spode bone china cup and saucer, pattern 1216. Marked Spode in red.
Photograph Douglas Chadbone

Colour Plate 20. Spode bone china coffee cans, patterns 282 (left) and 2094 (right).
Photograph Douglas Chadbone

Colour Plate 21. Spode bone china basket. View of Grantully Castle with crest and motto Ne Cede Malis *of the Faith family. Mark Spode painted.*

Colour Plate 22. Spode bone china teapot, pattern 1108, marked Spode in red. Photograph Douglas Chadbone

in other trades acting as a spur. However, as a direct result of the unique way of paying pottery wages, it was to be many years before a trade union encompassing all processes and all workers would be formed. In 1824, the Union of Clay Potters was formed, whose members were throwers, handlers, plate makers and hollow ware pressers, while the printers formed another smaller union. Because of their fragmented nature, neither union had much power. If one group went on strike, the rest of the pottery could continue working, and without the power to bring the entire site to a standstill the strike was doomed to failure.

In 1825, there was an attempt at strike action. The demands were an increase in piece rates, the regulation of the sizes of the ware and the abolition of 'truck', this being the payment of workers in kind rather than in cash. It is not known to have been in operation at Spode; their workers were paid in coin of the realm. A strike committee met on 27 July 1825, but the timing of the strike was not good. Trade was so bad that the men were glad to have any job at any price and the strike petered out. Relationships between employees and masters were on the whole good and when, in 1831, the National Union of Operative Potters was formed with a subsequent membership of 8,000, most employers gave their approval and, indeed, gave encouragement to their employees to join. The master potters met to agree a fixed selling price for their goods in order to meet the rise in wages negotiated by the union. But old habits died hard and little agreement was reached.

Two old trade customs continued. One was the annual hiring on 11 November (Martinmas) and the other was the practice of paying the workers on production 'Good from Oven'. This meant that they were only paid for work which, after firing in the oven, was good, even though many of the items they had made which were not regarded as good enough were later sold as 'seconds'. The employer said that this system protected him from careless workers.

In spite of all these vicissitudes, the accession of William IV in 1830 showed the Spode works still flourishing, with about 800 workers employed. The tradition of Spode I and II continued with the production of fine blue and white earthenware with innovative patterns, superb dessert

Colour Plate 23. Spode beaded spill vase, pattern 1983. Marked Spode. Height 6in. (15.2cm). Photograph Mark Diamond, Private collection

Colour Plate 24. Spode bone china gadroon edged bread and butter plate, pattern 23 in black.
Photograph Douglas Chadbone, Private collection

services, stoneware or New Stone decorated with Chinese porcelain designs as well as fine white bone china. A vast variety of product was made, everything from garden seats to candle holders, all bearing the name Spode. Backstamps of this period show the name Spode with many variations, one of the most distinctive being Spode Felspar, c.1821. Spode's Imperial was used on ivory coloured earthenware. From about 1830, a few backstamps included the name of the pattern, and from 1833 all marks incorporate the name Copeland and Garrett. The shapes of the teacups, saucers and dessert plates continued from the days of Spode II, very much influenced by the silversmiths' designs of the day. Classic in design, as the influence of the Regency style faded, they were to be replaced by the more ornate fashions of the Victorians.

Both the manufactory and the London business continued to be profitable, while around the works the town of Stoke was developing fast. Spode I and II had been heavily involved in the expansion of the area, and William Taylor Copeland (son of William Copeland, Spode II's partner in London), having bought the Spode works, now invested in property in Stoke. He bought 189 houses and land for £11,000 from Spode's executors and in the late 1830s began to develop the north side of the manufactory between Liverpool Road and Peel Street (now re-named Elenora Street). These were superior houses, having a yard, a wash-house, a privy and an ash pit, and would have commanded a good rent.

In the town the building of a new town hall was commenced in 1834, though not completed until 1850. The old market hall was built by sub-scription and housed the town's fire engine. When finished, the new hall, in Glebe Street, held the market on the ground floor, while on the next floor there was a courtroom, the Stoke Athenaeum and the School of Design attended by many of the Copeland artists. There was gas lighting in the town provided first by the British Company Gaslight Works at Shelton but by 1839 by the new Stoke, Longton and Fenton Gas Company. The early 1830s were once again a time of industrial unrest and in 1834 the pottery workers went on strike. Some pottery owners in Tunstall, one of the six towns, wanted to hire their workers on the low rates of 1833, some 30-35% lower than the union rates. Relations between master and men deteriorated but, after a ten week strike the union prevailed, securing a wage increase of 20-25%.

In March 1836 the pottery manufacturers re-formed themselves into a Chamber of Commerce, to protect trade and to fight the union. The trade union campaigned again in 1836 for an end to 'annual hiring' and payment 'good from oven'. This led to a 'lock-out' by many manufacturers and strikes at other works from autumn 1836 to January 1837, twenty weeks in all. Eventually, all parties reached agreement. The annual hiring now meant that each worker was guaranteed sixteen days' work each month and the right to give his employer a month's notice. After much argument the system of paying 'good from oven' was altered a little. All the poor ware made by the worker was to be broken without pay, but he was to be paid for all ware that was damaged in subsequent processes.

The 1833 Parliamentary Inquiry into the employment of children brought the Factory Inquiry Commissioner to the Spode works. He reported that the factory was in the 'best of order'.

In the 1830s the decorating department at the Spode works was still run on the lines laid down by Henry Daniel, but unfortunately it has not been discovered to date who was responsible for running the department after he left. It is not even known how many of Daniel's artists stayed on with Mr. Spode, but some of them did stay as the Special Order Reference Books prove. The work of R. Greatbatch and Mr. Ball (see Chapter 6) shows the quality and deftness of design produced by Daniel and it is reasonable to assume that they would be training young painters in the Spode way. Their artistic ability can be seen in the pieces which have been collected from this period.

The head of the decorating department was responsible for all hand painting and gilding as well as designing new patterns. Hand painting was done by both men and women, often being recorded in the Special Order Reference and pattern books as 'painted by women' or 'painted by men', sometimes 'painted by lads'. Hand painting could be simply filling in the printed design of a pattern, for example Pattern No.2118, Peacock. This pattern was used to teach the female apprentice paintresses. When they could complete it all perfectly, they had earned the right to be called journeywomen and could then progress to more intricate floral designs. Some of these painters and paintresses only ever painted one pattern, and even after they had left the works were often called back when an order came in for 'their' special pattern. Many apprentices were employed at Spode and Copeland under an indenture similar to one dated 1864 for R. Wallace (Appendix 13). Most artists would have served an apprenticeship and spent years gaining the skill and experience which gave them the right to be called artists.

The other large branch of the decorating department was that of the gilders, both branches being under the direction of the Art Superintendent, who was responsible for appointing the foremen of these branches and who negotiated the rates of pay with the foremen. They then negotiated with each painter, paintress, artist and gilder as they allocated the work.

In 1833 there were three decorating kilns surrounded by painting shops. The shops were long rooms, usually on the second or third floor, as near to clear daylight as possible. This was important in an age when the air was foul with fumes and smoke at ground level. Perhaps as many as twelve paintresses would work together in one room with a similar number of men in the other, for men and women never worked together.

The rooms were heated by coal stoves, known as stove pots, on which they also cooked their breakfasts, but otherwise conditions were primitive. It was not until a painter had been dignified with the title of artist that he would work in a superior room with only two or three fellow artists. The apprentices were allocated minor parts of the painting at first until their skill improved enough for them to be given more important parts. In the pattern books which we can see today many of the designs have been painted by apprentice painters.

Gilders worked in exactly the same conditions, but it must be said that their skill has rarely been appreciated. When we examine the scales on pattern 1166 (Colour Plate 13), we can see the dexterity with which the gilder wielded his brush.

Artists and gilders sat at benches on three-legged stools. Although these

photographs (Plates 39 and 40) were taken in the late 1800s and early 1900s, they show the painting shops just as they would have been in the days when the Spode works was owned by the Spode family.

The great variety of ware produced at Spode up to the 1830s is exemplified in the variety of cup shapes, the main ones being still the ones created by Spode I and II.

Bute shape was the most classical clear line which was to be followed in the early 1800s by Porringer, Dresden, Etruscan and Bell. London shape was one of the most popular, particularly when decorated with the many now famous blue and white patterns on earthenware. In fact Spode is still today making London shape decorated with Blue Italian. Gadroon, Pembroke and Octagon

remained standard cup shapes for many years. The diversity of cup handles gives an added fascination. It is interesting to remember that while it was the custom to order twelve tea cups and twelve coffee cups, it was not thought necessary to have more than twelve saucers to serve both types of cups. Fashions and tastes were changing, so that by the 1830s Spode was producing many embossed patterns, with cups decorated with fine landscapes and floral studies.

Much of our information has been gained from the Special Order Reference Books. The first of these that survive are dated 1835. Entries record the date, the type of body, the name of the article, the shape, the pattern number, the customer and the artist or gilder, They record the cost of painting and gilding. Each entry shows a combination of these details, but rarely all of them. For example, an entry for Ball on 10 October 1845 shows that he painted a dessert plate on Turk shape pattern number 7871 with a view of Mount Pilatus. Another entry for Barrett on 5 December 1845 reads that he was paid 2s.6d. for painting a watermill landscape (Colour Plate 25).

Colour Plate 25. The Pattern Book shows that this watermill centre was painted by Barrett on Plain Victoria shape, entered on 5 December 1845. The cost of painting was 2s.6d. and of gilding 1s.8d.

Also in the Spode archives are a series of little black books which seem to have been kept for easy reference. They had no costing at all in them but show a short description of the pattern. The pattern books, too, have additional information. Two sets of pattern books were kept, one for the use of the decorating department while the other was kept in the Master's office to be shown to customers. A separate set of illustrated record pattern books was kept for 'B' numbers, featuring underglaze decorations. Blue and white prints were in the main not recorded in pattern books – they were named, not numbered, and the only records were kept by the Engraving Department. Even with detailed analysis of all this information, it is still not possible positively to identify any of the artists and gilders who were employed at the Spode works before 1835. Only the ware, so highly prized by collectors, remains as a lasting testimony to their artistry and hard work so long ago. However, after 1835 artists are named and the photographs of patterns from that time on are all taken from the pattern books with the costing book information added. (See Chapter 6.)

The finished ware was now not only being sent to London by road and canal, but also to the of port of Hull and to North America via Liverpool. With the accession of a new young Queen in 1837, the Spode works had entered into an exciting period under new management, a new partnership and now traded as Copeland and Garrett. Tracing the changes and ownership of both the London business and the Spode works starts back in 1811. Orders from all levels of society were pouring into the London showroom and the scene was set with father Spode in Staffordshire and son in London. The management of the

London business by William Spode, Josiah II's son, and William Copeland had been a great success, so in 1805 Spode II decided to make his son and William Copeland equal partners, trading as William Spode and Co.

We know little about William Spode, only that he stayed a partner in the business until 1811, when he retired, wealthy but still a young man. He went to live with his sister Elizabeth and changed his name to William Hammersley. His father left him money under that name in his will.

Spode's younger son, Josiah III, only a year younger than his brother, trained as a potter under his grandfather. His career at Spode was brought to an unhappy end when he lost an arm in an accident, caused, it is thought, by getting it caught in the beam engine. He retired to his estate at Great Fenton, his already wealthy state increased by an annuity of £500 from his father. He and his wife had one son, Josiah IV, who was to have no part in the future of Spode. But times were changing. William Spode retired in 1811 and a new partnership agreement was drawn up between William Copeland and Spode II. William Copeland was to have a 75% share in the London business and Spode II the remaining 25%. The firm now traded as Spode and Copeland. In 1824, for the first time, the name Copeland was seen on the backstamp of Spode ware.

How and when William Copeland became involved with the Spode family is still not known, although his grandson Alfred[5] records in his diary:

> My grandfather was a traveller in the tea trade, thinking to associate the sale of cups and saucers with tea, entered into some arrangement with Mr. Spode, got on, made money by speculation I expect.

Obviously William was an astute opportunist and a canny businessman. There is little doubt that William Copeland and Spode I and II had an amicable and successful association. It was not unusual for travellers to become partners in the firm they worked for. The travellers were of the utmost importance to their employers. They found, met and catered for their customer's needs, they would pass on orders for special patterns and needed to be able to forecast accurately market trends, often reaping rich rewards for themselves in the form of promotion within the firm. William Copeland's hard work and merchanting skills were rewarded by the Spode family. As a partner in the London business he had become a wealthy man and bought a large and prestigious estate at Leyton in Essex. Spode II was able to leave the London business in his capable hands and concentrate on 'potting'. This partnership continued until the death of William Copeland in 1826. His only son, William Taylor Copeland, was admitted into the partnership in 1824, taking one part of his father's shareholding.

The years from 1826 to 1830 were ones of great change in the firm. William Taylor Copeland and Josiah Spode II formed a seven year partnership, becoming equal partners in the London business. At this stage, Josiah II was still in total charge of the Spode works. But, on 29 April 1827, Josiah Spode II died and his son, Josiah III, came out of retirement to run the Spode works.

5. Alfred Copeland Diaries 1895-1908. Copeland Trelissick Archives, Cornwall.

Josiah III had been well trained by his grandfather and had the able assistance of his father's confidential servant, William Outrim. Sadly, this arrangement was to be short-lived as on 6 October 1829 Josiah III also died. His son, Josiah IV, was only six years old when his father died and was never to be a part of what had been until then a great family concern. This triple blow to the business would have destroyed many another firm, but Spode was in such good shape that it ran smoothly under the care of the two trustees, Hugh Henshall Williamson and Thomas Fenton. Both were related to the Spode family by marriage. Williamson was Spode III's brother-in-law and Fenton had married Spode II's sister Anne, but there is no doubt that William Outrim, who had joined the firm in 1813 and had worked so closely with Josiah Spode II, was in charge of running the works.

We know that when Spode's executors, Hugh Henshall Williamson and Thomas Fenton, went to the Special Court of the Lord of the Manor of Newcastle-under-Lyme on 1 March 1833, they met William Taylor Copeland and John Capper. Here the transfer of ownership of the Spode works and Spode properties was sanctioned to William Taylor Copeland for £13,491.

The years 1830-33 were the transitional period between the end of the Spode family era and the beginning of the Copeland era. Until 1833, William Outrim and the two trustees carried on the business with little change on the site. William Taylor Copeland continued to produce lucrative orders from London and initiate new designs and the Spode works continued to prosper.

Then, in 1833, came a major change. There were new masters, Messrs. Copeland and Garrett, who were to control the works until 1847. It had taken W.T. Copeland four years to raise the money to buy the Spode enterprise. He succeeded only after much financial manoeuvering. In 1826, when his father died, W.T.C., as he was known, was faced with a serious problem. As the only son, he inherited all his father's business interests, but William Copeland's will clearly specified that all properties were to be sold. His widow Mary was most unhappy and pleaded with the executors of the will to find a way out of the problem. Quite how this was achieved is not known; we know only that one of the trustees resigned and was replaced with a sympathetic member of the Capper family (Emma Marion, W.T.C's sister, had married Samuel Capper).

Alfred, W.T.C.'s son, records that W.T.C. borrowed monies from his sisters, at 4% interest, to buy the whole of Spode's interests, both at Stoke and in London. He also says that the rent book was kept at the Spode works, but it has never been found. Only two receipts for £41.13s.1d., which were payments of interest to William Taylor Copeland's sisters, Emma and Selina, remain as evidence. William Taylor Copeland paid £1,091 out of his own money and the remaining £12,400 was paid by William Taylor Copeland and John Capper jointly. The property was described as:

> All these potworks and buildings used as a manufactory of China and earthenware situated at Stoke upon Trent aforesaid and within the township of Penkhull aforesaid, hitherto occupied by Josiah Spode the elder Esq. deceased, the late

Colour Plate 26. Felspar china punch bowl. Its story, printed in a reserve panel on the outside within a frame of laurel leaves, is as follows: 'At the suggestion of MR THOMAS GROCOTT this punch bowl was MANUFACTURED from the BONES collected after the Entertainments given to MESS COPELAND & GARRETT Stoke upon Trent To their work people on the 13ᵗʰ & 14ᵗʰ Nov 1834 to commemorate their taking the ESTABLISHMENT 1ˢᵗ March 1833. To be considered as a permanent appendage to the Wheat Sheaf Inn'. Another bowl was produced for the Talbot Inn which is now displayed in the Spode Museum. On the base of the bowls in a pink panel inscribed in paint are the words 'This Specimen of Porcelain manufactured by Messrs Copeland & Garrett. Stoke upon Trent 1834. The celebrations were widely reported in the local papers and the bones were taken from the ox which was roasted at the entertainments.* Copeland China Collection, Cornwall

father of Josiah Spode the younger and now by the said Hugh Henshall Williamson and Thomas Fenton, with all the workshops, warehouses, hovels, fire engines, stables, sheds and other erections whatsoever appertaining to the said potworks and occupied therewith and also all the land lying about and behind the potworks, mills and other buildings which was formerly part of a close called Madeleys Meadow on which land has been converted into a reservoir of water and other parts are used for a lime kiln and for wharves, roads, railways yards and other purposes connected with the said manufactory.

Having achieved his ambition, W.T.C. asked Thomas Garrett to become a partner in the enterprise since he needed someone to come to Stoke and

Colour Plate 27. Felspar bone china cup and salver bearing the Copeland coat of arms. Mark Copeland & Garrett in sepia. The inscription on the base of the salver reads: 'This cup and salver presented to alderman copeland ESQ.ALD.M.P MANUFACTURED from the BONES collected after the Entertainment's given by MESS⁰ COPELAND & GARRETT STOKE upon TRENT to their work people on the 13ᵗʰ & 14ᵗʰ Nov 1843 in commemoration of their taking the ESTABLISHMENT 1ˢᵗ MARCH 1833". Another cup and salver was produced for Thomas Garrett and both are now on display at the Copeland China Collection, Cornwall. Copeland China Collection, Cornwall

manage the pottery while he continued his political life in London. Thomas Garrett, born in 1784, had worked for the London business for some time. When he witnessed William Copeland's will in 1826, he was described as clerk to Spode, Copeland and Son, but he was originally employed as a traveller for the firm where he had been very successful.

From 1833 to 1847 the firm traded as Copeland and Garrett, which is to be seen on the backstamp of that period. When Garrett came to Stoke he lived first at Trent Vale, but by 1843 had built himself a large house in Cliff Vale known as Cliff Bank Lodge. The partnership was marked with a grand celebration in 1834. An ox was roasted and from the bones two large punchbowls were made, one for the Talbot Inn (now in the museum at the Spode works) and the other for the Wheatsheaf Inn. Each partner had a goblet and salver on which were painted their coats of arms. These (Colour Plates 26 and 27), with the Wheatsheaf bowl, are now displayed in the Copeland China Collection at Trelissick, Cornwall.

Until the discovery of Alfred Copeland's memoirs there was no evidence to suggest that this partnership was other than successful, but Alfred[6] writes:

My father bought the whole Spode interest in the potworks which had been the best in the Potteries and he carried on at 37 Lincoln's Inn Fields; at the back an extensive warehouse for wholesale, foreign and retail trade. This required money so he borrowed the portions, handsome ones £20,000-18,000 of his sisters and paid 4-½% to them. good interest too and paid punctually, monthly. But, trusting to subordinates he was pillaged. He took a partner who nigh ruined him. He knocked the 37 Lincoln's Inn Field house where my brother Charles and I were born into the warehouse; to my mother's disgust. In 1847, he got rid of his partner and took 160 New Bond Street for all purposes.

Although Thomas Garrett may have proved to be a disaster, his son Spencer became invaluable to the Spode works, participating in the creation of Parian. He was a great friend of Alfred Copeland,[7] who wrote of him:

Garrett had to leave to look after a brickworks, son of Tommy Garrett, a good little fellow in every way, a good little potter, a gentleman, tried at home sorely, impecunious. I recollect giving him ten pounds for some Wedgwood ware, I sold most of it for forty pounds.

Spencer Garrett was also involved in the experiments at the Spode works to make encaustic tiles. William Taylor Copeland spent nearly £5,000 on trying to perfect the technique and is said to have been quite upset when Mintons got it right and made a fortune.

However the years 1833-1847 were to prove to be not only profitable for the firm but also the starting point of many new innovations which were to keep the name of Copeland and Garrett at the forefront of the pottery industry (Colour Plates 28-37).

6. Ibid.
7. Ibid.

Colour Plate 28 (opposite). Copeland & Garrett earthenware lidded jug. Mark 143.
Copeland China Collection, Cornwall

Colour Plate 29. Copeland & Garrett earthenware Toby jug. Copeland China Collection, Cornwall

Colour Plate 30. Copeland & Garrett china dessert plate, pattern 8093. The view of the Castle of Chillon was possibly painted by Plant. Mark 143.
Copeland China Collection, Cornwall

Colour Plate 31. Copeland & Garrett china small flower encrusted vase.
Copeland China Collection, Cornwall

Colour Plate 32. Hand-painted decoration on a Copeland & Garrett china dessert plate. Artist not named, but possibly W. Ball.

Colour Plate 33. Copeland & Garrett china cup and saucer, Wellington embossed shape. Hand-painted panels, artist unknown. Mark 141. Photograph Douglas Chadbone

Colour Plate 34. Copeland & Garrett octagonal shape plate, pattern 'Parrot'. Mark 132. Photograph George Worlock

Colour Plate 35. Copeland & Garrett felspar porcelain plate, 'Dragons' pattern. Marks 133 and 18. 7⅜in. (18.7cm).

Colour Plate 36. Copeland & Garrett earthenware plate decorated with the Warwick Vase pattern. Marks 135 and 102a (22). 10⅛in. (25.7cm). Photograph W. Coles

Colour Plate 37. Copeland & Garrett low Egyptian creamer, basalt body, size 36. Raised enamel pattern 5595. Mark 101a. Photograph W. Coles

Chapter 3

COPELAND & GARRETT TO W.T. COPELAND

1830s to 1868

The period from 1833-1868 was an exciting one for all connected with the names of Spode and Copeland. They were involved in the invention of the new body known as Parian or Statuary Porcelain with the associated argument over just who had invented it. The factory played an important part in exhibitions, at home and abroad. The changes in fashion from the Georgian style to the more elaborate taste of the Victorians had a profound effect on the pottery industry, as it did on all aspects of design, and led to the coming of highly talented artists from all over Europe. Add to these yet another change of management and we can see that these were indeed heady days at the Spode works.

At the same time, it should be remembered that the Spode works were in essence a commercial enterprise, producing a functional product for use in the home. The range of articles covered every aspect of life in the Victorian home, whether cottage, mansion, suburban villa or elegant town house. Fortunes made from the railways, iron, coal and the building trade had increased the demand for all kinds of pottery.

Below stairs, the well-equipped kitchen would have a range of moulds for jellies, aspics, blancmanges, meat and fish pastes, basins, bowls and jugs of all sizes for every culinary purpose. Here too were the plates and dishes for the

Colour Plate 38. Unusual Copeland & Garrett jug with the pad mark of the period. Mark 111.
Photograph George Worlock

*Colour Plate 39. Copeland &
Garrett earthenware basin
pattern B171 showing ship
border pattern with bouquet
centre. Mark 132.*
Private Collection.
Photograph W. Coles

*Colour Plate 40. Copeland & Garrett dessert plate
c.1842, pattern 6903, named on the reverse 'LAKE
URI', attributed to the artist Plant.*

servants' meals, with the service for the upper servants being more decorative
than that for the lower staff. Great quantities of ware were necessary, for these
were the days of enormous breakfasts, lunches and dinners, with afternoon teas
to fill the gap between early lunches and late dinners, and supper laid out to
await those members of the family who had been to the theatre or to one of the
many balls held in the Season (Colour Plates 38 to 45 and Plates 41 and 2).

Colour Plate 41. Copeland & Garrett earthenware plate. Marks 105 and 148 with +. Clay maker 36. 8½in. (21.6cm). Photograph W. Coles

Colour Plate 42. Copeland & Garrett earthenware plate, Chinese Plants (later Aster) pattern. Marks 102a and 135. Clay maker No. 7. 8½in. (21.6cm). Photograph W. Coles

Colour Plate 43. Copeland & Garrett china door plate and door knobs. Painting attributed to W. Ball. Mark 143. Plate 11⅛in. (18.2cm). Copeland China Collection, Cornwall

Colour Plate 44. Copeland & Garrett sucrier (left) and sugar box (right). Note the change from Spode's classical shape to the more ornate style.

Colour Plate 45. Copeland & Garrett china donkey. Mark 143.
Copeland China Collection, Cornwall

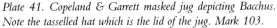

Plate 41. Copeland & Garrett masked jug depicting Bacchus. Note the tasselled hat which is the lid of the jug. Mark 103.

Plate 42. One of a pair of Copeland earthenware blue sprigged vases with cameo inserts. Mark 244. Height 4in. (10.2cm).

The dining-room showed the most exquisite results of the potter's and the decorator's art in the flatware and hollow ware laid out on the gleaming mahogany table and sideboard, from tiny place card holders to huge soup tureens. Fish services were an innovation, many fine examples being produced in the late 1860s, and dessert services comprising tall, medium and low comports and plates were decorated with botanical studies or landscapes which provided a topic of conversation as well as a receptacle for fruit.

The drawing-room held many objects to delight the eye: vases, matchpots, garnitures, candleholders, figures, from the tiles in the fireplace to the door plates and handles. In the study, library or smoking room would be found ashtrays and tobacco jars.

The bedrooms were not to be forgotten. As well as bedside candles and the ornaments on the mantelshelf there was the washstand set, a large jug and basin with its attendant soap dish, toothbrush holder and mug, while hidden discreetly in its cupboard or under the bed was the matching chamberpot and slop pail. The Victorian passion for collecting plants for the conservatory and garden gave the Potteries the opportunity to produce garden pots, jardinières and garden seats. (Colour Plates 46 to 51.)

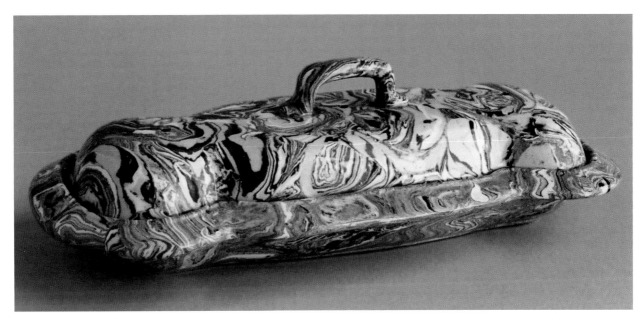

Colour Plate 46. Copeland & Garrett toothbrush box and cover, agate body. Mark 111. 8⅜in. (21.2cm).
Photograph W. Coles

The Art-Union[1] of November 1846 shows pictures of the output of the factory, starting with Etruscan ware, followed by Grecian designs, saying:

> Messrs Copeland and Garrett have taken the neglected flower pot under their essential guardianship, humble as its fate has been hitherto, they have seen that it is worthy and susceptible of ornamentation and they have thus commenced to bring our conservatories and green houses within the range of decorative art.

A collection of just one of each of the articles produced in this period would be most impressive, but we can imagine the size and range of activities of the Spode works when we read the words of a reporter on the *Penny Magazine*[2] of May 1843 when he was sent to describe a 'Day in the Staffordshire Potteries'. The reporter wrote that the manufactory was, he believed, the largest in the district, employing 1,000 hands and having 120 separate workshops,

> the department of the works apportioned as the porcelain manufactory surrounds a large neatly gravelled area and is much cleaner than most other parts of the works.

William Taylor Copeland's partnership with Thomas Garrett was dissolved in 1847. There is no documentary proof as to why it was so short lived, but this entry in Alfred's diary leads to conjecture: 'My father had a partner who near ruined him'.

William Taylor Copeland was not, of course, alone in seeking the major share of the market and there was much fierce rivalry between pottery firms, not least between Copeland and Minton, who became involved in an argument over just who had invented Parian, an argument which has not been resolved over one hundred years later.

1. *The Art Union*, November 1847, page 1287.
2. *The Penny Magazine* Supplement, May 1843, page 201.

Colour Plate 47. Copeland & Garrett bone china tea service commissioned by the Corporation of London for Sir Sills Gibbons, then Lord Mayor. Pattern 5866. Copeland China Collection, Cornwall

Many views have been expressed attributing the invention of this new body both to Copeland and to Minton; certainly Minton called it 'Parian', Copeland referring to it as 'Statuary Porcelain' in their Special Order Reference Books. But, whoever invented it and whatever it was called, it was an enormous success for both Copeland and Minton, as well as other potters. Simulating marble, it was ideal for producing portrait busts of the famous, classical figures and many other ornaments of the type beloved of the Victorians.

When John Mountford left the Derby manufactory, he and Spencer Garrett, Thomas Garrett's son, worked on the new body under Thomas Battam, the art superintendent, and developed a satisfactory recipe. Battam claimed he had been the originator of the body and perhaps it would be more truthful to say that Copeland's Statuary Porcelain was invented under his direction. However,

Colour Plate 48. Copeland & Garrett china double candlesnuffers, mark 143. Copeland China Collection, Cornwall

Colour Plate 49 (above). Copeland & Garrett unusual shaped hand-painted, jug, pattern 5193. Rare mark 137.
Private Collection. Photograph Douglas Chadbon

Colour Plate 50 (right). Copeland & Garrett garden seat, basalt and raised enamel. No marks.
Photograph W. Coles

he had great faith in it and knew it would be a commercial success. Cheverton's reducing machine had made it possible for modellers to reproduce small scale copies of classical figures. These were already being made at the Spode works in felspar porcelain, and at Sèvres and Derby in biscuit porcelain. Battam could foresee a market for these figures in his new body.

Such was his confidence that he was able to persuade the Duke of Sutherland to allow him to use one of the sculptures at his country estate, Trentham, only three miles from the works. When the Duke was shown the resulting figure, Wyatt's Apollo as the shepherd boy of Admetus, he was so impressed that he bought it on the spot. In 1845, at the Manchester Exhibition, many small figures were exhibited and in the official catalogue of the Great Exhibition of 1851 Thomas Battam described the process:

> The articles under the heading of Statuary Porcelain including Carrara etc. are produced by 'casting'. as the most direct method of illustrating this process, let us suppose the object under review to be a figure or group, and this we will assume to be two feet high in the model. The clay, which is used in a semi-liquid state, about the consistency of cream, and called 'slip' is poured into the moulds forming the various parts of the subject (sometimes as many as fifty): the shrinking that occurs before these casts can be taken out of the moulds, which is caused by the absorbent nature of the plaster of which the mould is composed, is equal to a reduction of one inch and a half in the height. These casts are then put together by the 'figure maker'; the seams (consequent upon the marks caused by the subdivision of the moulds) are then carefully removed and the whole worked upon to restore the cast to the same degree of finish as the original model. The work is then thoroughly dried to be in a fit state for firing, as, if put in the oven while damp, the sudden contraction consequent to the great degree of heat instantaneously applied would be very liable to cause it to crack: in the process it again suffers a further loss of one inch and a half by evaporation and it is now but one foot nine inches. Again, in the 'firing' of the bisque oven, its most severe ordeal, it is diminished three inches, and is then but eighteen inches high, being six inches, or one-fourth less than the original. Now, as the contraction should equally affect every portion of the details of the work, in order to realize a faithful copy, and as added to this contingency are the risks in the oven of being 'overfired', by which it would be melted in a mass, and of being 'shortfired', by which its surface would be imperfect, it is readily evident that a series of difficulties present themselves which require considerable practical experience successfully to meet.

There is no doubt that this new process needed new workshops and would account in no small part for the expansion of the Spode works at this time. Despite considerable investigation it has been impossible to find even one oven which was used solely for firing Parian – one which was thought to have been used for this purpose was found, to the researcher's great disappointment, to have been a privy!

Colour Plate 51. Copeland & Garrett pair of small china vases decorated with lily of the valley. Mark 143. Copeland China Collection, Cornwall

The success of Parian was assured when, in 1844, the Art-Union of London chose 'Narcissus', the famous sculpture by John Gibson R.A. exhibited at the Royal Academy, as a prize for their subscribers. The order was secured by Thomas Battam. Mr. E.B. Stephens was commissioned to produce the

Plate 43 (far left). 'The Veiled Bride' modelled by Rafaelle Monti. This Parian bust was commissioned by the Crystal Palace Art-Union from Copelands and is marked on the base. Copeland China Collection, Cornwall

Plate 44 (left). Copeland Parian 'The Greek Slave' after the sculpture by Hiram Powers. 18½in. (47cm). Mark Copeland impressed on the base. The original marble statue is at Raby Castle, Co. Durham, the home of Lord Barnard.

reduced figure. One slight problem had to be overcome to cater for Victorian prudery: Narcissus was a nude figure, so a tasteful fig leaf was designed by Mr. Stephens who, however, insisted that the first model produced should be without the fig leaf, and he would take this in part payment for his services – all the others had the fig leaf in the correct place!

Battam had heard that Gibson, who spent nearly all his time in Italy, was coming to England to work on a sculpture for Queen Victoria. A visit to the Spode works was arranged for a party consisting of members of the Art-Union,[3] Mr. Gibson, Alderman Copeland (William Taylor Copeland) and Thomas Battam. The party toured the works and saw for themselves the expertise of the Spode workers. The visit resulted in the Art-Union placing an order for fifty figures at a cost of £3 each and later another fifty at £2.5s.

Parian figures were also commissioned by the Art-Unions of Scotland, Liverpool and Ireland. Many of them are clearly marked on the back of the bust or figure with the name of the original sculptor, the date, the factory mark of the time and often the Art-Union which commissioned the work (Colour Plates 52 to 63 and Plates 43 to 49).

3. Lyndel Saunders King, *The Industrialization of Taste, Victorian England and the Art Union of London* (UMI Research Press, Ann Arbor, Michigan, 1985), page 81.

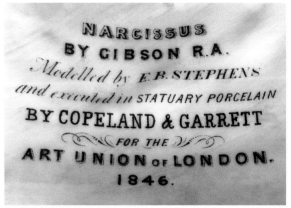

Colour Plate 52A. The inscription on the base of the 'Narcissus' statue. Backstamp 2in. x 1½in. (5cm x 3.8cm), position 1in. (2.5cm) from base.

Colour Plate 52. Copeland & Garrett Parian 'Narcissus' after the marble statue by John Gibson, R.A.

Colour Plate 53A. Mark for the Beauvais jug.

Colour Plate 53. Copeland & Garrett Parian Beauvais jug. Mark 113. Photograph W. Coles

Plate 45. Parian covered centre ornament vase with goats' heads modelled on either side supported by puttis, richly gilt. Height 8¾in. (22.2cm).

Plate 46. Parian jug, Renaissance decoration with masked heads, impressed COPELAND on the base. Height 8½in. (21.6cm)
Private Collection

Plate 47. Parian group 'Chasse au Lapin' after the bronze by P.J. Mêne, exhibited at the Paris Exhibition, 1855. Impressed COPELAND at the rear. Height 7¼in. (18.4cm).

Plate 48. Parian group, Paul and Virginia, after the sculpture by Cumberworth. Impressed mark Copeland Copyright. Height 14in. (35.6cm).

Plate 49. Parian figures of Ruth after Theed (left above) and Rebecca (left). Both names on the base and impressed COPELAND at rear.

Battam's faith in his product had been proved and by 1851 orders were flowing in. As a man of vision he must have been delighted with the thought of an international exhibition to be held in London and took the opportunity of creating the finest Copeland products for exhibition. The idea for an exhibition, which was to be known as The Great Exhibition, was first promoted by Henry Cole, a prominent civil servant and owner of Summerly's Art Manufactures, who in 1852 took over the management of the School of Design in London, with great effect. He is also credited with the founding of the South Kensington Museum, later to be known as the Victoria and Albert. Cole was impressed with an exhibition he had visited in France and persuaded

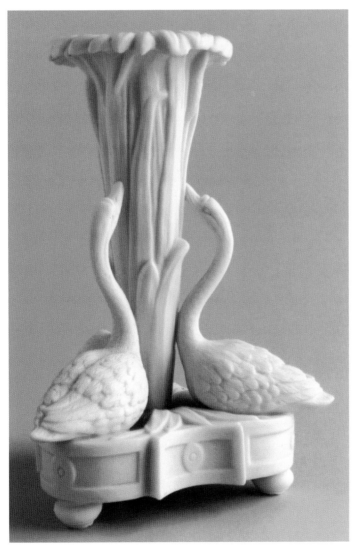

Colour Plate 54. Parian vase with swans, impressed COPELAND on the base. Height 7½in. (19cm). Private Collection

Colour Plate 55. Copeland Parian long-eared owl (Asio otus). Mark Copeland impressed. Height 7in. (17.8cm). Photograph W. Coles

Colour Plate 56. Left: Parian group of boy with rabbit, c.1850, impressed COPELAND on the base. Right: original marble figure. Copeland China Collection, Cornwall

Prince Albert that Britain would gain both prestige and fame by holding an exhibition and inviting other countries to send exhibits.

So 1851 could be regarded as one of the highest points in the history of the Spode works. William Taylor Copeland and Herbert Minton were chosen by their fellow potters to represent the pottery industry at the meetings called by Prince Albert to organize the Great Exhibition of All Nations, the Festival of Peace. Between this honour and the actual opening of the Exhibition at the Crystal Palace lay many months of hard work and planning, the design,

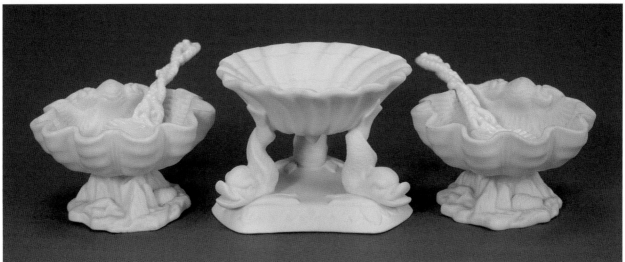

Colour Plate 57. A group of small Parian animals, all impressed COPELAND on the base. Left to right: rabbit; Assyrian lion sculpt. A. Hays; sheep.

Colour Plate 58. Parian salts, pink tinged spoons, all impressed COPELAND on the base.
Copeland China Collection, Cornwall

Colour Plate 59. Parian group 'Cavaliers Pets' after the painting by Edwin Landseer, impressed mark COPELAND on the base. Height 5in. (12.7cm).

Colour Plate 61. Coloured and named Parian model of Jumbo, the elephant famous at Barnum and Bailey's circus. Impressed COPELAND on the base.

Colour Plate 60 (left). Parian gothic style pierced vase with red glass liner, impressed COPELAND.
Copeland China Collection, Cornwall

making and decoration of the special ware, the selection of the artists and gilders, and the excitement, jealousy and anxiety which must have pervaded every aspect of pottery life. Much was at stake, for this was the first time that the art of the Spode works would be seen beside that of their competitors of, amongst others, France and Germany. The implications for the future of the Staffordshire potteries were great and the whole of the Potteries was infected with exhibition fever.

Thomas Battam had now moved from London to live in a large house not too far from the Spode Works at Herons Cross and toured the six towns exhorting all pottery manufacturers to take part. Special trains were laid on to

Colour Plate 62. Decorated Parian bottle vase painted with roses by Gregoire c.1860. Impressed COPELAND.
Copeland China Collection, Cornwall

Colour Plate 63. Coloured Parian jug with dragon handle.
Private Collection

cope with the numbers of pottery workers who saved hard for the price of a ticket so that they could go and see their work in Paxton's Crystal Palace. Meanwhile the Exhibition pieces were displayed in the works showrooms and discussed in pubs, shops and homes throughout the area. Remember that the throwers, turners, printers, etc., having finished their part of the production of a piece, may never have seen a completed article. Now they could; now they could feel that their small unit in the works was a significant part of a much larger whole and they could be justly proud of themselves and the firm for which they worked.

In March 1851 the *Staffordshire Advertiser* reported that both Copeland and Minton had put their exhibits on show in their works showrooms. The Duchess of Sutherland visited the Spode works to view the display. These pieces are described in the Exhibition Catalogue. There were at least twelve Parian busts and groups, including one of the Duke of Sutherland by Francis. There were also garden vases and pots, while fine porcelain was well represented by sumptuous dessert services, tea and coffee sets, in fact, something of every type of ware (Colour Plates 64 to 67).

On 15 July another group of people visited the Spode works. They were the

foreign Jurors who, with their English counterparts, would judge the exhibits of each competitor and make the awards. W.T.C., now known as Alderman Copeland, did not approve of the constitution of this panel of Jurors and said so, emphatically!

When members of all crafts had been asked to join in the first International Exhibition, little had been said about prizes or, indeed, about a competitive spirit. The idea was that each manufacturer would put his best ware alongside that of his foreign rivals. This was bound to give rise to an unofficial competition, but it seems to have come as a surprise when it was announced that medals would be awarded.

Both Minton and Copeland had assumed that a medal would be awarded for

Colour Plate 64. Copeland bone china low comport with a view of Messina, made especially for the Great Exhibition of 1851. Note the rich gilded border. Mark 235. Copeland China Collection, Cornwall

Colour Plate 65. Copeland bone china Madras shaped jewelled bottle which was exhibited at the Great Exhibition of 1851. Mark 235 in green.
Copeland China Collection, Cornwall

Colour Plate 66 (left). Copeland bone china vase made for the Great Exhibition of 1851 and also shown at the Paris Exhibition, 1889.
Copeland China Collection, Cornwall

Colour Plate 67 (opposite). Copeland bone china dessert plate with a view of the Tower of Comares attributed to Daniel Lucas Junior. Possibly exhibited at the 1862 exhibition. Mark 238. Copeland China Collection, Cornwall

their Parian exhibits but, as the dispute over the invention of the body was at its full height, the Council of Judges decided in their wisdom that this area of production would have no medal and stated so in their report. They also, foolishly as it proved, awarded two medals for excellence. Their mistake lay in calling one the Council medal and the other the Prize medal. The immediate result was that they were regarded as first class and second class medals, which was not the judges' intention.

Alderman Copeland, according to Alfred's account,[4] had been led to believe that his firm would be awarded the Council medal, instead of which he was awarded the Prize medal and Minton gained the Council medal. If the worthy

4. Letter in the Trelissick archives written to Alfred from his youngest brother Richard, asking about the Great Exhibition and why they did not win a medal, and Alfred's reply. 1895.

Alderman was upset, it was nothing to the anguish of his workers who wrote the following address which they presented to him. On 1 November 1851 it appeared in the *Staffordshire Advertiser*.

> Worthy Employer, we your servants beg to express our sympathy with you on the position in which you have been placed by the decisions of the Jurors in connection with the late Exhibition.
>
> We most earnestly beg of you not to accept the medal which has been awarded to you, considering as we do, that it would be an acknowledgment that you only hold a secondary place in the manufacture of those articles which constitute the staple trade of this district.
>
> Your eminence as an employer has long been acknowledged and the extensive patronage which has been so profusely lavished among you by the persons of acknowledged taste will of itself be sufficient to deter you from receiving any such award

The epistle was signed by over four hundred workers.

Alderman Copeland refused the medal and tried in vain to find out why the firm had not got the award. Many theories have been aired by members of the Copeland family even into the twentieth century, but no satisfactory answer has been found. However, those interested may find in the Spode Museum, among the gold and bronze medals awarded at later exhibitions, one small bronze medal awarded to Alderman Copeland for his work at the Great Exhibition of 1851.

The Jurors printed report comments on the Copeland exhibits:

> This exhibit is remarkable in several respects, especially for the great beauty of the Parian groups and figures, several of which are eminently successful, and show complete mastery over this material in its best and most legitimate application. The jury especially desire to mention the large porcelain slabs or panels decorated with flower painting and other patterns and now much used for fireplaces, panels and tables and a variety of other purposes connected with useful and ornamental furniture. The large flower painting on some of these has a very handsome effect and some Pompeiian patterns are particularly pleasing.

Copeland's new jewelled ware was described by some critics as lacking in taste and was not to be appreciated until the 1880s, but bat printing was regarded as important enough for Thomas Battam to write a description of it for the official catalogue of the Great Exhibition:

> The "bat printing" is done upon the glaze and the engravings are for this style exceedingly fine, and no greater depth is required than for ordinary book engravings...The copper plate is first charged with linseed oil and cleaned off by hand, so that the engraved portion alone retains it. A preparation of glue being run upon flat dishes, about a quarter of an inch thick, is cut to the size required for the

Plate 50. Copeland bone china seaux, floral studies painted by C.F. Hürten, c.1860s. The gilding is superb.
Spode Museum

subject, and then pressed upon it, and being immediately removed, draws on its surface the oil with which the engraving was filled. The glue is then pressed upon the ware, with the oiled part next the glaze, and being again removed, the design remains, though, being in a pure oil, scarcely perceptible. Colour finely ground is then dusted upon it with cotton wool, and a sufficiency adhering to the oil leaves the impression perfect, and ready to be fired in the enamel kilns.

This process was recently re-discovered by Mr. Paul Holdway, engraver at Spode.[5]

Although Copelands sent exhibits to five more international exhibitions throughout this period (Dublin 1853, Paris 1855, the Anglo-French 1860, London 1862 and Paris 1867), it was the Great Exhibition of 1851 which caused the greatest storm in the field of design. Highly acclaimed though they might be, English potteries could not compete in the field of intricate patterns as exemplified by Sèvres and Meissen. The potters turned to the practice known today as 'head-hunting' and persuaded some of the best foreign artists to come to England and turn their talents to the benefit of English pottery design.

In 1858 William Taylor Copeland welcomed to Stoke Charles Ferdinand Hürten, who was born in Cologne, trained at the Cologne School of Art and then employed by the Sèvres manufactory. He was offered a contract, which still survives in the archives at Stoke, and it states that if at any time Hurten wanted to return home, Copelands would pay his fare and that of his family. In fact, although Hürten complained continually in letters home about the weather in the Potteries, he stayed at Copelands until 1895. He was given a studio of his own and his every wish was granted, even to his own choice of the ware he painted. His floral studies on all shapes and bodies of ware show absolute excellence of design and artistic skill (Colour Plate 68 and Plate 50).

5. Drakard and Holdway, *Spode Printed Ware*.

Colour Plate 68. One of a pair of Copeland bone china ginger jars painted all round with wisteria, signed C.F. Hürten. No backstamp. Copeland China Collection, Cornwall

During this period it appears to have been the fashion to pay a visit to the Spode works to see the ware being made. Many important personages and customers were escorted round the works by the management while the workers patiently explained to them the intricacies of their craft. One such visitor was Charles Dickens who visited the Potteries in 1852. While he was not impressed by the town of Stoke, he wrote an article[6] in which he looks at a plate in his hotel, remembers his visit to Copelands and imagines the plate to be talking to him:

And don't you remember [says the plate] how you alighted at Stoke – a picturesque heap of houses, kilns, smoke, wharfes, canals and river, lying (as was most appropriate) in a basin – and how, after climbing up the sides of the basin to look at the prospect, you trundled down again at walking pace and straight proceeded to

6. Charles Dickens 'A Plated Article' in *Household Words,* 24 April 1852, pages 117-21.

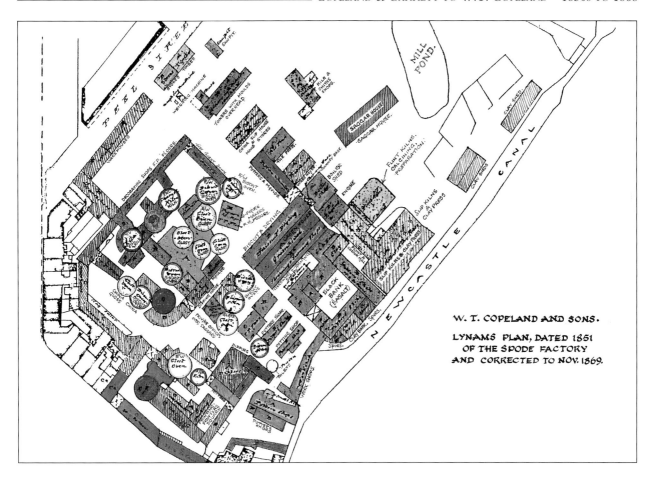

my father's, Copeland's. where the whole of my family, high and low, rich and poor, are turned out upon the world from our nursery and seminary, covering some fourteen acres of ground? And don't you remember what we spring from:- heaps of lumps of clay, partially prepared and cleaned in Devonshire and Dorsetshire, whence said clay principally comes and hills of flint, without which we should want our ringing sound, and should never be musical. I had been shown, at Copeland's, patterns of beautiful design, in faultless perspective, which are causing the ugly old willow to wither out of public favour; and which, being quite as cheap, insinuate good wholesome natural art into the humblest households. When Mr. and Mrs. Sprat have satisfied their material tastes by that equal division of fat and lean which has made their *menage* immortal; and have, after the elegant tradition, 'licked the platter clean', they can – thanks to modern artists in clay – feast their intellectual tastes upon excellent delineations of natural objects…

Colour Plate 69. Plan of W.T. Copeland & Sons, November 1869. This plan was first completed in 1851 by Charles Lyam and updated in 1869. It shows the purpose of each building at that time.

The backstamps Dickens may well have seen on his plate, from 1847-1868, are impressed Copeland. Printed marks on earthenwares between 1847 and 1890 are Copeland late Spode, but one of the most commonly seen marks on china of the period is the crossed Cs 1850-90 with or without Copeland underneath.

Pattern numbers had reached 9999 by 1852, when a new series, known as D numbers, was started, running until D9999 was reached in December 1874.

Certainly Dickens would not have recognised the factory from the earlier plans but this next plan (Colour Plate 69) shows the separate buildings for

7. Charles Lynam, J.P., F.R.I.B.A. (1829-1921). Due to Alderman Copeland's influence, he attended the Christ Church Hospital School in London and said this was the greatest benefit of his life. Lynam returned to Stoke to assist his father in the family practice. In 1850 he was chosen by the Stokeville Building Society to design twenty-four houses which became known as 'The Villas'. Alderman Copeland bought No. 14 but whether he ever lived there is not known.
8. Alfred Copeland Diary from 1895-1908.

china making, and the decorating shops. All the plans have been colour coded: blue for china, green for earthenware and yellow for the glost ovens. It shows the evolution of the site from the early evidence of the Spode plate mentioned in Chapter 1, and we can now see the different areas, with the beginning of the development of a system of production. The plan is entitled 'Messrs. Copeland and Sons Manufactory, Stoke-on-Trent, copied from Mr. Lynam's plan dated 1851, corrected to November 1869'.[7] From this it has been possible to identify the many changes since the 1833 plan colour-coding them in grey to show the many changes in manufacture. The names of the various areas are now marked. The main alterations are the addition of the Needham and Kite clay press in the slip kiln area by the side of the Newcastle Canal (Plate 51). The tile press can now be seen where Spencer Garrett experimented with the production of encaustic tiles and where he invented his brick cement. Here the tiles were made when Copelands took on the task of tiling the Reading Room ceiling of the Imperial Library in Paris in 1868. Alfred's diary[8] says:

Doubtless my father was essentially not a potter but he and Mr.Garrett set the encaustic tile trade going and having lost three thousand pounds Herbert Minton took it up and made a success of it.

Output at the works was increased as a result of the adoption of the Needham and Kite filter press in 1856-7. Before this the clay had been put into the slip kilns, described in the *Penny Magazine M*ay 1843 as:

the slip kiln, a remarkable and very long building. This place consists of a very low room, 120ft in length, having on either side shallow slip kilns and a passage

Plate 51. Removing the clay from a clay press, 18 July 1899.
Photograph by William Fowler Mountford Copeland

Plate 52. A composite pen and ink drawing of the china slip house and mould stores, c.1880s. Harold Holdway, 1993.

down the middle. The kilns are merely open troughs 60ft long and 5ft wide and one foot deep formed of fire brick and heated with flues underneath. Here the slip, or clay cream, remains exposed to heat for 24 hours by which time it evaporates to the stiffness of clay.

In the new filter presses the slip was pumped into each section surrounded by a fine cloth and 'pressed' to force the water out of the cloth and so achieve the same result as the old slip kiln in less time. William Taylor Copeland, having assessed its capabilities, became the agent in the Potteries for this process. Printing output, too, had been greatly increased in 1847 as a result of the invention of the Fourdrinier brothers' roller printing machine. They also patented a new transfer paper which was much superior to the old type.

It would even have been possible in the early 1850s to mechanise plate making by the use of a jigger driven by belting from the steam engine. However, as in other industries, the workers at the Spode works strongly objected, nicknaming the machine 'the Scourge'; such was the outcry that the management did not dare install it until the 1870s. The Black Bank area shown on the map has been completely altered; the two basalt ovens are no longer shown and more warehouses have been built.

Another Clay Bank had been added, on either side of which were workshops to make kiln furniture. When firing the glaze it was essential to prevent the articles sticking together so 'thimbles' and 'spurs' (consisting of three legs and a central point support) were used. The clay drying area had been increased by building a new shop between the two existing ones. The china making area now had its own slip house (Plate 52). Near to Peel Street (now

93

Elenora Street) a weighbridge machine and a timber store had been added. Three earthenware ovens had been pulled down, one replaced by a figure making shop, no doubt because of the success of Parian, while on the site of another a new Master's office was built. This is still used today by the Managing Director of Spode, who has restored the old Board Room to its former glory. The third oven was pulled down and a larger and better dipping shop for glazing was erected. The printers' area was modernised, becoming larger and better planned, and the decorating area was also enlarged.

In the decorating area, the plan says 'just burnt down', referring to a fire which caused terrible damage. The report in the *Staffordshire Advertiser*[9] stated that the fire started in the paintresses' shop on the first floor and the store place on the ground floor was set alight. It went on to say that, as the building was old and made of wood, even two fire engines could not put out the fire. The smoke drifted into the gilding and painting shops and all the ware there was badly damaged. Chief Superintendent Sweeting used the Spode fire engine and the Stoke engine but, even though there was a good supply of water from the mill pool, the building could not be saved. The letters F.P.F on the plan of 1869 mean Fire Proof Floors, obviously after the fire improvements had been made. Here was the opportunity to build well-lit decorating shops, giving the girls who worked there better working conditions.

Thomas Battam, who served the Copelands faithfully throughout many of these changes, contributed to their success using his undoubted flair for design and decoration, introducing many new shapes and carrying out his belief that pottery design should be an art form. Possibly one of his greatest achievements was The Prince of Wales Service commissioned by the Prince of Wales on his marriage to Princess Alexandra of Denmark in 1863 (Colour Plate 70). Unfortunately Battam died before it was completed. There are two entries in the Special Order Book relating to this service – on 15 July a cup and saucer, orange blossom and fruit, roses in the initials of the Prince of Wales, and on 22 May a comb tray painted with a wreath of orange blossom and roses, chased gold border and monogram in roses and chased gold, painted by Hürten. A further entry on 23 May refers to what may have been additions ordered after the Prince of Wales had seen the completed service – an 8in. (20cm) pillar candlestick painted with oranges and roses and a covered toilet rose knob similarly decorated.

The *Art Journal* of April 1866 stated:

The result of this commission is a triumph of ceramic art; perhaps the greatest that has been achieved in this country. It may certainly be accepted as the evidence of the utmost extent to which art can be carried in England. Of the painting we may first speak. There has been nothing of the class so exquisitely perfect; the groups of flowers are arranged with consummate skill, and are marvelously true to nature. The centre of the service is a double assiette montee; the principal comport being supported by figures representing the four quarters of the globe (Asia, Africa, America and Europe), each figure with its appropriate

Colour Plate 70. Copeland bone china dessert plate from the Prince of Wales service, painted by C.F. Hürten.

symbol. These have been modelled by the eminent sculptor Joseph Durham from those which support the statue of the good Prince Albert in the memorial place in the garden of the Horticultural Society. The four raised fruit dishes are elevated upon groups, each consisting of three figures, which typify, by their several zodiacal signs and the diversities of their ideal occupations, the twelve months of the year. These are from the admirable models of Mr. F. Miller, and four smaller comports are of great beauty and very original in design. These represent the elements, fire, air, earth and water and are the production of Mr. G. Halse. The remaining pieces of the service comprise, ice pails, cream bowls, and dishes for fruit and confiture, the ice bucket covers surmounted by a bacchanal. The design by which they are ornamented is principally derived from the vine. The plates are of the purest porcelain perforated with great skill and care, each containing the four panels in which are grouped fruit, oranges and blossom and flowers surrounded by festoons and ribbons of raised and chased gold. In the centre is the monogram of their Royal Highnesses, the initials of the Princess being of festooned roses those of the Prince in raised and chased gold. We do not believe there is an artist living who can surpass these pictures, either in design, arrangement or execution; and Mr. Hurten is entitled to a large share of the honour which the service is certain to receive for the manufacturer and those who have been his aides in the undertaking. The late Mr. Thomas Battam conceived the plan which others have carried out.

The Prince of Wales granted Copelands the following Royal Warrant:

Alderman Copeland, you are hereby appointed China and glass Manufacturer to His Royal Highness the Prince of Wales. Given under my hand and seal.
Marlborough House, this 6th day of August 1866.
W. Vinolloys, Controller.

Battam was a man of many talents from writing articles to controlling a large art department. His early death in 1864 at the age of fifty-four must have been a terrible shock to the Copeland family. However, like Henry Daniel, he left a legacy of fine design and diversity of product which kept them at the forefront of the market place.

Throughout this period of expansion shown on the map the Spode works was owned solely by William Taylor Copeland following the dissolution of the partnership with Thomas Garrett. From 1867, when William Taylor took his sons into partnership, the firm traded as W.T. Copeland and Sons. William Fowler Mountford Copeland, the eldest son, served the family business for nearly sixty years. He seems to have never been given overall authority for one department but his sound advice (although not taken by his father!) proved invaluable to the company after William Taylor Copeland's death. He had no children of his own but was very fond of his younger brother's family. Many of the photographs in this book were taken by his nephew, also William Fowler Mountford Copeland, in the 1890s and early 1900s. Alfred James Copeland, who became the family historian, ran the London office for a number of years, retiring in 1881. Edward Capper Copeland started with great promise, being sent to the works at the age of nineteen to learn the business. His father's intention was that Edward should supplant Horton Yates, then Super-intendent of the works (and a cousin of William Taylor Copeland's wife Sarah Yates). Yates lived in a house on the south side of Victoria Square, Shelton. He was known as a jolly, genial and entertaining man who died of a fever at sea. However, although popular with his contemporaries, he and the Copelands must have had some disagreement as he was given a cash settlement of £500 and persuaded to leave, making room for Edward. Unfortunately Edward was to prove no more satisfactory than Yates, because of his fondness for fortified wine, and his brothers reluctantly had to ask him to leave. None of his children joined the family firm.

The youngest of the four brothers, Richard Pirie Copeland, had always been interested in all aspects of making earthenware and china. He was the first Copeland to make his home in Staffordshire and was to be seen driving his pony and trap from Kibblestone to Stone station to take the train to Stoke every morning, often accompanied by his two younger sons.

In 1868 William Taylor Copeland died suddenly at his home, Russell Farm, Watford, Hertfordshire (Plate 53), leaving the business to his sons. Alfred's c.1895 description of his father is his best epitaph:

Well with all his faults my father was a godly specimen of a manly English gentleman. He could write well, speak well and was not vulgar, but he had not received education at a public school, nor could he speak French. A firm friend, a bad enemy. Very nice looking and inclined to be corpulent, having a fair complexion and parting his hair down the middle. No forgetfulness of old friends, no snobbishness about him. So died the senior alderman of London, spoken of to this day as a great man and he was. We cannot all be prime ministers; but for active public duty, no better existed. Faults he had, but why not, but he was kind, amiable, contented and spent a good unselfish life.

Plate 53. Russell Farm, Watford, Hertfordshire, the last home of William Taylor Copeland.

Chapter 4

W.T. COPELAND & SONS

1868 to 1900

Plate 54. Packing the ware,
13 July 1899.

The death of William Taylor Copeland was not, as far as the Spode site was concerned, such a cataclysmic event as the death of Josiah Spode II. There was no hiatus in the overall control and running of the works. William Taylor Copeland had left the firm in the hands of his four sons, all well trained, experienced and capable of maintaining its position at the forefront of British pottery design and manufacture.

From the days of the first Josiah Spode to the first part of Queen Victoria's reign, there was little change in the processes which went into the making of earthenware and fine china. In the mid- and later years of the Victorian period great advances in mechanisation speeded up those processes, although there was no change in the basic elements of production, in the making of the clay bodies, and decoration of the ware.

However, the buildings and the number of ovens and kilns at the Spode works underwent considerable alteration. Potting shops were similar in appearance to those of the West Yorkshire woollen mills, being two or three storeys of long sheds. Study of the plans raises the question of why a pottery needed so many warehouses and why, as it changed, was warehouse space one of the first considerations?

After being made, the clay ware was taken to a greenhouse to be dried and sorted ready to be fired to the biscuit state. Next, the ware was taken to another warehouse to be sorted again, this time for glazing and then glost firing, then to the decorating warehouse and finally to the packing warehouse (Plates 54 and 55). In each warehouse the ware was carefully checked for imperfections; some was returned to the various processes where it could be reclaimed, still achieving the high quality standard required; some, totally unacceptable, was destroyed. Ware known as 'seconds' was sent to the seconds bench where the faults would be carefully examined. Seconds found in each process would then be attributed to the relevant department and either the culprit or the foreman sent for, to explain why. Some of these imperfections could be rectified, then sent with the best ware off to the next stage of production, after which the whole procedure was repeated.

The expertise of those at the seconds bench could save a pottery a lot of money. Much has been written about the skills of the workers in the making and decorating processes, but one of the vital components of production was the skill and speed of the selectors who could spot imperfections at a glance.

The final, but by no means the least, stage in the long and complicated process of pottery production came in the packing house. The warehouse man was responsible for the making-up of the orders. Meticulous packing was essential to make sure the goods arrived in perfect condition. He was also responsible for their final despatch to the customer, who, on receiving the order, would then pay the pottery for it.

Plate 55. The glost sorting room, 30 August 1899.
Photograph William Fowler Mountford Copeland

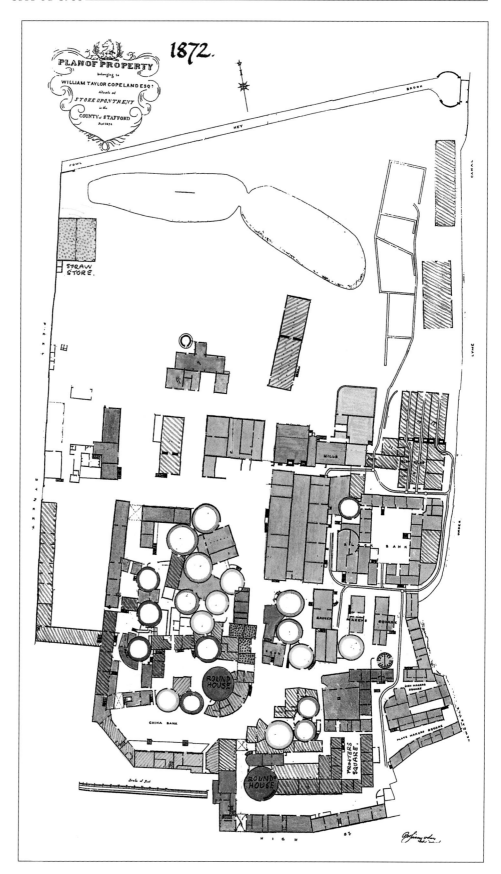

Colour Plate 71. Plan of property belonging to William Taylor Copeland Esq. situated at Stoke-upon-Trent in the County of Stafford September 1872.

There was, from time to time, a change in the usage of some of the long, low rooms (for example, from warehouse space to apprentice painters' shops), but warehouse space was always of prime importance. Large buildings were also needed to store the vast quantity of moulds used in the production of holloware and Parian.

The 1872 plan (Colour Plate 71) shows many alterations to the site, naming for the first time the china bank and the saucer makers' square. New bottle ovens and kilns were built by the pottery's bricklayers. These men could make or mend a kiln with equal facility, so were among the few who could count on full employment.

The plan shows ovens previously marked as for the firing of biscuit earthenware now being used for the firing of glost ware, a change made possible by the skill of the fireman who could respond to the demands of a changing market. Around these ovens rose more and more potting shops, which benefited from the heat generated by the ovens. The alleyways between the buildings were very narrow and even now old employees remember walking around the works in the depth of winter enjoying the warmth from the smoking ovens and kilns.

From the plans and from old photographs taken by the Alderman's grandson, William Fowler Mountford Copeland, it has been possible to build up a clear idea of how the pottery would have looked at this time.

After the fire of 1867 (Plates 56 and 57) which destroyed one of the decorating shops, a new decorating shop was built on the site of the old one.

Plate 56. Fire practice at Copelands, 1899.
Photograph William Fowler Mountford Copeland

Plate 57. The Copeland fire engine coming out, 1899.
Photograph William Fowler Mountford Copeland

Plate 58. A composite pen and ink drawing of the decorating shops with the biscuit oven on the left and on the right Mr. Daniel's enamelling kilns, c.1870s. Harold Holdway, 1992.

Plate 59. Wooden truck on a piece of the old 'plate way' still surviving at the Spode works as late as the 1950s. Photograph Robert Copeland

It is thought that the new building was two storeyed. Harold Holdway's artist's impression (Plate 58) shows the building as it would have looked in the 1870s.

Visitors to the Spode works can see by looking at the brickwork that another storey has been added, probably in the early 1900s.

The 1872 plan shows the 'China Bank' – this is known as the Terrace. Below was the clay cellar with three fire-proof storeys above which were housed workshops and a mould chamber. It is possible that here Spode II made bone china.

The clay had been mixed in the slip kilns at the other end of the site, and was taken to the china clay cellar by pony and cart. Tracks were laid around the site and the wagon had iron wheels which fitted the tracks, making the transport of earthenware clay easier and quicker (Plate 59). The tracks did not reach to the china clay cellar and at the end of the track the clay was taken by labourers to the cellar. The 1872 plan shows clearly where these 'plate ways' started and finished. The cellar was at the correct temperature for the storage of clay, eventually being lined with tiles made on the site. The clay was wedged here by hand as late as 1934. The date when the de-airing pug was installed is not known but after its installation the throwers and plate makers did not have to wedge the clay by hand to get all the air out, because this de-airing pug mill did it for them.

In the new building the clay was taken to the next floor to the china throwers and turning shops. Plates were made by the flat makers on the floor above, while on the third were the mould chambers and the mould makers. These processes continued on the Terrace until the 1960s. Another storey was added in the 1900s and was a subject of controversy between William Fowler Mountford and Richard Pirie. When William was shown the new 'height' by his brother, he asked what it was to be used for. Richard replied proudly that the new height had been added for the engravers and modellers. William's retort, which has been handed down in the family, was: 'height of damned nonsense Richard'. The workers who have worked up there do say that the top floor appeared to sway in the wind, so perhaps William was right!

Harold Holdway's impression of the Terrace without the extra storey shows the doors and steps of the building and the wooden casks (which were made on the site) in which the ware was packed ready for despatch (Plate 60). Here, too, was the studio of the great floral artist Charles Ferdinand Hürten.

The fine arcaded building adjacent to the Terrace may have been converted in the 1870s from a warehouse into one in which the company could

Plate 60. A composite pen and ink drawing of the china terrace building c.1890s. The two windows top right were the artist C.F. Hürten's studio. Harold Holdway, 1993.

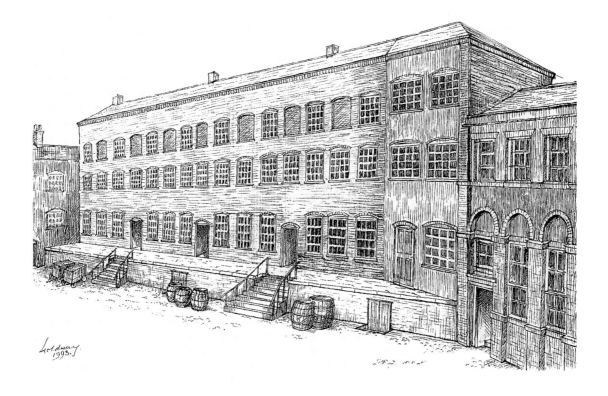

Colour Plate 72. Copeland bone china candle snuffer in the shape of a bishop's mitre, c.1880s. Mark 235.
Photograph George Worlock. Private Collection

Colour Plate 73. Copeland earthenware lidded sauce tureen with stand decorated with the 'Country Scenes' pattern, 1878. Copeland China Collection, Cornwall

Colour Plate 74. Copeland bone china teapot, Crichton shape, decorated with the 'Burns' pattern. Copeland China Collection, Cornwall

entertain their most important clients. By this time it was obvious that it was no longer suitable to take eminent guests to the North Stafford Hotel, so an elegant and comfortable reception room was necessary. Carriages were sent to Stoke Station to meet important guests and convey them to the pottery. These would include the many travellers and agents who sold Copeland's ware, as well as important retailers like Thomas Goode of Mayfair and Mr Daniell of Wigmore Street, London who came to be shown the latest designs (Colour Plates 72 to 75). The carriages would draw up at the central door which is shown on the plans and the visitors would be entertained in the long room, suitably impressed by the furnishings and the displays of superb porcelain. New ideas and designs and orders for existing lines would be discussed here in

Colour Plate 75. Copeland bone china nightlight lighthouse. Mark 235.
Copeland China Collection, Cornwall

Plate 61. Heads of departments, names unknown, taken c.1900 in front of the Parian statue of Cupid and the Swan.

comfort and privacy. The building was originally used to keep special pieces of ware which were design samples for the decorating department. Later fine examples of many factories, such as Sèvres, Meissen, early oriental and saltglazed pieces collected by the Copeland family, were displayed here. Now the building is part of the Spode Visitors Centre.

A large Parian sculpture of Cupid and the Swan, of which many photographs have been taken, used to stand in front of this building (Plate 61). It was thought to have been moulded by George Perry, the father of Arthur Perry, one of Copeland's famous artists. A family story tells of how the sculpture was damaged one night by a night-watchman who had imbibed too freely. Catching a somewhat bleary view of the figure he challenged it. Naturally it did not respond so the pot-valiant guardian fired his blunderbuss at it, badly damaging an arm. This story may be apocryphal, but it is one of the legends of the old pottery.

We have seen that throughout this period there was more mechanisation and more changes in the site itself, but the main changes came in the working conditions. It was a time of growing concern and action to improve the health and safety of factory workers, both adults and children; laws were passed and inspectors appointed – not always to the satisfaction of the workers who were very much inclined to resent any change in working practices which had been the norm in their fathers' and grandfathers' days. The workers did, however, approve of the new system of payment of wages. The old days of the annual hiring had gone; workers were paid a weekly wage at piece work rates with a month's notice on either side. Trade disputes were dealt with by the Joint Board of Arbitration and Conciliation from 1868, though the awards made by them were not regarded as satisfactory and in 1892 it was dissolved, being replaced by a Joint Committee of Conciliation. This lapsed in 1897 because the pottery workers had little faith in it. The National Order of Potters was revived in 1883, merging with the Hollow Ware Pressers Union in 1898, but on the whole the pottery workers preferred to negotiate their pay with their own masters.

In the late 1800s the Home Office produced a series of statistics which showed that the lead used in glazing was indeed a health hazard. The reported cases of plumbism (i.e. lead poisoning) in 1898 were stated as 386 out of the 4,703 workers who were exposed to the risk No details of the illness were given but directives were sent to manufacturers and workers to alert them to the dangers.[1] The other disease, which became known as Potters' Asthma, locally called Potters' Rot, and which was due to the dust generated in many departments, was stated in a report as not being so prevalent as it had been in the 1840s, because of an improvement in food and working conditions, but was still a health hazard, the dust particles causing irreparable damage to the workers' lungs. The Home Office was adamant that workers must be taught better hygiene. They must no longer eat or cook their meals in the affected departments. Washing facilities must be provided by the employer and the workers supervised to ensure that they washed thoroughly before leaving the workplace so that they did not carry dust into their homes or the works dining room. This caused some friction with the workers, who took the view that these diseases would happen to someone else and, in addition, their wages would suffer as a result of all this washing.

The Home Office appointed a Select Committee to look into conditions. They proposed that brooms should be provided in all areas and there must be no cooking or food in the following areas: dipping house, dippers' drying room, scouring room, glost placers' shop, ground laying shops or the majolica painting room. In addition, all rooms must be ventilated to remove the dust in the air. This had, in fact, been attempted in Spode's day. A fan had been installed in the ground layers' shop which collected the loose ceramic colour and sent it to a box under the bench. All the loose colour was mixed together in the box and it is said that the colour was collected and used again, the resulting hue being known as Spode's Green. One is tempted to think that the fan was installed more in the name of economy than for the benefit of the workers.

The Home Office decreed that after August 1899 no person under the age of eighteen should be employed in the danger areas. All workers employed in the designated areas must be examined at the factory every month for signs of lead poisoning, a practice which continued well into the 1950s. No food or drink was to be taken into the workplace and protective clothing, supplied by

1. W. Burton, *The Use of Lead Compounds from the Potter's Point of View* (London, Simkin, Marshall, Hamilton and Co., 1899).

Colour Plate 78 (Opposite, above left). Unusual earthenware transfer printed piece thought to have been a wig warmer but often shown as a doorstop, 1880s. Mark 147, pattern B573.
Photograph George Worlock. Private Collection

Colour Plate 79 (Opposite, above right). Copeland bone china spoon warmer, impressed 1883. Photograph Robert Copeland. Private Collection

Colour Plate 76 (above). Copeland majolica vase. Impressed Copeland mark 202. Height 9in. (23cm).
Photograph George Worlock

Colour Plate 77 (right). Copeland vase with sprigged scene of Columbus landing in America in 1492 produced for Burley & Co. of Chicago in 1892 to commemorate the 400th anniversary. Copeland England impressed. Mark 349.

Colour Plate 80. Copeland bone china jewelled tray. A family piece displaying the family crest with jewelling and raised and chased gold. Copeland China Collection, Cornwall

the employer, must be worn. A list of workers in the danger areas must be kept ready to be shown to the Factory Inspectors. The order also insisted that every effort must be made to find a lead-free glaze.

The boards on which the ware was carried were to be scrubbed by being fed through a machine with two rotating brush rollers (Plate 62). This method of cleaning the boards also continued long into the 1950s. Personal hygiene in all areas was updated with the compulsory provision of soap and towels in the lavatories.

In common with all industrial towns, the atmosphere surrounding the pottery towns was foul with thick black smoke from factory and household chimneys. Washing hung out to dry often came in dirtier than when it went out and lung ailments were rife, even in people who did not work in the local industries. In Stoke there was a body of men called the Smoke Commissioners, whose task it was to investigate all complaints regarding smoke emission from the pottery chimneys, with the power to fine all offenders. The potteries were each allowed a certain time in the day in which to fire their ovens – a rule which was often broken. Copelands, in spite of having Edward Copeland as one of the Smoke Commissioners, was one of the worst culprits. On one occasion Edward promised to deal with the problem, but the Commissioners were not impressed, and sent a formal complaint to the board of Copelands. The problem of smoke belching from the ovens was not to be completely solved until the 1950s when coal was largely replaced by gas and electricity. The health of the community suffered to such an extent that even many years

Plate 62. Workers carrying the ware on a board, September 1900.
Photograph William Fowler Mountford Copeland

Weekly Wages in the Pottery Industry c.1750

Worker	Wage		Earnest★	
	s.	d.	s.	d.
Thrower	8	0	42	0
Turner	8	0	42	0
Handler	7	0	10	6
Ornamenter	6	6	15	0
Ovenman	5	6	2	0
Placer	5	6	3	0
Fireman	5	3	5	0
Boy Lathe-treader	2	0		6
Girl Flowerer	1	0		

Based on Thomas Whieldon's Notebook in The Potteries City Museum
★ Money given on token of a bargain made

Weekly Wages in the Pottery Industry 1769

Worker	Wage
Gilder (man)	12s.
Gilder (woman)	7s.6d.
Painter	10s. to 12s.
Engine Lathe Man	10s. to 12s.
Thrower	9s. to 12s.
Handler	9s. to 12s.
Ornamenter	9s. to 12s.
Presser	8s. to 9s.
Plaster-of-Paris Moulder	8s.
Washer and Breaker	8s.
Grinder	7s.
Modeller	one of £100 a year

Based on A. Young, A Six Months Tour through the North of England (1770), iii, 306-9 (wages paid at Wedgwood's factory)

Weekly Wages in the Pottery Industry 1841

Worker	Wage
	s.
Thrower	40
Painter of landscapes and flowers	40
Platemaker	38
Turner	32
Dipper	32
Presser	30
Slipmaker	29
Warehouseman	24
Gilder	24
Groundlayer	24
Ovenman	18
Sliphouseman	18
Lathe-treader	10
Scourer	10
Transferrer	10
Thrower's woman	9
Children	2s. ½d (average)

Based on 2nd Rep. Com Child. Emp., App, Pt. I [431], H.C. (1843), xiv.

Weekly Wages in the Pottery Industry 1877, 1908 and 1924

Worker	1877		1908		1924★	
	s.	d.	s.	d.	s.	d.
Thrower	37	6	27	10	76	2
Turner	29	0	26	10	58	9
Handler	28	0	28	2	52	4
Hollow-ware Presser	28	0	24	9	48	5
Flat-ware Presser	28	0	28	9	55	5
Mouldmaker	28	0	38	0	68	0
Printer	24	0	24	3	51	0
Jiggerer			35	1	67	9
Ovenman			30	0	56	4

Based on Warburton, Trade Union Org. in N. Staffs. Potteries, 244-5, 247.

★The average earnings in 1924 in these trades were 59s.4d.; in the same year the average possible earnings (for a 47-hour week) were 73s.8d.

Average Earnings in the Pottery Industry 1938-63

	1938	1947	1963
Men	116s. 8d	127s. 2d.	317s.11d.
Youths and Boys	40s. 5d	53s. 4d.	156s. 1d
Women			
full-time	48s. 4d.	65s. 9d.	154s. 6d
part-time		32s.11½d	88s. 2d.
Girls	21s. 9d.	45s. 1d.	107s. 7d.

Based on figures in Min. of Labour Gaz. April 1948 and February 1964. The figures for 1938 have been deduced from the percentage increase stated for 1947.

Minton Artists' Annual Salaries 1868 and 1882

	Occupation	1868	1882
		£	£
Leon Arnoux	Art Director	1,200	1,500
Marc Louis Solon	Pâte-sur-pâte Artist	400	800
Antonin Boullemier	Figure -painter	400	205
Paul Comolera	Modeller	210	
John Henk	Modeller	151	
Edmund Reuter	Designer		250
W.H. Foster	Figure-painter	275	
Thomas Allen	Figure-painter	160	
Thomas Kirkby	Figure-painter	156	
Aaron Green	Gilder	117	
Richard Tilsbury	Flower-painter	117	
Charles Toft	Ornamenter	164	

Based on Salaries Book at Mintons

(See page 116)

Colour Plate 81. Copeland bone china jewelled vases. Left: height 8⅛in. (20.6cm), mark 252a. Right: height 4¼in. (10.8cm), mark 235.
Photograph Robert Copeland

Colour Plate 82. Copeland bone china Gordon tray. Mark 235.
Photograph Mark Diamond. Private Collection

Colour Plate 83 (opposite). Copeland bone china Chatsworth shape vase exhibited at the London exhibition of 1871. Bird painting attributed to C. Weaver. Copeland China Collection, Cornwall

Colour Plate 84. Copeland bone china centrepiece, mark 241. This plain pure white form of statuary was most popular in the early 1900s. Copeland China Collection, Cornwall

Plate 63. Copeland bone china teapot, sugar, cream and cup and saucer, shape Charlotte. This service is hand painted in iron red and richly gilt. Copeland China Collection, Cornwall

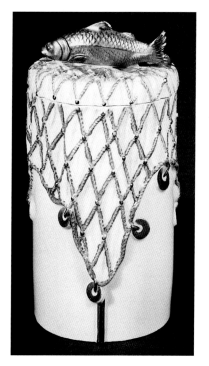

Plate 65. Copeland bone china fish paste jar. Mark 235. Private Collection

Plate 64. Copeland bone china bouillon set, print and enamel. Mark 235. Diameter 8in. (20.3cm). Photograph Jack Shaw. Private Collection

114

Plate 66. Copeland bone china revolving coffee set, Chelsea shape, decorated with the 'Willow' pattern. Mark 235. Copeland China Collection, Cornwall

after retiring old pottery workers had chronic chest complaints. They used to talk of how they managed to dodge the medical examinations and how they never really stopped eating at the workplace. It was only in later years that they realised the risks they were taking with their own health. Workers were encouraged, in their free time, to use the local amenities, to take advantage of cheap day returns to the seaside, run by the North Staffordshire Railway company, where they would benefit from fresh air and relaxation.

1868 was a particularly bad year for trade. Many of the potteries were taking orders at reduced prices in order to keep their works open, but the workers' wages were maintained at the usual level. It was hoped that the workers would remember this when trade picked up and they wanted to negotiate a rise in pay! The *Staffordshire Advertiser* of 20 November 1869 reported that few potteries were on full-time working but that the colonial trade had improved and that Italy, Russia and Turkey were increasing their orders for earthenware.

In 1871 there was an attempt by the pottery manufacturers to fix agreed prices for earthenware for the American market. The *Staffordshire Advertiser*

Colour Plate 85. Copeland china Gordon tray and coffee can decorated with the 'Trusty Servant', c.1890s. Mark 235. The original painting hangs in the entrance to the kitchen of Winchester College. Copeland China Collection, Cornwall

reported on 18 February that a meeting had been held in Hanley of all the earthenware manufacturers at which it was decided to raise the price of round flatware and jugs, ewers and bowls by 15%. Meetings similar to this were held throughout Victoria's reign, sometimes to raise the cost of ware and some-times to maintain or lower prices, depending on the vagaries of trade. But a common policy was easier to decide upon than to put into practice. Each manufacturer was fiercely independent and did not always stick to the agreed policy, which created many arguments.

The tables on page 111 show the wages paid in the pottery industry from about 1750 to 1963.[2] When carefully studied, they paint a picture of not only the different workers' jobs but, since they include the Minton artists' wages, they can be compared with those of the Copeland artists. Wages were always kept as secret as possible, but it is reasonable to assume that these tables provide a rough guide to the changes in pay throughout the industry. There is little doubt that employers always claimed that they paid higher wages than was the norm and that the unions always asked for greater rises than they were prepared to accept. Also, some processes could demand higher rates than others. Even though piecework rates were low, a decent living wage could be earned when orders were coming in and by the efforts of the individual worker. After the jigger and jolley were introduced in the platemaking and hollowware departments, a jiggerer was thought to have earned 7s. a day in 1883, but by 1908 this had gone down to 35s. a week.

Child labour was as prevalent in the Potteries as it was in other industries. Children were sent to work at the age of five or six and were expected to work for as much as seventy-two hours a week for a wage of sixpence or a shilling a week. We have no details of child labour at the Spode works but there is no reason to assume that it was any different from other factories. The child's tiny wage brought in much-needed money.

2. *The Victorian History of the Counties of England: A History of the County of Stafford*, ed. M.W. Greenslade and J.G. Jenkins (London, O.U.P., 1967), pages 47-51. Or *The Victorian History of the Counties of England* edited by R.B. Pugh (The University of London Institute of Historical Research University Press, 1967).

Colour Plate 86. Copeland bone china cup and saucer, pattern D1188. Mark 235. Copeland China Collection, Cornwall

In 1879 The Forster Elementary Education Act brought compulsory education for all children, even though it was limited to part-time schooling. The Act established School Boards, members of which were elected by the local ratepayers. The Boards had the power to order the building of schools and to appoint an attendance officer to compel parents to send their children to school. The School Board Man was known and disliked by parents who felt that their children were better off earning money and learning a trade, but successive Factory and Workshops Acts brought full-time education for all children under the age of eleven, as well as improving the conditions and hours of young workers.

It is difficult to give accurate figures for artists' wages in this period. For example, the Special Order Reference Books at the Spode works do from time to time give the pay for some hand painting. Artists could earn 10s.6d. to 15s. for landscape work, but it is not shown how many dessert plates they painted for this sum, or how many hours' work was involved. Special exhibition vases could have earned the artist 10s. or more for each painting. If the vase had a landscape on one side and a floral study on the other, each would have been done to a different price. This also applied to the gilders, who were paid for the piece and for the intricacy of the decoration. Charles

Plate 67. Advertisement from the Staffordshire Advertiser *5 January 1895.*

Ferdinand Hürten, Copeland's acclaimed floral artist, was given a contract which states that he was to be paid £350 a year, a substantial sum of money in those days.

The advertisement from the *Staffordshire Advertiser* of Saturday 5 January 1895 (Plate 67) contains material quoted and referred to in this chapter, and, in addition, Parian figures and jewelled ware. The claim that Copelands could make 'non-crazing' ceramic ware caused problems, because some of it did craze.

This was the era when the aristocracy ordered not only special dessert services, beautifully decorated and hand painted, but also the 'bread and butter' products of the manufactory – jelly moulds and cooking dishes of all shapes and sizes. The traditional blue and white earthenware remained a firm selling line. It would be impossible to record the total range of pieces made in this period, but one which deserves special mention is the repeat order in 1888 for the Prince of Wales Service, again commissioned by Thomas Goode, the famous London showroom in South Audley Street, Mayfair, for the Corporation of the City of London as a present to H.R.H Albert Edward, Prince of Wales. Hürten was still working for Copelands and was able once again to create his renowned floral studies.

Thomas Battam, who died in 1864, had been succeeded by George Eyre, although exactly when is not known with any certainty. It is thought that he was Art Director from 1868-1880. The *Art Journal* catalogue of the 1868 Paris Exhibition gives special praise to the Copeland exhibits, particularly emphasising the use of nature on the china decoration, saying that Mr. Eyre was a worthy successor to Mr. Battam. Eyre in turn was succeeded by Robert

Frederick Abraham, who worked closely with Richard Pirie Copeland. Together the two men created a display for the Paris Exhibition of 1889, which so impressed Thomas Goode that they bought every exhibit before the exhibition opened.

The influence of Thomas Goode, with their luxurious showrooms in Mayfair, cannot be over-estimated.[3] Established in 1827, they had, within six months, secured orders from such exalted names as the Earl of Sefton and Prince Esterhazy. This early success was maintained and by 1858 they were supplying china to Queen Victoria. Their forte lay in the field of special orders, some of which were supplied by W.T. Copeland & Sons bearing the backstamps of Thomas Goode and Copeland. In the Spode archives there still exists a special order book for Thomas Goode alone. Special sample plates were prepared with new patterns to show the buyers in the hope of large orders, for no effort was spared in the battle to wrest Goode's business away from Copeland's great rivals Minton. So, Richard Pirie Copeland must have been highly delighted when Goode's bought all the exhibits at the Paris Exhibition, though there was one slight problem – the clash of personalities between Robert Frederick Abraham and William Goode. However, this letter, found in the Goode archives, shows that it was not allowed to stand in the way of business. Written by William Goode to Richard Pirie Copeland from the Hotel Continental, Paris, 28 September 1889, it reads:[4]

Dear Copeland

Mr. Abraham's trite remark made several months that 'if l could make Minton's when a boy I could do the same for you now I am a man' has been verified by the result of the Exhibition for as l telephoned to you this morning you have gained the Grand Prix…This important fact is due, I consider, to your readiness to back my efforts and to your last appearance here to meet the jury.

The remark about Minton's no doubt alludes to the Paris Exhibition of 1878 when it was Minton's who were awarded the Grand Prix and whose exhibits were sold to Goode.

The following extracts from the correspondent of the *Staffordshire Advertiser,* 28 May, describes Copeland's exhibits at the Paris Exhibition of 1889 and makes an interesting reference to the feeling that artists' names should be known.

MESSRS COPELAND & SONS, STOKE-ON-TRENT,

who exhibit in their name but whose splendid collection has been purchased by Messrs T. Goode and Co., South Audley Street. The last named house is acting as agent for several other leading firms, and fills with a superb display of pottery and glass not fewer than three large courts. Messrs Copeland's collection is in every respect – novelty, variety, technical skill and artistic merit – worthy of their historic reputation. We had the advantage of the courteous guidance of Mr. Herbert Goode, for it is a distinct advantage to the newspaper correspondent to be

3. P.M. Raynor, *Thomas Goode of London* (London, privately published).
4. Letter in the Trelissick Archives.

119

Colour Plate 87. Copeland bone china Goldsmith shape vase painted and signed by C.F. Hürten. Mark 235. Note the fine gilded decoration to the handles and gold border of the vase. Private Collection

relieved to some extent of that embarrassment which comes of artistic riches (newspaper correspondents are seldom embarrassed with any other kind) and to have his attention directed with intelligence and celerity to the object most deserving of notice. Before we go any further let one explanatory word be permitted. We strongly favour the publication of the names of artists and never with hold them if once they come to our knowledge. This seem to us to be a matter of the simplest justice, and if in these articles, or at any other time, an artist misses the mention of his name he will kindly remember this declaration of our own feeling on the subject. Having said that we find that the explanatory word must be explained. We had not Messrs Copeland specially in mind in the remarks just made.

Colour Plate 88. Copeland bone china framed plaque. The scene of Warwick Castle is painted and signed by W. Yale.

Of its kind, the most distinguished and novel among Messrs Copeland's exhibits is a china dessert service, entitled the 'Midsummer Night's Dream' service. It has been specially modelled by Mr. Owen Hale. The centrepiece is composed of a sleeping figure of Titania, canopied over by the branches of a tree, and surrounded by foxgloves and other wild flowers. There are eight tall comports, the dish in each instance being supported by a composition of a tree-stem, covered with clinging or trailing plants, and a graceful fairy form. The comports are taller than usual, so that the artist has free play in modelling the figures. There are many low comports, supported by elves and pixies. All the figures are pure white, and the other accessories are touched with half-tones of colour. Each plate bears a named subject from the play, and these illustrations have been beautifully painted by Mr. S. Alcock. The whole was designed and arranged under the superintendence of Mr. R.F. Abraham.

Two plates, painted by Mr. Alcock, have subjects after Angelica Kauffmann; immediately outside each plate is a band of turquoise blue, while the whole is enclosed in a richly painted and jewelled rim. These choice specimens are daintily bestowed in velvet-lined cases. The same artist has on a pair of oviform vases two figure subjects a lady playing on a guitar and another lady for whose thoughts one might be induced to offer the customary penny were there any doubt as to the nature of her pleasant reflections.

Robert Abraham had in his department some of the finest ceramic artists in the industry at that time – for example, Alcock with his figure painting, Hürten with floral studies and Yale with landscapes. Many of Copeland's artists' finest pieces do not bear their names and it is only by style and quality that we can give credit to their skill (Colour Plates 87 to 89).

Plate 68. Copeland earthenware service, gadroon, game subjects with Tower border. Impressed Copeland, c.1880s. Each plate has a different bird depicted.

Plate 69. Copeland earthenware dessert service, Chelsea shape, impressed 1884.
Copeland China Collection, Cornwall

When Robert Frederick Abraham died in 1895, Alfred Copeland[5] wrote of him:

> Abraham from Coalport came on through Fred Painter the traveler, son of old Painter in ancient days and known as Copeland's Elephant. Abraham died this September, an excellent man knowing the styles and intricacies of Sevres, Dresden and Chelsea.

Plate 70. Copeland eggshell porcelain jewelled vases made for the 1872 London exhibition.
Copeland China Collection, Cornwall

Abraham was succeeded by his son Francis Xavier Abraham.

Despite difficult trading conditions, W.T. Copeland & Sons were prosperous. The fame they acquired at the exhibitions and a reputation for fine quality ware served them well. As well as fine china, Copelands had produced for the earlier London Exhibition of 1871 large earthenware slabs, some measuring 40in. x 18in. (102cm x 46cm). Painted by Hürten, they were praised by the critics as the body and glaze was so good that it was thought that they were made of porcelain. Another curiosity at the same exhibition was a special section in which Copelands were showing hand-painted tea and coffee services of a very high standard of painting. All painted by women, they were less expensive to buy than those done by men and were a great success. At this time ware was marketed with the impressed backstamp of COPELAND, sometimes with the name of the body added – Copeland White Body used on hotel ware, Copeland with a crown denoting Crown body 1860-1869. Sometimes Spode was added on ivory coloured earthenware bodies, Copeland Spode Imperial c.1890, Copeland with the crossed Cs, seen on bone china, and on earthenware Copeland late Spode. An impressed date mark can often be seen as well.

5. Alfred Copeland's Diaries 1895-1908.

Colour Plate 89. Copeland bone china dessert plate, Richelieu shape, painted by Samuel Alcock c.1880s, part of a large dessert service decorated with one of the paintings called Gainsborough heads that were very popular in America. The jewelling on the border is attributed to Coxon.

This advertisement (Plate 71) for a Mandarin cream jug (Colour Plate 90) shows not only the variety of ware available, for it was made in china and in majolica, but also illustrates the selling techniques of the time.

The steady flow of orders received at the factory for everyday ware and prestigious services kept the firm in good heart. However, if Richard Pirie Copeland had taken the advice of his brother William and expanded the range

FOUND IN A MANDARIN'S POCKET

A little china figure on a little bracket sat,
His little legs were always crossed, he wore a little hat,
And every morning, fair or foul, as shine a shadow dim,
A pretty little housemaid came and softly dusted him.

She took him up so gently and with such a charming air,
His china heart was melted quite, he loved her to despair;
All day he sat and thought of her until the twilight came,
And in his china dreams at night he softly breathed her name.

One day while being dusted, in his joy he trembled so
To feel her little fingers, that alas she let him go,
In vain she tried to grab him back, fate willed that they should part,
He fell against the fender edge and broke his china heart.

She gathered up the fragments and told a little lie,
Expounding to her mistress how the cat had made him die,
And on the following morning, when the shutters back were thrust,
She spoke his little epitaph, "there's one thing less to dust."

W. T. COPELAND & SONS, MANUFACTURERS,
STOKE-UPON-TRENT

WHITE CHINA,
1/- each.

WHITE
WITH GOLD EDGE
AND SOLID
GOLD HANDLE,
2/3 each.

TURQUOISE AND
GOLD, 0349,
2/9 each.

SLIGHTLY
DECORATED, 0650,
1/9 each.

RICHLY
DECORATED
12/- each.

THE "MANDARIN" CREAM JUG

Colour Plate 90. Copeland bone china 'Mandarin' milk jugs, impressed date 1874. Photograph George Worlock. Private Collection

Plate 71 (left). Advertisement for the Mandarin cream jug.

of products into sanitary ware, the business would have been even more prosperous at the beginning of the new century. Alfred Copeland says (October 1904)

Had my brother gone into sanitary ware a large lucrative business had been established but the opportunity slipped by, we were behind the times.

Things did not always run smoothly. The trade in 'consignment goods' had been, in theory, very lucrative in the early part of the century when operated by William Copeland, but it had one serious drawback. The various china houses and agents abroad placed orders but only paid on receipt of the goods. If the ship carrying those goods went down, as was highly likely on voyages to Brazil or Peru, the enterprise was literally a dead loss, to be borne by the firm. Alfred wrote in 1905:

Plate 72. Mrs. Bruce,
9 October 1901. A paintress
at Copelands for over fifty
years, she specialised in
painting cornflower studies.
Photograph William
Mountford Copeland

Consigning goods to Bahai, Lima and Army colonial ports upon indents furnished by the houses abroad, was a disastrous proceeding. Money being wanted my brother William loaned some to my father and the consigning trade was stopped not a minute too soon and the ship [the business] righted itself.

William Fowler Mountford Copeland was a good enough businessman to see the dangers and had to take the necessary steps.

Another problem arose in 1878 with the realisation that the trade figures for Copeland's warehouse at New Bond Street were far below what they should have been. Investigation led to the admission by the then manager, Mr. Andrews, that he had been using the firm's money to bet on horses. As he had been a personal friend of the family, no one had had any suspicion of his embezzlement until after the Alderman had died. Eventually he paid back £3,000 or £4,000, but admitted to Alfred that the total sum was £33,000. Auditors were called in and found a deficit of £27,000. Andrews had also been in charge of Selina and Emma Copeland's affairs, but there seems to have been no dishonesty there. He was not taken to court because, as Alfred wrote:

Had we prosecuted, disagreeable matters with the family affairs might have crept out?.

Despite more research the 'disagreeable family matters' still remain a secret to this day. Alfred implies in his diary that the knowledge of his guilt shortened Andrews' life for he died shortly afterwards.

After the 1889 Exhibition the next ten to fifteen years were a period of steady success as the orders flowed in. There was the opportunity for artists

Plate 73. Mrs Edith Blackburn, a highly skilled gilder, 18 July 1899. Photograph William Mountford Copeland

and gilders to exercise all their various skills to the full (Colour Plate 91), but by 1892 their numbers were decreasing. Highly decorated ware was becoming too expensive and less fashionable. In 1895 the showroom stock shows a description of the piece, the cost of manufacture and the selling price.[6] A Goldsmiths' shape vase, painted by Hürten, with roses on one side and chrysanthemums on the other on an ivory and chocolate background richly gilt, cost £2.17s.6d., yet was put for sale at fifty-five guineas. There is also a document which implies that Mr. Alcock had some of his private stock on show at the Copeland showroom at the Spode works; when it was sold the factory would get 25% of the selling price.

In January 1897[7] the Prince and Princess of Wales paid a private visit to the Duke and Duchess of Sutherland at Trentham Hall. The Prince of Wales had been asked, in his capacity as Grand Master of English Free-masons, to lay the foundation stone for the new Sutherland Institute at Longton, which was to be the new library and technical school for the borough. The Princess of Wales, meantime, was to visit W.T. Copeland's & Sons and the Minton, Hollins & Co. Tile works. The report mentioned the heads of department unfortunately without naming their departments, but some of them we know. Mr. Bennett was in charge of the showroom, F. Hammersley (Fred) was one of the foremost floral artists of his day and F.X. Abraham was the head of the art department. Mrs. Bruce (Plate 72), well known for her cornflower and poppy painting, was head of the paintresses and responsible for the quality of their painting which had been so praised at the 1871 Paris Exhibition. Mrs Blackburn (Plate 73) was head of the burnishing shop, Mr. R. Wallace

6. Keele University Library: Spode MS. 109.
7. *Staffordshire Advertiser,* 6 January 1897.

Colour Plate 91. Copeland bone china St. George shape dessert plate c.1880s, attributed to Lucien Besche. Private Collection

was the gilder whose indenture is mentioned in Chapter 2, while Mr C. Brough (Charlie) was an excellent artist who was with Copeland's for many years.

In 1895, this notice appeared in the *Staffordshire Advertiser* announcing the retirement of William Fowler Mountford Copeland, much to everyone's surprise:

OCTOBER 1895.

Notice is hereby given that the PARTNERSHIP which has for some time past been carried on by WILLIAM FOWLER MOUNTFORD COPELAND and RICHARD PIRIE COPELAND under the style of firm of W.T. Copeland & Sons at No 12 Charterhouse Street London & Stoke upon Trent in the trade or business of China and earthenware Manufacturers and Merchants was this day DISSOLVED by mutual consent and the business will in future be carried on under the same style by the said RICHARD PIRIE COPELAND alone. As witness our hands the first day of October 1895 WILLIAM FOWLER MOUNTFORD COPELAND AND RICHARD PIRIE COPELAND.

Witness to the signatures of the said W.F.M. & R.P. COPELAND –
GEORGE F. PADDOCK,
Solicitor Hanley.

He retired to Quarry House, St. Leonard's-on-Sea, where he indulged his hobby of gardening, leaving the firm in the hands of his youngest brother. Richard Pirie Copeland was now sole owner of the pottery. The next few years were ones of continued success, with 1899 recording one of the best years' trading in the industry. The following excerpts from selling brochures show the variety of ware being produced.

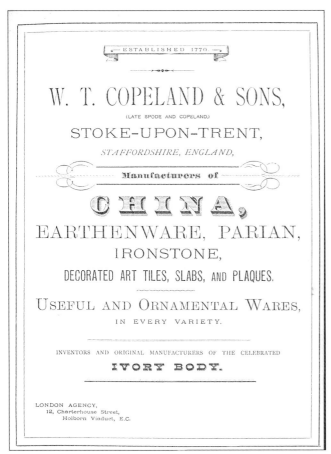

c.1900

c.1910

W. T. COPELAND & SONS, STOKE-UPON-TRENT.

"DAISY & GRASS"
BLACK, BROWN,
SAXON BLUE OR PINK.

"CAIRO"
BLACK, BROWN, GREEN, PINK,
OR SAXON BLUE

"STORK"
BROWN OR COBALT BLUE

Y^E STORK
INVITETH
Y^E FOX
TO DINNER

"FABLES"
BROWN OR BLACK

"DUNCAN SCENES"
BLACK, BROWN OR BLUE

"FERN"
BROWN OR BLACK

"PRIMROSE"
BLACK, BROWN, BLUE OR GREEN

"STRAWBERRY"
BLACK OR BROWN

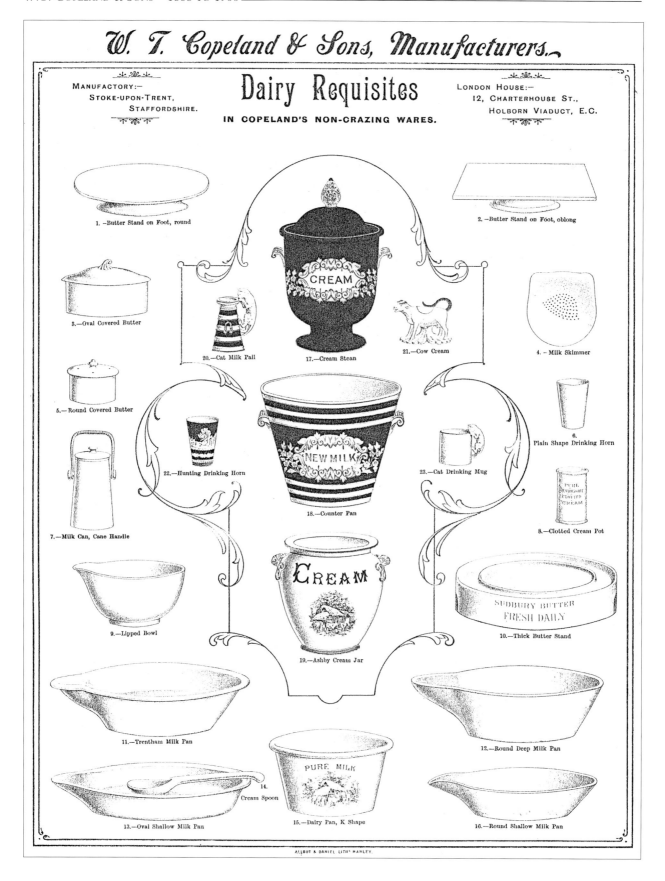

COPELAND'S NON-CRAZING CHINA.

9

$\frac{1}{9333}$

$\frac{1}{9554}$

$\frac{1}{9554}$

$\frac{1}{9555}$

$\frac{1}{9554}$

$\frac{1}{9105}$

$\frac{1}{6237}$

$\frac{1}{7767}$

$\frac{1}{6237}$

$\frac{1}{8760}$

$\frac{1}{9546}$

W. T. COPELAND & SONS' China Dessert Services Burnished Gold Decorations.

67. Gadroon Dessert

66. St. George Shape

68. Nemo Shape

69. Coventry Dessert and Fruit Basket

71. Bow Flute
Dessert Dishes and Plate

70. Richelieu

72. Madrid

73. Primula Dessert and Fruit Dish

75. Belinda Dessert and Fruit Basket

74. Queen Anne

76. Chelsea Shape

Manufactory: STOKE-UPON-TRENT.   London Address: 12 Charterhouse St., E.C.

Octagon

Napier

Dresden

Melon

Steamer

Beaufort

Low Dutch

Florentine

Avon

TEA POTS

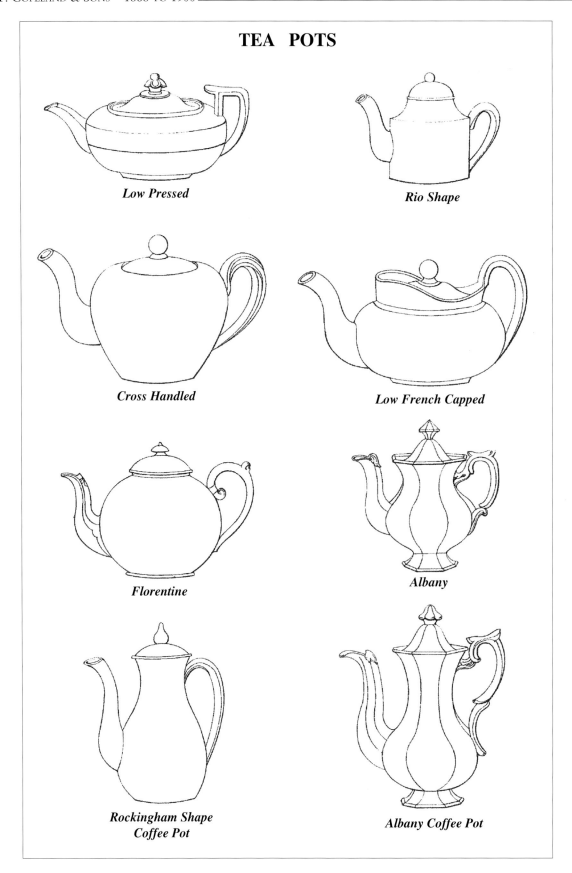

Low Pressed

Rio Shape

Cross Handled

Low French Capped

Florentine

Albany

*Rockingham Shape
Coffee Pot*

Albany Coffee Pot

In July 1900 another Royal visit occurred, this time by the Duke and Duchess of York, who drove with the Duchess of Sutherland in two open carriages from Trentham Hall. Richard Pirie had printed a booklet entitled Copeland (late Spode) China in which the Royal visit is recorded.

Much interest was evinced in the throwing, turning and china casting, and by the desire of the Duchess of Sutherland, the dipping house was also visited. His Royal Highness found this department of captivating interest, particularly the application of the glaze to the bisque. Many were the practical and searching inquiries to various technical parts which the Duke addressed to the head of the firm, and a thorough explanation was given. The improved system of the Home Office as embodied in the new rules – viz.: the cleaning of the glaze when dry over water – called forth expressions of approval. The next move took the party to an earthenware bisque oven which was in course of being filled. Their Royal Highnesses entered the oven and the various processes of placing the ware were explained. The contraction of a Parian figure in the course of firing, illustrated by the comparison of an unfired and fired figure called forth surprised comment from the party. The groundlaying shop was next inspected and here the new fan for drawing the dust away from the worker suggested by Mr. Osborne of the Home Office, was seen in operation and fully explained. Its efficient and beneficial working greatly pleased their Royal Highnesses as an ingenious and valuable factor in minimising the dangers of the work.

Millicent Duchess of Sutherland (Meddling Millie to the Master Potters) was a keen advocate of the new lead regulations, hence the interest shown on the tour of the works. The article also describes many pieces which were on display as well as the special pieces presented to the Royal visitors.

Richard Pirie Copeland took the family business into the new century, still at the forefront of British pottery making, thanks to his unrivalled grasp of the art of potting and his business brain. It was to be a century which was to see many upheavals and changes, changes that would alter both society and the potting industry in ways which could never have been dreamed of by Josiah Spode I.

Chapter 5

TWENTIETH CENTURY COPELAND AND SPODE

1900-1970

Richard Pirie Copeland (1841-1913), the third generation of the Copeland family, was the first member to make his home in Staffordshire. He married Emily Henrietta Wood of the Wood potting family. He became Mayor of the Borough of Stoke-upon-Trent from 1875-1877 and in 1881, as an Alderman of the town council, served on the General Purposes, Market and Works committee, and the Baths and Free Library committee. Richard Pirie served the County of Staffordshire as a Justice of the Peace and a member of the Staffordshire County Council for over thirty years. He became High Sheriff, and in 1902 a Deputy Lieutenant of the County.

Richard Pirie loved the Spode works and used every opportunity to improve the site. On 2 July 1902 a fire unfortunately broke out in the turning and throwing shops, and demolished the biscuit warehouse. The fire was so fierce that it took the combined efforts of Hanley, Longton, Fenton, Stoke and North Staffordshire fire brigades, as well as Copeland's own fire engine, before the blaze was extinguished. William Fowler Mountford, Richard Pirie's eldest son, took photographs which record the disaster (Plate 74). Copelands were awarded £1,500 damages from the Northern Insurance Company, which Richard Pirie used wisely to rebuild and improve this area.

Plate 75. The Spode factory decorated for the visit of King George V and Queen Mary, 1913.

On 22 April 1913 King George V and Queen Mary honoured the Spode works with a visit (Plates 75 and 76) and were escorted by Richard Pirie's sons, Ronald and Gresham. Their father, who had planned the visit, had unfortunately died only the month before, on 13 March 1913. He had been a fine Master Potter, well respected by the workers, and a friend to those in need. However, when his notebook, dated 1879, was found in the Trelissick archives[1] in the late 1980s, only then was it realised how Richard Pirie had improved the quality of the ware by the experiments he had conducted. He had analysed the well and canal water on the site which was used in the

1. Richard Pirie's notebook in the Trelissick Archives.

Plate 76. Copeland pen and ink set used by important visitors when they entered the old Spode showroom and signed the visitors' book.

139

Plate 77 (right). Plate making in the early 1930s at W.T. Copeland and Sons.
Photograph Harold Holdway

Plate 78 (below). Mrs. Ball's painting shop, c.1930s. Left Mrs. Ball, right Mrs. Wakefield (née Poppy Hall). Note the pattern book open at the side.

production of the clay, finding impurities such as lime which affected the clay bodies, and he also measured the hardness of the water which affected the water used by the boilers. It is interesting to note that as late as 1940 water from the canal was still used in the boilers and lavatories at the Spode works, although the well water was supplemented with water from the town supply.

After their education at Harrow, all three of Richard Pirie's sons had joined their father at the Spode works learning the art of becoming Master Potters. Richard Ronald John and Alfred Gresham were to became joint partners in the family business. The eldest son, William Fowler Mountford, whilst at Trinity College Cambridge (where he obtained a first class degree in chemistry), experienced a deep Christian conversion which was to change the course of his life. He stayed in the business until 1909 when he married Beatrice Eddes. He and his wife then devoted the rest of their lives to the service of God, preaching to children through the Christian Special Services Mission. Ronald and Gresham Copeland, the fourth generation of Copelands, had to meet the challenge of a changing world, both in trading practices and in new industrial processes.

The first great challenge was the state of the industry after the First World War of 1914-1918 when the value of the pound dropped to 8s.3d. Although there was a trade boom, due to the lack of all commodities, the markets lost during the war years were difficult to regain and in 1921 the great depression came with nearly two million unemployed.

The 'Land fit for Heroes' of post-war Britain saw the break-up of the class system. Many of the old aristocratic families had lost not only their sons, but also many members of their staff, and found they could no longer support an extravagant lifestyle. A

Plate 79. Putting handles on mugs, 18 July 1899.
Photograph William Fowler Mountford Copeland

once profitable market for the pottery industry was sadly depleted.

The status of the workers was also changing in Staffordshire. By 1919 the practice of paying the workers 'Good from Oven' had been abolished in some potteries and workers were being paid 'good from hand'. A working week of forty-seven hours was established and workers' pay strictly controlled. Each employee was given his own disc which he put on the board each morning. This was checked in by the lodge man, who closed the gates at eight each morning; those workers who were late were docked pay. A register was kept of the hours worked and checked by the wages office. At the end of the working week the wages to be paid were put into numbered tins, on trays, and collected by the head of the various departments, who then gave them to his workers in return for a numbered metal disc corresponding with the number on their tin. Each worker checked his pay carefully and secretly, as even now no one knew how much the other had earned. The empty tins were thrown into a large bin, ready for the next week, but were often used by the apprentices as footballs! By 1919 many workers had joined the National Society of Pottery Workers, whilst the Master Potters formed the British Pottery Manufacturers Federation.

As conditions at the works had improved by the early 1900s, changes were taking place in the art department, which were to have far reaching effects. In 1912 Francis Xavier Abraham, a fine figure and floral artist who had followed in his father's footsteps as art superintendent, decided to leave Copelands. Ronald appointed Thomas Hassall as the new Art Director. He was the son of Joseph Hassall, a fine floral artist who worked at Copelands for over thirty years. Thomas was made foreman of the decorating department when only twenty-three years of age, where his duties included passing out the day's work to each painter and fixing the price, just as in the early days of the factory.

However, the role of a twentieth century art director was very different.

Hassall had to be a proven designer and a man of business acumen. His department had to be profitable. His relationship with Ronald was also unique, more that of a works manager than an art director. Hassall's ability to keep his department cost effective in difficult trading conditions was essential to Copeland's success and he turned to old Spode patterns as sources of design. Hassall had a skilled team of artists and gilders including Arthur Perry, Harry Hammersley, Charles Brough and Thomas Sadler, with Charles Deaville in charge of the gilding department.

In 1920 Copelands held a banquet for their work-force to celebrate the 150th anniversary of the founding of the firm.[2] After the celebrations the Copeland brothers turned to the modernisation of the site and in 1923 replaced the old Watt steam engine with a new Bellis and Morcam engine to supply the works with electricity to drive the machinery and provide electric light.

In an article entitled 'Potters of Today', the trade magazine *The Pottery Gazette and Glass Review* wrote of Copelands:

Improvements have been made from time to time during the last eight years and the latest innovation is that of putting down an electric generating station to supply power and light. Each shop has a motor installed, sufficient to supply the power needed for that particular shop. Thus, each workshop is – for power purposes – independent of its neighbour, the current to drive the motor coming from the central station. Any manufacturer who still uses the pulley and rope system will understand and appreciate the immense advantage of such installation.

The brothers now turned their attention to the marketplace. Gresham ran the factory, making sure the quality and tradition of Spode was maintained. This was no mean task: he spent hours on what was known as the 'seconds bench' assessing below standard ware and asking why.

Ronald, however, realised that although trade in America and Canada had always been a significant part of Copelands' success it must be expanded. In 1923 he appointed Sydney Thompson as Copelands' sole agent in America, and in Canada W.A. Duncan. Two new trading companies were set up as Copeland and Thompson Inc., New York, and Copeland and Duncan Ltd., Toronto, Canada (Plate 80). Sydney Thompson insisted on using the name Spode, ordering traditional patterns which were hand printed and painted, and emphasising the factory skills handed down by the Spodes. Sydney Thompson and representatives from Thomas Goode and Daniells of London came to see new patterns for the coming season, many ideas were produced and discussed and sample plates made during their stay until the final decision was made. Some of the artists were allowed to sign their work – examples are appearing in antiques fairs which show the diversity of their talent.

However, unlike his predecessors, Hassall had to cope with a diminishing market for prestige ware. Some of the new more successful patterns, such as Indian Tree, were transfer printed and hand painted by paintresses, working in a shop called 'The Villa', a temporary wooden building. This pattern kept the

2. Celebrations of 150 years of the founding of the firm, 1920, Spode poem and menu, Trelissick Archives.

Plate 80. The management photographed with the American salesmen of Copeland & Thompson, 1950s. Left to right: Ted Hewitt, Spencer Copeland, Robert Copeland, Henry Carlin, F.L. Thorley, Henry Cortez, John Carlin, R.R.J. Copeland, Gordon Hewitt, Gresham Copeland.

paintresses busy the whole of the year; the girls there painted only this one pattern. Hassall was responsible for appointing skilled paintresses to train the young female apprentices. He continued to run the art department throughout the many changes which were to take place on the old site.

Ronald Copeland and his wife Ida toured America and Canada, speaking of the Spode tradition.[3] The new market no longer bought the vast variety of ornaments so beloved by the Victorians. Also, the widespread use of the water closet and piped water meant that toilet sets, once a large part of the market, were now no longer ordered. The way ahead was to cater for the bridal market. Ronald started the idea of selling 'place settings' so that a full dinner or tea service could be built up, decorated with new and traditional designs which, although expensive, would always be available. This was to prove be a lucrative market.

In the early 1900s Richard Pirie had printed a small book *Copelands Late-Spode China*[4] which, using his elder son's photographs, told the story of how the ware was made and the firm's history. Ronald adopted his policy, encouraging authors and collaborating with them; e.g. *Spode and his Successors* by Arthur Hayden. In 1925[5] Ronald produced a small hard-back book with coloured photographs, *The Hunt,* the story of the coachman artist, John Frederick Herring Senior. Herring had been at school with Alderman Copeland who, finding him in financial difficulties, paid off his debts and lent him a cottage on his estate.[6] Herring repaid him by painting some of his successful racehorses. In 1931 the sketches Herring did of the hunt were adapted as decoration on earthenware services which proved very popular; later they were also used on china. The pattern became a best seller, known in Britain as 'Herring Hunting Scenes', but in Germany solely as 'The Hunt'. The European market could not cope with the Herring name, associating it

3. *Milwaukee Journal* Sunday 4 November 1923. Report of Ronald's series of lectures to the Chicago Art Institute. *The Globe,* Toronto, Thursday 18 October 1923. Headed 'Praise for Toronto by English visitor'.
4. *Copeland's (Late Spode) China* (Hanley, privately published c.1900).
5. *The Hunt* (Hanley, privately published c.1900).
6. Alfred Copeland's Diary 1895-1908.

Plate 81. Pieces of Copeland bone china tea service in Stafford shape decorated with 'The Hunt' pattern designed from sketches by J.F. Herring, Senior.
Copeland China Collection, Cornwall

with the fish and not a pattern (Plate 81).

The factory at this time was still using the showroom opened in 1857 and built by Alderman Copeland. Spode I's old façade had been redesigned in the early 1800s by Spode II and a more impressive building was added to the original. It was in this part of the factory that the Alderman created his impressive showroom. Harold Holdway's pen and ink drawing (Plate 82) shows the frontage before it was to be altered yet again in 1929, when Stoke High Street was widened and modern shops were built. However, part of the old buildings were saved and the entrance of today is still part of the original 1800s building.

In 1931 the *Pottery Gazette and Glass Trade Review,* reporting on the visit of the Duke of Kent to the Spode Works, commented on the new façade:

The frontage of the Spode Copeland works has been altered, there has disappeared from view the old archway and the lodge, which controlled access to the factory by inner and outer double gates as well as the warning bell and the

Plate 82. A composite pen and ink drawing of the Spode factory frontage before it was altered in 1929.
Harold Holdway, 1993.

Plate 83. Aerial view of the Spode works c.1950s. Note that very few bottle ovens remain and new buildings can clearly be seen.

rustic stone stump to which Mr Spode and the original Copeland were accustomed to tie up their horses at the beginning of the earlier century. In their place now stands a modern designed brick and stone structure. In other words through the exigencies of town improvements, the factory covering close upon eleven acres has recently receded somewhat from the main thoroughfare and tucked itself in so to speak behind a modern row of shops.

Two years later in 1931 W.T. Copeland and Sons became a limited company when they bought Jackson and Gosling, a Longton factory owned by Arthur Edward Hewitt. The amalgamation was reported in the *Pottery Gazette and Glass Trade Review* on 1 December:

> Our readers will be interested to learn that the well known historic firm of W.T. Copeland and Sons, manufacturers of Spode Copeland china and earthenware has decided to link up and join forces with the firm of Jackson and Gosling Longton, manufacturers of Grosvenor China.

Arthur Edward Hewitt had joined his grandfather's firm of Barker Bros. Ltd., run by his father and uncle, in 1910. In 1915 he was commissioned in the Royal Artillery and had a distinguished service record, being awarded the Military Cross and twice being mentioned in dispatches. After the war he decided not to return to the family business and with borrowed money bought the ailing Jackson and Gosling's factory which produced bone china tea and coffee wares. He soon turned it into a profitable concern. Hewitt entered into local politics and, as Treasurer of the local Conservative party, he met Mrs. Ronald Copeland and helped her to become Conservative M.P. for Stoke on Trent in 1931 She introduced him to Ronald and Gresham, and they invited him to join the board of W.T. Copeland & Sons to reorganise production.

By the early 1930s methods of production changed dramatically and the old bottle kilns shown in this aerial photograph of the 1950s (Plate 83) were slowly to disappear. New kilns using gas and electricity would be the ovens of the future.

Arthur Edward Hewitt

145

Plate 84. China figure making, 2 August 1899. Photograph William Fowler Mountford Copeland

Plate 84a. Mr. Arthur Steel, china figure maker, making Chelsea figures c.1930s. Photograph Harold Holdway

In 1933, to celebrate the bicentenary of Josiah Spode's birth, Ronald Copeland decided to reproduce a range of figures called Chelsea Figures, producing a coloured brochure to launch them. William Taylor Copeland had bought these moulds in 1852 from Derby, but they had scarcely been used and it was no mean task to piece together all the different parts of each figure. The true story of each figure had been lost, but some were called 'The Ranelagh Figures,' originally made at Chelsea to depict merrymakers at the party of the year given on 24 May 1759 for the Prince of Wales at Ranelagh Gardens, London. The most expensive were retailed at £1.10s.0d. in 1933 and the cheapest 16s. Some of the figures were made again in the 1950s. The original 1930 ones were marked Chelsea Derby Spode and have the name and number of the figure on the bottom; the later editions have only the factory backstamp. (Plates 84 and 84a and Colour Plates 92 to 96).

Ted Hewitt, after his appointment,[7] had proposed a three year project to streamline and increase earthenware production. By 23 March 1934 the company had commissioned Gibbons Bros. to install a new electric Rotolec kiln, which was to be used as a hardening on kiln, i.e the transfer printed ware went into the kiln to have the oils fired off so that in the next stage of production (glazing) the glaze would adhere to the surface. This kiln was estimated to fire some sixty thousand pieces of tableware per week. Manpower, time and money were saved, and greater levels of production achieved. To be cost effective the kiln had to be in constant use and three shifts were worked throughout a twenty-four hour period.

As early as 1903 experiments were being made into the use of gas for firing pottery and by 1906 The Longton Gas Company installed a small muffle furnace and reduced the price of gas, to show that firing with gas was both practical and economical. The Royal College of Art at South Kensington had also installed a

Colour Plate 92 (above left). Copeland bone china figure No. 15, 'French Shepherd Boy'. Mark 242. Photograph Mark Diamond. Private Collection

Colour Plate 93 (above right). Copeland bone china figure No. 16, 'The Shepherd Girl'. Mark 242. Photograph Mark Diamond. Private Collection

7. Hewitt Family documents.

Plate 85. The dipping house before demolition in 1936.
Photograph Harold Holdway

Plate 86. Mrs. Turner's shop behind the kiln in December 1935, just before the area was demolished.
Photograph Harold Holdway

Plate 87. Demolition of the earthenware glost oven, 1936. On the left are the wooden steps curling round the hovel of the kiln which was built in 1856.

Plate 88. Thomas Hassall collecting shards from old Chinese pitchers from the foundations of the top big oven when it was being demolished to make room for the Davis kiln in 1936.
Photograph Harold Holdway

similar kiln. The Davis Gas-fired Glost Tunnel Oven was a far cry from those small beginnings when Copelands erected it on their site to fire the glost ware. The oven was 107ft. (32.6m) long, and could produce over six thousand dozen glazed wares per week. This new tunnel oven came into full production on 17 August 1936, replacing some of the old bottle ovens (Plates 85 to 88).

Later in 1936 another decorating Rotolec kiln was built, as it was now realised that by changing the temperature this kiln could be used for enamel firing, i.e. firing the colours on to the ware. It was so successful that another

Plate 89. The pressing shop in the early 1930s. Note the board resting on the three-legged stool which, when full, was taken to the biscuit kiln to be fired.
Photograph Harold Holdway

149

Colour Plate 94. Chelsea Figures No. 3, 'The Sportsman'. Mark 276. Photograph Mark Diamond. Private Collection

Colour Plate 95. Chelsea Figures No. 2, 'Mistress Robinson'. Painter's mark D, mark 276.
Photograph Mark Diamond. Private Collection

Colour Plate 96. Copeland china figure No. 27, 'Simon, The Fisherman". Mark 242. Photograph Mark Diamond. Private Collection

one was built in 1938. The workers at the Spode Works adapted well to the new methods. Frank Simpson, previously employed to fire the old enamel bottle kilns, now was put in charge of the Rotolec kilns and found yet another use for them. The true story is told at the works that he used to fry his breakfast eggs on the top of the new kiln with great success (Plate 91)! A new dipping house, printing shop warehouse and packing house were built to cope with the increased output and by the end of 1938 this stage in the modernisation of the plant was completed.

The name Spode was now being used far more frequently and with great effect in North America; backstamps on the ware show this shift in policy. Ronald Copeland and Sydney Thompson returned to the great achievements of Josiah Spode I and II in their marketing literature, stressing the importance

Plate 90. Ground laying shop, Spode works, c.1950. In the background is Harry Hundley, manager of the department, and in the foreground Jack Booth.

Plate 91 (right). Mr. Frank Simpson, enamel kiln head foreman, still working at Copelands at seventy-five years of age.

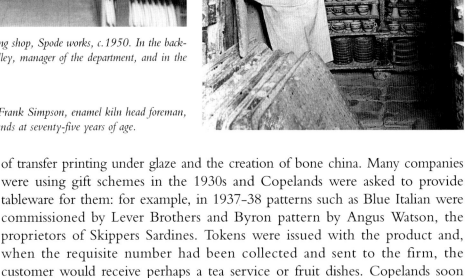

of transfer printing under glaze and the creation of bone china. Many companies were using gift schemes in the 1930s and Copelands were asked to provide tableware for them: for example, in 1937-38 patterns such as Blue Italian were commissioned by Lever Brothers and Byron pattern by Angus Watson, the proprietors of Skippers Sardines. Tokens were issued with the product and, when the requisite number had been collected and sent to the firm, the customer would receive perhaps a tea service or fruit dishes. Copelands soon found that the retail china houses were being asked for these patterns and ordering a variety of ware, which proved very profitable for the company.

The sales team of the 1930s consisted of Frank Thorley (previously at Wedgwoods) as Home Sales Manager and in 1934 Ted Hewitt introduced August Warnecke of Hamburg (his principal European agent at Jackson and Gosling's) to cover the important German market (Plate 92). New sets of literature were printed in German showing the whole of the Copeland range, the most popular patterns being Blue Italian, Blue and Pink Tower, Blue and Pink Camellia (Plate 93), Blue and Pink Rhine, Chinese Rose and Eden. Warnecke had an impressive showroom in Hamburg and was a dynamic man full of ideas.

Although Copelands did design art deco patterns, such as 'Reindeer' designed by Harold Holdway (Colour Plate 97) and 'Autumn 'designed by Ronald Copeland (Plate 94), most of their customers preferred the traditional hand-painted ware. More new products were introduced: an earthenware body called Onyx, a soft grey colour, and two new matt glazes on ivory body called Velamour, a vellum textured glaze, Royal Jade a green glaze, ideal for the sculptured animal figures of the Norwegian designer Eric Olsen (Colour

Plate 92. August Warnecke.

152

Plate 93. Examples of Spode Copeland earthenware of Hamburg shape decorated with the 'Camellia' pattern, c.1960s. The pattern was available in pink, green and blue.

Plate 94. Copeland earthenware pieces with 'Autumn' pattern designed by Ronald Copeland, 1930s. Mark 441. Copeland China Collection,

Colour Plate 97. Spode's 'Reindeer' pattern designed by Harold Holdway, 1930s.

Plates 98 to 100) which are as popular for collectors of today as when they were first produced. Eric Olsen had his own studio but the other principal modellers, Tom Barlow and Max Henk, worked together.

In 1934 Harold Holdway joined the firm as a designer. Thomas Hassall, the art director, was not consulted and was not impressed with his new member of staff whom he regarded more as a threat than an asset, giving him little opportunity to design until Ronald intervened, recognising Holdway's designs would sell. His faith in his judgement was rewarded when in 1938 Holdway designed a pattern called 'Christmas Tree', originally for the American market, which was later to become a best seller and is still produced today (Colour Plate 101). In 1937 a Holdway prototype of a stylised bird with a Dutch influence, on stone china, was shown at the Ideal Home Exhibition and seen by Queen Elizabeth, who ordered a dinner service (Colour Plate 102). Each piece had a different design on the same theme and the pattern was named appropriately 'Queen's Bird'. The third pattern, Y5257, also on stone china and called 'The Little Fisherman', was influenced by Chinese art and shows an oriental fisherman catching fish; again each piece of the service, just as in the days of Spode, had its own unique design.

Further modernisation of the factory was now completed, with a china printing shop, warehouses and new showroom which, although altered, is still used today, and a new Art Gallery where Ronald's collection of Sèvres, Chelsea, Spode and Copeland were displayed. To show that many of the old Spode patterns had been designed for use in candlelight, Ronald had special alternative day and candlelight lighting put in the cases.

The next planned stage of modernisation at the works was a six year project. First the old canal which ran alongside the works was to be bought (for no more than £700) and two tunnel ovens were intended to be built there. A new, two storeyed building would provide a greenhouse and a warehouse on

Colour Plate 98. Spode Copeland onyx earthenware rabbit designed by Eric Olsen. Mark 281. Photograph George Worlock

Colour Plate 99. Spode Copeland Velamour cat designed by Eric Olsen. Mark 281.

Colour Plate 100. Spode Copeland onyx earthenware polar bear designed by Eric Olsen. Mark 281. Photograph George Worlock

155

Plate 95. Architect's drawing of the proposed new earthenware potting area, including the site for the gas-fired tunnel ovens 'Black' and 'Canal', c.1952.

the ground floor, and a jolley shop, and mouldmakers' department on the first floor (Plate 95). However, war clouds were gathering and in 1939 war was declared on Germany. The European market was lost and further modernisation deferred. The management fought for their key men to be exempted from active service, but as the war went on they all had to join up, some never to return. Women now were to play a key role in the factory proving, in many cases, just as competent as the men.

Home entertainment was provided at the factory. There was a Copeland concert party and a Copeland choir. Facilities were provided for the teams of fire watchers who played snooker and darts throughout the long night watches, when not required for duty. During the war the new works canteen was opened by the Rev 'Tubby' Clayton (the army chaplain who founded Talbot House known as Toc H, a rest home for troops). Its splendid stage saw performances by many well-known artists such as the contralto, Kathleen Ferrier. The radio programme 'Workers' Playtime' was relayed to all departments, some of the programmes being recorded at the works.

Although the London showroom was bombed, the Spode Works fortunately survived. Workers remember when special metal covers were made to fit over the top of the ovens to keep in line with the black-out regulations, as their glow could still be seen by enemy aircraft. The coal now available was of a much poorer quality than in the days when thirty-two tons of Great Row coal were used to fire two bottle ovens for one week, and one china biscuit oven used seventeen tons of Bowling Alley coal. An extra couple of feet was added to the top of the ovens to increase the draught which made the ovens more efficient.

In 1941 morale was boosted when King George VI and Queen Elizabeth visited the Spode works. They were escorted by Ronald and Gresham Copeland and Ted Hewitt, who was then Lord Mayor of the City of Stoke on Trent. Although the war prevented the new proposed buildings being erected it did not stop the Copeland staff producing new ideas. In 1942 Arnold Woollam, who had joined the company when Max Henk was called up, designed a utility teapot with an easy clean spout. He had also designed a scolloping machine (patent no. 585291), which produced perfect scolloped edges on earthenware cups, previously done by hand. The company, like its competitors, was banned from producing decorated ware for the home market, a restriction not lifted until 1952, although exports continued to America.

Throughout the war many articles were written by eminent potters and superintendents of art schools forecasting the way ahead after the war, urging the industry to be ready with innovative designs which would reflect the spirit of the people. Ted Hewitt was a member of a working party organised by the Government to visit factories in the U.S.A. to bring back new ideas.

Spode was very conscious of the loss of many of their trained staff. 'Boy painters' such as Arthur Gaskell, Eric Bates, Billy Eccles and Harry Wakefield, to name just a few, all in their early teens but with journeyman status, had already been called up (Plate 96). Many of the fine paintresses had also been drafted into the local munitions factory. When Thomas Hassall died suddenly in 1940, Geoffrey Chollerton and Harold Holdway established a new training system for young apprentice artists under Mr Fred Robinson and Michael Brennam which proved to be an attractive prospect for artistically inclined young school leavers. Frank Thorley was appointed to the board of the company to take Hassall's place, but because of the war it was not until 1947

Plate 96. Apprentice painters c.1930. Left Geoffrey Chollerton, top left Arthur Gaskell, top right Eric Bates.

Colour Plate 101. Imperial Cookware – Stone China Oven to Table. Spode, c.1970. Christmas Tree pattern designed by Harold Holdway, 1938.

Colour Plate 102. Spode 'Queen's Bird' on Lowestoft shape.

that Geoffrey Chollerton, a trained artist in the old school, was appointed Art Director with Harold Holdway as assistant.

After the war the management saw the return from active service of the next generation of Copelands. Spencer, son of Ronald, and John and Robert, sons of Gresham, embarked on a departmental tour to learn all aspects of the business. Spencer became head of Research and Development, closely involved in the new technology on the site, and was to become Managing Director. John ran the Earthenware Department and Robert, after managing the China Department for five years, joined Frank Thorley in the Sales Department, becoming Sales Director on Thorley's retirement. Ted Hewitt's son Gordon, who like his father had been mentioned in dispatches, went to Jackson and Gosling on his return and eventually became Copeland's Export Sales Director, having spent eighteen months with August Warnecke in Hamburg. In 1952 Spencer, John and Gordon were appointed directors of the company and in 1955 Robert joined them. Also in this year a new showroom was opened at 66 Grosvenor Street, London, to replace the one bombed during the war.

After reassessment the pre-war plans for modernisation were slowly put into operation, hampered by restrictions on new buildings and scarcity of materials which were the legacy of the war. In 1946 an electrically fired glost tunnel oven for bone china was installed on part of the old Madeley Meadow site and aptly called the Meadow oven. New machinery brought its own problems, however, both large and small. Spencer's Research and Development Department was busy not only overseeing new machinery, but also keeping a constant check on the supply and quality of the raw materials. Spencer developed a method for drying clay on the moulds by the use of high frequency radio waves which was

Colour Plate 103. Copeland bone china match box hand painted with pattern number 1/7500, 1893.
Copeland China Collection, Cornwall

much faster than using steam heating, The invention was patented but not used at the factory as it was thought to be too expensive.

In April 1951 Ronald laid the foundation stone for the building of new twin gas muffle tunnel ovens for the firing of biscuit earthenware, and new potting and printing shops. One tunnel oven was called the 'Black Oven', built on the old Black Bank site and the other the 'Canal Oven' built over the old Newcastle canal site. The project was completed by 1952, the year when Ronald had completed fifty years' service with the company.

Modernisation now turned to creating a better flowline production for making and printing under-glaze patterns. Transfer printed goods had always been one of the most lucrative markets for Copelands. In 1954 Ted Hewitt brought in Guy Murray to design a new printing machine, based on bat printing. Developed in conjunction with Spencer Copeland and Ian Forse, this was called The Murray Curvex and was used for printing on flat ware. The copper plate was fixed on a small table and the machine then applied colour to the copper plate and transferred it on to the biscuit ware by means of a gelatine 'cushion', so cutting out the use of the old roller printing machine, Before it could be used, however, a complete new range of cold colours had to be developed by the Research and Development Department. 'Blue Italian' and 'Tower', still the most popular patterns, were printed by the new method. The Art Department was asked for new designs for the process and Harold Holdway designed 'Olympus'. For the first time different coloured bodies of clay were used – white and green. The plate centre was white with a green rim and the saucer was green, the white cup having a green handle.

Plate 97. Nobby the railway horse used at the Spode works in the 1940s with the company's nursing sister holding the bridle. Note the wooden barrels for packing the ware in the background.
Photograph Harold Holdway

Plate 98. An old corner of the Spode works c.1950s, just before the bottle ovens were pulled down and the area modernised. Robert Copeland served his apprenticeship as a dish presser in the workshop at the top of the steps.

The central motif pattern was printed by the new Murray Curvex machine. Wix, the makers of Kensitas Cigarettes, used the new pattern for their gift schemes. The design was made available on tea- and tablewares and became a best seller in the home market. A new decorating department and design block was built to complete this stage of the factory development.

In 1956 the senior members of the Board retired, leaving the factory in the hands of their sons. Spencer was appointed Managing Director and made Harold Holdway Art Director. Robert was appointed Sales Director on the retirement of Frank Thorley in 1958. In 1959 Robert appointed Leonard Whiter as Home Sales Manager. He resigned in 1966 but was to rejoin the company in 1967 as Contracts and Commemorative Ware Sales Manager.

The factory was now producing a complete range of ware, including oven to tableware called Alenite developed by Spencer Copeland and Cyril Allen, the works chemist. Many new shapes on earthenware and china were now available. Stone china was produced on one shape only, Lowestoft.

K1177

K1219

K1175

K1174

K1241 – 9"

K1176

K1244

K1242

K1241 – 5"

K1173

K1214

K1213

K1215

Plate 99. Examples of Copeland's range of Lavender coloured earthenware with hand-painted embossed Prunus blossom design with a matt glaze. Designed by Harold Holdway c.1960.

Plate 100. Spode Copeland bone china Royal College shape coffee pot, cup and saucer and plate. Pattern Y7869 'Green Velvet' designed by Harold Holdway.

Plate 101. Spode Copeland bone china Royal College shape Gothic pattern by Michael Kitt, the first design on Royal College shape accepted by Heals of London. It became very popular in the 1960s.

Plate 102. Loading the gas-fired intermittent oven in the 1950s.

Plate 103. The Copeland biscuit oven called 'The New Un' in the process of being fired. The smoke was emitted for about ten minutes every four hours. Stoke church is on the left and next to the oven are the china making shops.

In 1960 the company entered a new range of china for the Design Centre awards. The Royal College of Art shape was designed by Neal French and David White, both students at the Royal College of Art, and developed under the direction of Professor Baker of the Royal College of Art and the design team at the Spode works. All were delighted when the shape won the Duke of Edinburgh's award (Plates 100 and 101) For the new shape Pat Albeck designed the pattern 'Provence', Roger Young 'Golden Fern' and Harold Holdway 'Green Velvet'. David Jackson designed 'St John' pattern, a soft grey printed design based on a botanical study of St John's Wort.

Finally bone china production was modernised by the installation of the Jubilee gas-fired oven for bone china biscuit ware (Plate 102) and the last firing of one of the old bottle ovens was celebrated. No longer did smoke pour out of the Spode site. New methods had proved their worth (Plate 103) and slowly all the potbanks turned to the new firing methods. Clean air could now be breathed across the Potteries.

By the end of the 1960s W.T. Copeland & Sons Ltd. offered the buying public a choice of fifty-five patterns on bone china, fifty-three on earthenware and six on stoneware. The ware was skilfully and widely advertised in the most popular magazines of the day. Many well-known stores, such as Harrod's in London and Tiffany's in New York, continued to request patterns to be sold

Colour Plate 104. Examples of Spode Copeland fine stone earthenware on Jubilee shape, transfer printed and hand enamelled, c.1960s. The pattern is the old Spode one known as 'Peacock'.

Colour Plate 105. Copeland earthenware Toby jug c.1900. Mark COPELAND impressed.

Colour Plate 106 (opposite). Copeland Spode plate commemorating the 250th anniversary of the Royal Artillery, 1966, designed by Harold Holdway.

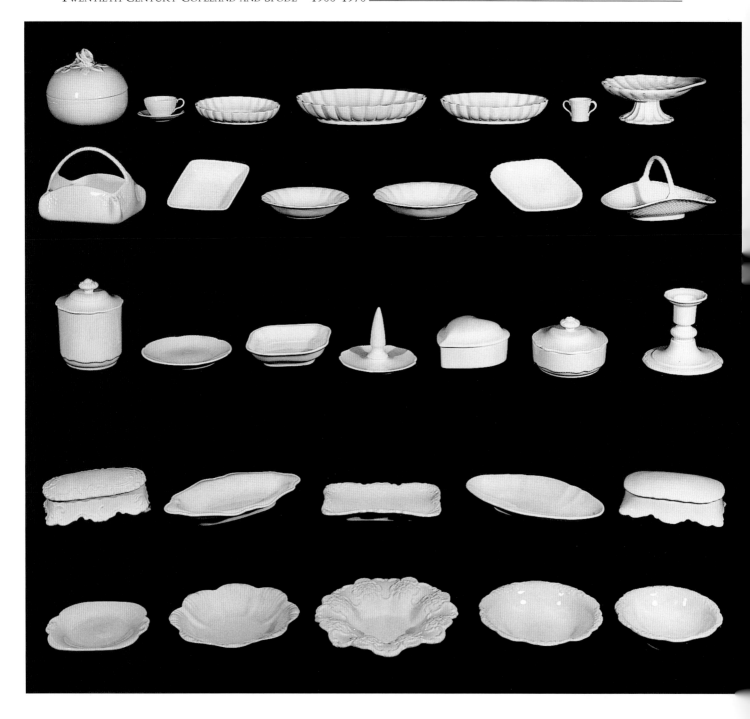

Plate 104. Spode Copeland's range of bone china fancy goods, c.1960s.

solely by them and had their own special backstamps on the ware, making Spode tableware exclusive.

In 1965 a new challenge was asked of the Art Department when Gordon Hewitt had the idea of designing a special limited edition plate to commemorate the 900th anniversary of the foundation of Westminster Abbey by St. Edward, King and Confessor. With the approval of Her Majesty Queen Elizabeth II and the authority of the Dean and Chapter of Westminster Abbey, nine hundred plates were produced, their final design being approved by Her

Plates 105 and 105A. A series of designs by Frederick Robinson of hand-painted New Zealand birds on bone china, c.1960s.

Plate 106. Spode Copeland bone china dinner service, flower embossed shape, pattern Y7195 'Lady Blessington'. Spode Museum

Plate 107. Copeland Spode bone china commemorative plates. Left to right: Iona plate; limited edition St. Edward plate with colour and gold; Westminster Abbey plate.

Majesty the Queen (Plate 107). The plate was a great success and other specially commissioned plates were ordered by cathedrals and also regiments throughout the country – for example, The Royal Artillery Plate, commissioned to celebrate the 250th anniversary of their founding (Colour Plate 106). Over the next ten years many more special commissions were received and designed by Harold Holdway and his team of young designers.

The 1960s saw more new methods of production and new machines on the Spode site and, by 1966, new management when the Spode works became part of the Carborundum group of companies, although the members of the family remained to guide the new regime. Spencer became Deputy Chairman and Robert was in 1979 appointed Historical Consultant. Gordon remained as Export Sales Manager.

In 1970 the Bicentenary of the founding of the firm by Josiah Spode I was celebrated (Colour Plate 107). For the first time the Royal Academy allowed a commercial firm to hold an exhibition in their hallowed halls. The exhibition was organised by Spencer Copeland and was visited by H.R.H Princess Margaret; a Celebratory Banquet was held in Goldsmiths' Hall attended by H.R.H. Princess Anne. The exhibition traced the history of the firm, showing examples of its products over the last two hundred years, and included a special small belt-fed tunnel kiln. This kiln caused great consternation with the London fire brigade who were finally persuaded that it was perfectly safe! Visitors to the exhibition were delighted to take home as a souvenir a coaster with their own initials printed on it.

The circle was completed in 1970 after two hundreds years. Spode had grown from the small pottery on Benjamin Lewis's fields in the small village of Stoke bought by Josiah Spode I, had been expanded by his son Josiah Spode II

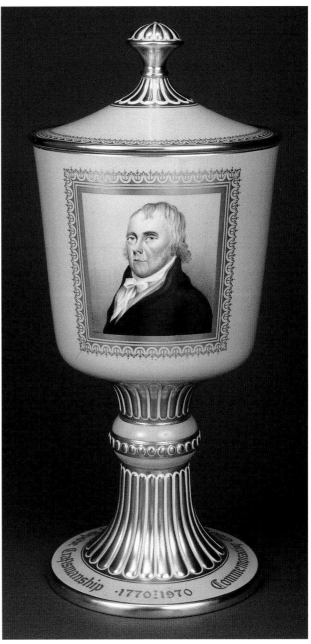

and continued by five generations of Copelands. To mark the event the company reverted to their old name Spode, trading as SPODE LIMITED, and a new company logo was designed.

Now in the twenty-first century the Spode works continues the great traditions set by its founder all those years ago, still on the same site and keeping pace with new techniques, producing Spode fine china and earthenware. Visitors can still walk under the old archway and on to the Terrace, explore the Visitors' Centre and see members of the staff demonstrating china casting, engraving and hand painting, and enter the museum where over two hundred years' of SPODE - COPELAND - SPODE products are displayed.

Colour Plate 107. Goblet made to celebrate Spode's bicentenary. It is inscribed in gold lettering 'Commemorating Two Hundred years of Spode Craftsmanship 1770-1970'.

169

Chapter 6

DESIGN AND DECORATION

Throughout the long history of Spode and Copeland, design and decoration has always had to keep pace not only with competitors, but with the changing fashion, economic and trading conditions of the time.

Spode I, when he started his own business, made redware, basalt ware, and fine earthenware. All these types of bodies lent themselves to different design and decoration. Redware was often decorated with black sprigging, the most notable example being the jar decorated with Egyptian motifs that became popular after Nelson's victory of the Nile in 1798 (Plate 12). Basalt ware decoration was achieved by turning and earthenware was often sprigged. Spode used either white sprigging on blue bodies or blue sprigging on white bodies (Plate 16) to create his designs.

It was the earthenware range, however, that produced the most notable patterns. Most potters, in those very early days, were trying hard to emulate the success of the Chinese. Josiah Spode I offered to the buying public not only earthenware showing the Chinese influence of design, but also simple hand-painted border designs which sold well. When he perfected the art of underglaze blue transfer printing his range of patterns started with the Willow type pattern and eventually more than seventeen variations upon this theme were produced.

On his death in 1797, the name Spode was one of the foremost in the country. But who was responsible for running the decorating department for Spode in those early days? Did he have a liaison with a decorating firm that so far has not been found, or did he rely on the skills of the various craftsmen he employed? So far no real evidence has come to light to answer these questions and there are no surviving documents which could provide an acceptable answer.

When Josiah Spode II went to London to start a retail business in 1778, selling not only his father's products but also ware from other potteries, there is no doubt that he would explore all possibilities open to him. He may have met the Battam family who had a decorating business nearby in Gough Square or the other Battam business listed in the London trade directories as late as 1845 as Thomas Battam and Son of 2 Johnson's Court, China Decorators and Enamellers.

The only evidence for their early contact is in Thomas Battam's obituary printed in the *Staffordshire Advertiser* of 5 November 1864:

> Mr Battam entered the services of Messrs Copeland in 1833-34, succeeding his father and grand father both of whom held similar positions under the late Mr Spode.

On page 44 of *Spode* Len Whiter quoted Simeon Shaw:

> For some years the branch of Enamelling was conducted by persons wholly
> unconnected with the manufacture of the Pottery; in some instances altogether
> for the manufacturers: in others on the private account of the Enamellers; but
> when there was great demand for these ornamented productions a few of the
> more opulent manufacturers necessarily connected this branch with the others.

He followed the quotation with the words:

> We have a picture of potters taking their ware for enamelling in rather the way
> that a housewife of the time would have taken a goose to the local baker. A potter
> in a large enough way of business could have monopolised the output of even a
> substantial enamelling establishment.

It is possible therefore that the Spodes had such a relationship with the
London Battam firm. Here could be the source of some of the early earthenware patterns both before and possibly after Spode II formed his business
liaison with Henry Daniel at Stoke in the early 1800s.

Spode I and II established a market for the vast range of blue and white
earthenware printed patterns which have become so collectable today. They
were taken from the engravings of books, for example, the Indian Sporting
Scenes patterns from *Oriental Field Sports* by Captain Thomas Williamson and
the Caramanian series taken from the three volumes of *Views in Egypt,
Palestine and the Ottoman Empire* by Luigi Mayer published in 1803, chiefly in
Volume 2. Sydney Williams wrote in his book *Antique Blue and White Spode:*

> The use of engravings as subjects for the potter's art was not a new idea. All the
> potters of this country and also on the continent were using them for their
> decorations, some were using paintings and also sketches. The originality of the
> Potter is to be observed in their choice and the adaptation of these originals.

This the Spodes did with great effect, changing borders on their blue and
white patterns, yet maintaining a central theme.

In the 1800s Spode II needed to complete his range of goods with finely
decorated pieces in his new body, bone china, a fine white translucent porcelain.
One example is a deep oval tray c.1810 (Colour Plate 108) marked on the back
Morlands Winter after the artist George Morland (1763-1804) and another is a
pair of vases with the scene described on the base. One has inscribed *The Earl of
Lindsey when a prisoner, Visited by Sir William Balfour after the Battle of Edge Hill*
whilst the other vase has *The joyful reunion of Olivia and her Father, whom Alphonso
releases from the Prison of the Inquisition Vide. Adventures of a Guinea Vol. II
Chap.52.* Both examples are finely painted (Colour Plate 109).

When Spode I died and Josiah Spode II decided to return to Stoke-on-Trent
and run the Spode Works, he left the London business in the capable, trusted
hands of William Copeland, sure in the knowledge that it would prosper.

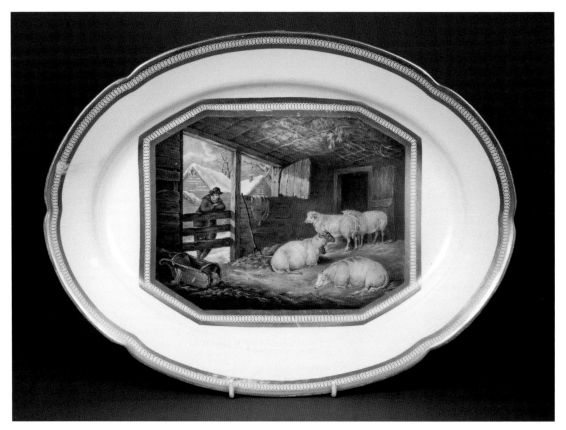

Colour Plate 108 (above). Spode deep oval tray. The scene of 'Winter' is copied from the painting by George Morland (1763-1804).

Colour Plate 109 (opposite above). Spode beaded vases, the scenes described on the bases. Left: the Earl of Lindsey, when a prisoner, visited by Sir William Balfour. Right: the joyful meeting of Olivia and her father, whom Alphonso releases from the Prison of the Inquisition, vide Adventures of a Guinea, Volume II, Chapter 52.

Colour Plate 110 (opposite below). Spode china vase and barrel scent jar (pot-pourri), pattern 967 (one of the most popular Spode patterns). Mark 21.

A new era began. Spode II gave Henry Daniel the opportunity to create new colours, to teach the art of ground laying, supervise decorating and enamel and gold firing, and to train a team of painters, artists and gilders, whilst Spode II secured the services of a fine craftsman who would produce new and innovative designs for his fine china. The two men worked together in close harmony, and when in 1822 Daniel decided to leave the site the parting was amicable. It was clearly stated that any of his staff could either go with him or stay with Mr Spode. Fortunately for the future history of the company, many did stay, to teach new hands to continue decorating the ware to the same high standard that they had been set by their master.

The Daniel period of design and decorating is one of fine hand painting and gilding on many and varied shapes of ware from teasets and dinner services to the small ornamental ware. The two most notable examples are patterns 967 (Colour Plate 110) and 1166, still the most collected Spode patterns to this day.

The names of three of Daniel's artists are known from the fourteenth stanza of *The Progress of Enamelling* found by Len Whiter: Sherwin, Burgess and Hancock. Sherwin is shown as painting pattern number 3449 in an old pattern book, Burgess and Hancock are in Daniel's recipe book of 1812 and John Hancock junior was hired by Spode II on 11 November 1805.

Spode produced classical shapes of elegance which appealed to the buying public who came to the London showroom. Tea cups could be bought in Bute shape, the first shape shown in the pattern books, followed in 1812 by London shape. The year 1813 saw embossed shapes coming into fashion, starting with New Dresden Embossed and Flower Embossed. These designs, by skilled modellers, moulded in the clay, were as effective on tea and coffee cups as on dinner services. All subjects were used to decorate the ware from every then known species of flowers to birds, landscapes and scenes taken from the old masters (Colour Plates 111 to 115).

Stanza 15 of the *Ode* shows clearly the range of decoration that was popular at the time:

The Ornamental Gilders they have charms,
The Herald Painters practise nought but arms;
The Landscape Painters they are fix'd in herds.
Here's others that do nothing paint but birds;
For figure painting theres but little call,
By this you see my case is worst of all.

By 1833 the buying public demanded more elaborate shapes for both tea and dinner prestige ware. It must always be remembered, however, that the blue and white printed designs of Spode on earthenware, such as 'Blue Italian', were in constant demand and provided much of the capital necessary to change and experiment with designs and decorations on fine vases and ornamental china. The ware suitable for use in cooking was decorated with transfer printed hand-coloured patterns and also ornamental garden furniture, suitable for the garden and the conservatories of Britain, which was both popular and lucrative. As the fashion in Victorian Britain was to clutter their rooms with ornaments, let alone birds, Copeland and Garrett could supply their need (Colour Plates 116 and 117).

William Taylor Copeland, now owner of the Spode works and London showroom, was no more a potter than his father. His contribution to the future development of the company was the ability to choose men of vision who would note the changing fashions in design and decoration and incorporate them into new designs. Decoration and shapes of ware lost the classic lines of Spode. They were now much more elaborate, following the rococo scrolled style used with great effect on the base of ornaments or incorporated in the design of tableware. More embossed shapes were introduced and this period became very distinctive. Lowther embossed the first shape under the new name of the company with a large scrolled foot. By

1837, two years after Thomas Battam joined the company as art super-intendent, the shape had become even more ornate, the scrolled cartouche around the cups lending itself to many styles of decoration from fine floral studies to gilded birds. Battam was responsible for introducing the Etruscan and Greek style of design into the Copeland and Garrett range.

Throughout Battam's tenure as art superintendent for the Copelands, designs were still influenced by the special services commissioned by the aristocracy of the day, who bought ware for both upstairs and down. The decoration on them was influenced by the experiences of members of the families when they undertook their Grand Tour of Europe. They would possibly choose famous scenes from Switzerland, or have a service showing the exotic plants they had collected and brought back to grow in their orangeries and gardens.

One such service, known as the Lubbock Service, was commissioned by John Lubbock, a banker in the City of London who was created a baronet in 1806 (Colour Plate 118 and Plates 108 and 109). This banqueting service was brought to the attention of Len Whiter and Harold Holdway in 1965 when the then owner wished to sell it. By special arrangement, the surviving pieces of the service were brought to the Spode works and carefully examined. The service dated from 1800 to 1847. Pieces showed both Spode and Copeland and Garrett marks, an example of an original order being added to over the years. It consisted of 313 pieces made of Spode bone china, Spode Felspar Porcelain and Copeland and Garrett Felspar Porcelain. The hand-painted botanical border designs were the work of a number of skilled artists, none named, and each item had a botanical description on the back in script lettering. It was thought that the decoration was taken from some published work, but the source was not discovered.

Plate 108 (above left). Spode bone china dessert plate from the Lubbock service.

Plate 109 (above right). Spode bone china Stilton cheese dish and stand from the Lubbock service.

Colour Plate 111. Spode encrusted vase, pattern 4649. Mark 22 in red. Height 5in. (12.7cm).

Colour Plate 112. Spode oval dish, pattern 282 'The Tree of Life'. Mark 22.

Colour Plate 113. Spode large double-handled dish, part of the 'White Bait' service used at the White Bait dinners held at the Ship Inn, Greenwich.

Colour Plate 114. Spode china sugar box, octagon shape, pattern 2528. Photograph J. Mathews. Copeland China Collection

Colour Plate 115. Large Spode handled tray inscribed 'Jan Van Huysum'. Mark 23a. Copeland China Collection, Cornwall

There are no entries for this important service in the Special Order Reference Books which shows that many were commissioned but not recorded. The Copeland and Garrett customers listed in the Special Order Reference Books record the members of the aristocracy who ordered services from them and the emergence of new retail houses.

The business liaison with the famous London showroom of Thomas Goode in Mayfair was also of paramount importance to the firm. The company was started in 1827 by Thomas Goode and their customer list very soon began to read like the pages of Debrett. The population in London expanded from 900,000 in 1801 to 1,655,000 in 1831, and many of the wealthiest people living in the fine new houses of Mayfair and Belgravia vied with each other in collecting china and porcelain, both to use and to have as cabinet pieces. They came to Thomas Goode and to the Spode showroom where they would see pattern books of the latest designs and many would then adapt them to their own ideas. Thomas Battam had to have new designs ready for them and his team of artists and gilders at the Spode works did not let him down.

Competition in Stoke between Mintons and Copelands no doubt spurred both potteries on to greater efforts. One can imagine the chagrin at the Spode works when they heard that Mintons had just had a prestigious order from Goode and the redoubling of their efforts to make sure that they got the next one. Thomas Goode's son, William, is known to have come to the Spode and Minton works with designs. He was a talented artist and by 1857 a partner in the firm.

Battam's first truly impressive order must have been that from Prince Albert when he built Osborne House on the Isle of Wight in 1845. Battam designed many of the fireplace slabs for the new house and also the door furniture, which consisted of the door knobs, finger plates, and keyhole covers. The Special Order Reference Book entry of 5 April 1849 reads: 'Slabs Pompeian border black and fawn The Prince of Wales' and later on 20 June 'Set of Slabs Crimson scroll and border in white and gold alhambra blue ground with royal crest on the side tiles and V.A. the initials of Queen Victoria and Prince Albert.'

By 1845 Battam had perfected his statuary porcelain body and gained the approval of the Art-Union of London who placed orders with him for busts of famous people in the new fabric. He also designed small attractive useful pieces: small vases for floral decorations and salts for the dinner table, which had glazed insides and small spoons lightly tinted with pink (see Colour Plate 58), so that the guests could see just how much salt they had on the spoon!

The Victorians loved animals. Battam's range included large groups and also small animals on rococo scrolled bases. King Charles spaniels were very popular at this time and he designed the group called 'Cavalier Pets' (see Colour Plate 59), which is one of the best examples.

Battam recognised the need to use the work of the noted sculptors of the day for his statuary porcelain ware. Competition with Minton was fierce; their range in this field of design was impressive. Copeland's most sought after examples are those of 'The Veiled Bride' by Raffaele Monti (1818-1881) and the sculptures of William Theed the younger (1804-1891), whose work of the Three Graces was often used to support china comports. This combination of bone china and statuary porcelain (now called Parian) was very popular.

Theed was born in Trentham in Staffordshire, the son of William Theed who was then working as a modeller for Wedgwood. William junior was sent to Rome in 1826 and studied under Gibson. When in 1844 Gibson was asked by Prince Albert for marble statues for Osborne House, he recommended Theed's designs and two were accepted. Theed continued to have commissions from the Queen and Prince Albert.

There were many superb examples of statues, busts and groups from other excellent sculptors which Battam then reduced with the Cheverton machine into models for small Parian replicas. Figures now were decorated with fine gold edging and vases were painted with floral patterns. Decorated parian became popular. By the early 1870s Gregoire had come to Copelands, painting roses on Parian (see Colour Plate 61), but unfortunately little is known about this artist. The market for all types of Parian remained good until it suddenly lost its popularity in the 1900s, but it is now once again avidly collected.

Thomas Battam's ability to recognise the changing market and to design for it was the secret of Copeland's success. He saw the establishment of Art Unions in the major cities of Great Britain and designed for that market. The prizes which were available to the subscribers brought art to the public in a form they could afford, either in small sculptures, engravings of the work of well-known artists or bronzes, all of which provided many sources of inspiration for design.

Battam also played a significant part in the development of Schools of Design, first in London and later in the provincial towns of Britain. They were to improve dramatically the skills of the pottery artists. Previously they had learnt from other painters and artists in the pottery in which they worked, being influenced solely by them and taking their sources of design from work handed out to them in the decorating department. Very few would have had the talent to 'see' the many flowers and plants growing around them and be able to adapt what they saw into suitable designs. The work of the ceramic artist was mainly that of copying, with great accuracy, the picture which was put before him, be it landscape or floral. By the 1850s the art world realised that design taught to artisans should reflect the trade in which they would be employed. This was to open new vistas for talented artists and gilders.

William Taylor Copeland was now well known in political circles, being elected M.P. for Coleraine in 1828 and serving as Sheriff of London and Middlesex in the same year. In 1829 he was elected Alderman for the Bishopsgate Ward in the Corporation of London and in 1835 became Lord Mayor of London. In 1836 Copeland became involved in the setting up of the London School of Design in Somerset House, sitting on the Select Committee on Art and Manufacture, which found that there was no overall direction in the teaching of art throughout the country. The London School, run by the Board of Trade, opened in 1837 at Somerset House. By 1842, the Board of Trade decided that the school should be run by a director and a committee of twenty-four eminent citizens selected by the Board.

In 1852 Henry Cole took over the management of the Schools of Design. He established a new Department of Practical Art under the Board of Trade, which was to become the Department of Art and Science, and the School was moved to more suitable premises, Marlborough House. Cole thought that some of the profits of the Great Exhibition should be devoted to a College of Arts and Manufacture, which was eventually agreed. A Museum and School was established at South Kensington which was to become the Victoria and Albert Museum. Cole contributed much to training artists from the Potteries who in the years to come were to win scholarships and train in London.

It was not until 1847, however, that Schools of Design were opened in Stoke and Hanley. The fees were 3s.6d. for men and 3s. for women per three months. The Schools were equipped with casts of models, both ancient and modern, from which the students learnt to appreciate good proportion and to draw a likeness. They also learnt historical ornament, ideal for using in designs on pottery, and saw for the first time a range of books on art. The schools were backed by the Government but administered by local committees. Battam's artists, if their parents' could afford it, now had the benefit of this further education, bringing new ideas and skills to the pottery. Many of the artists who signed their work after 1870 had been trained at their local school of art and

Colour Plate 117. Copeland & Garrett bone china dog. Mark 143. Length 8in. (20.3cm). Private collection

Colour Plate 116. A pair of Copeland & Garrett candlesticks, pattern 531(6)? Mark R.C. 143. Height 9in. (22.9cm). Private collection

Colour Plate 118. Photograph taken in the Blue Room at the Spode works c.1965 of the Lubbock dinner service made for Sir John Lubbock, dating from 1800-1847.

won medals of which they were very proud. If they showed great skill, there was the opportunity to win a scholarship for further training at the London school.

In December 1852 Henry Cole came to Burslem to advise them on starting their School of Design. He suggested that the original school started the year before in a loft belonging to the Legs of Man Inn, where art had been well taught by William Muckley, should become a general school. Unfortunately the Government could only give £40 for the first year and the rest of the money would have to be raised locally. The pupils would pay 6d. for five evening lessons a week, but part time instruction would cost 1s. a month for men and 1s.6d. for women. Despite grave financial difficulties the school was one of the most successful in the country. It did have to close in 1858 through lack of funds but reopened in a new building called the Wedgwood Institute in April 1869.

Meanwhile in Stoke on 21 July 1858 the foundation stone was laid for a School of Art to be called the Minton Institute in memory of Herbert Minton who had contributed £500 to the project but unfortunately died before it was completed. The building was designed by the architects Pugin and Murray. Many of the art superintendents of the large potteries spoke at the Schools of Art prize-giving encouraging the pupils to stay and train and speaking of the advantages they would get when trained. They told the students to look around them at the changing seasons, to read the books provided and train as artists.

Robert Frederick Abraham, when he became Copeland's art director, encouraged his work-force to attend art school. He sent his sons Robert, Francis and John to the local schools, then to London for further training, Francis winning a travelling scholarship to Belgium. Copeland's artists and gilders were now well trained not only in their own art department, but if they had the talent were encouraged by the management to train further.

Abraham designed for a wealthy market and he designed many fine vases which needed the work of skilled artists. By the 1870s entries in the Special Order Reference Books show names of both artist and gilder, for example, 'May 17th 1873 Two handled Berrisford Vase, figure subject one side by Besche, flies and grass on the reverse, gilt by Potts, chasing by Salt'. Another entry is for 2 May 1873 showing painting of large flowers by Hürten taking nine days and gilding and chasing by Muller taking five and a half days. The entry on 23 April 1872 gives us the painting and gilding costs for a Magellan Vase: 'figure subject on side by Besche 21/- gilt by Potts raising and gold 10/- chasing by Salt 17/-.'

Before the Special Order Reference Books were studied, the work of the gilder was not truly recognised. Fine gilding enhances the work of many of the well-known artists. A gilder was trained at art school in the same way as an artist, but to appreciate the fine work they did they must be divided into two separate categories: precision gilders who painted fine gold decorative bands around the plates and painted simple designs in gold and artist gilders who were capable of using raised gold to produce a totally different effect of low relief embossment.

Jewelled ware shown by Copelands at the Great Exhibition of 1851 was regarded as being in poor taste, but from the late 1870s to the 1890s it became very fashionable. Its true artistic worth was recognised and, although very expensive to produce, it sold well.

Both artists and gilders used raised colour at this time. The artists had two preparations, a special mixture of white enamel, and a hard firing wax white. They used the enamels to gain the effect of depth in floral patterns, applying it lightly to highlight a leaf or a flower. They modelled the hard firing wax white into a decorative shape, be it landscape or floral, which after firing was decorated with low fire enamel painted decoration, giving a raised and more lifelike effect. This special form of design can not only be seen on the ceramic surface of the plate or vase, but can also be felt.

Artist gilders used a specially prepared powder colour for their work which was bought from colour manufacturers such as Wengers. This special colour was mixed very carefully into a paste, then applied to the design. Unlike other ceramic colours, being a paste it stayed exactly where the gilder put it on the design. After it had been fired the artist gilder would cover the embossed area with gold pigment which, after another firing, could be chased and burnished.

Pearling, done by the precision gilder, was achieved by using a special pearling enamel and applying it to the border of the plate in tiny pearl-like drops with great dexterity. Another form of pearling was achieved by using a water resist paste to make the 'drops' which were allowed to dry and then coated with gold. The border decoration was next completely covered with best gold, allowed to dry, and then taken to the kiln for firing. After firing the piece was carefully removed from the kiln and put on a white cloth on the bench. The 'pearls' were then carefully shaken off leaving a perfectly clean imprint of tiny circles. The little balls covered with gold were carefully collected and the gold recovered for further use. Pearling enamel was then applied to the spots and the pearl effect achieved within the gold border. This form of ornate gold border decoration was very popular in the late Victorian period.

Artist gilders were highly skilled craftsmen, designing gold decorations without which many patterns would not have been successful. They could be said to paint with gold just as their artist colleagues did with different ceramic colours. The jewelled effect on the ware achieved by these methods is seen on many examples of dessert plates painted by Samuel Alcock, who signed his work. The only names of gilders so far found who were allowed to sign their work are W. Ball and C.J. Deaville.

In 1873 Abraham decided to use this special type of gilding on Belinda shape, with great effect. The plates so far found have a cobalt blue groundlay on which the design of birds, fruit and flowers are worked, and are attributed to the artist Brayford. Later Brough continued to produce this kind of decoration in 1883.

Jewelled ware of this period should not be confused with *Jewel* shape created from moulds found in the old mould chamber and known to have been used in 1857 for a special decorated service (Colour Plates 119 and 120 and Plate 110). The surface of the pieces was embossed with tiny concentric rings into which mirror-backed simulated rubies, emeralds, and topaz gemstones were inserted. This service became known as The Shah's service as it was found in the Golestan Palace, Tehran. It is thought it was commissioned by Queen Victoria to give to Napoleon III. This is one of the finest services made by Copelands and is shown in the Special Order Reference Books in 1857.

In the 1920s Copelands took this jewelled shape and made it on Ivory Imperial earthenware decorated in the centre with a rose known as the Billingsley Rose, transfer printed and hand painted. It became a best selling pattern.

By the 1900s many of the old potting crafts were no longer used and the September 1908 *Pottery Gazette* laments their loss. The unknown writer of the article first transports the reader back to the 1860s-1870s.

Colour Plate 119. Copeland bone china jewelled dessert plates from the Shah's Service. Castle of Chillon.

Colour Plate 120. Copeland bone china comport, part of the Shah of Persia dessert service exhibited at the Bicentenary Exhibition, 1970. Height 16in. (40.6cm).

Colour Plate 120A. Copeland bone china comport bearing the profile heads of Queen Victoria, Prince Albert, Napoleon III and the Empress Eugénie in raised and chased gold. Height 16in. (40.6cm).

But to come to a closer inspection of our crockery stall, let us take a glance at the principal sources of decoration in vogue at this period. We shall see what seems destined to endure all changes of fashion, viz. the ordinary printed dinner, toilet and tea patterns, and in practically all the colours that we see them today.

Further we might see some of the identical patterns, pheasant, willow pattern etc. – which for some inscrutable reason seem gifted with immortality. We might see printing in two or three colours – a style that has apparently died an undeserved death. Elaborately tinted and enamelled printed patterns would form the principal feature of the next grade, while in fancy articles and dessert services ground laid colours with hand painted panels elaborately traced in gold. At that period the art of the pottery painter was at its height. The style was no doubt conventional, but it was undoubtedly clever. That it was original, we cannot claim, being inspired by Dresden and Sevres, but its dexterity of manipulation and the simple honesty of its effects are such that cannot be excelled today throughout the whole range of the British Potteries Groups and sprays of flowers, rose, poppy, anemone, forget-me-not, pansy, every painter had a list of flowers, each of which required certain stereotyped but elegant turns and strokes of the brush, which were never departed from. An artist painting groups of flowers, say, on a dessert service, would go through the entire service with the roses, then he would follow with the anemone or poppy, and so on, till all the flowers being completed, he would add leaves in two greens (light and dark), and afterwards put in the tracing and various touches to his flowers, all according to the rule. The principle was to work through in the various colours one at a time, and it was extremely curious to see how the parts of the different flowers which happened to be the same colour were touched in when he was working with that colour, having the appearance of a Chinese puzzle to the uninitiated.

Colour Plate 121. Copeland bone china cup and saucer commissioned by Spaulding & Co., Chicago and Paris. Pattern R1977, c.1903. Hand-painted and signed by T. Sadler.

Colour Plate 121a (below). Close-up of Sadler's signature on Colour Plate 121.

By the late 1890s hand-painted services became too costly to produce, but many transfer printed patterns were enhanced by the work of the artist gilders, a field of collecting well worth exploring.

By the 1900s the Copeland range of earthenware patterns was extensive. Lynne Sussman, who researched the Hudson's Bay Company sites in Canada, found evidence of 109 patterns supplied by Copelands from the mid-1800s to the 1900s. Some of the most notable patterns are: Aesop's Fables reproduced from Samuel Croxall's illustrations for *Fables of Aesop* published in 1793; Byron Views taken from engravings by Edward and William Finden published by John Murray in *Finden's Landscape and Portrait illustration to the Works of Lord Byron;* Continental Views; Rural Scenes derived from watercolours by Edward Duncan; and finally the Seasons pattern, which had two groups of centres, those derived from specific places such as Windsor Castle and the Alps and those depicting Italian garden scenes. The name of the Season can be found on the individual vase in each pattern. Many more floral patterns were produced and some designs with just simple border patterns are reminiscent of those of Josiah Spode I.

Spode-Copeland had become an established tableware house offering the best in traditional hand-crafted designs. Their designs fitted in perfectly with the definition of Art as something aesthetically pleasing yet suitable for practical purposes in modern usage. This interesting painting on a fine board (Colour Plate 121) shows how Copelands now provided sample designs for their customers. The board was called Bristol board and could be sent easily to

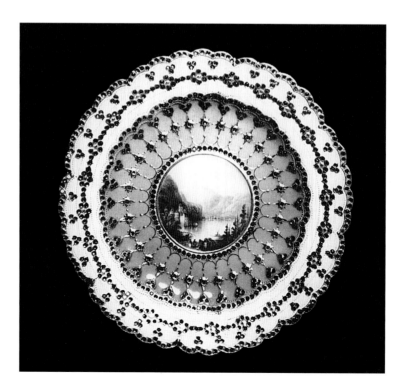

Plate 110. Copeland bone china jewelled dessert plate from the Shah's Service. Diameter 8¾in. (22cm).

Plate 111. Examples of Spode Copeland Crown body on Marlborough shape, pattern S3274 'Blue Bird' pattern.

all retailers, unlike the original sample plates of the early Spode, Copeland & Garrett and Copeland period. Bristol board had a fine drawing surface almost like glass and the resulting drawings, produced by the best artists of the time, were of excellent quality. Thomas Goode's boards had a small gold seal in the corner and no doubt other great retail houses had similar markings. Copelands re-issued popular old patterns with new colours, such as an early Copeland pattern called 'Cherry Picker' (Plate 111) which was renamed 'Blue Bird' pattern. The design was the idea of Herr Fuchs' son. Herr Fuchs, one of Warnecke's best customers, sent his son Hans to the Spode works to see how the ware was produced. When looking at the old pattern books, the son turned to Sam Williams (who was in charge of them) and asked if he could have a sample of the pattern but coloured in cobalt blue and sage green. Samples were shown to his father and Warnecke who approved the design and then ordered it in quantity.

The 'Blue Bird' pattern became a great success, an example of how a simple idea from a young man resulted in a best-selling pattern not only in Europe but also in America, for when Sydney Thompson came over to the works and saw the pattern, he too ordered it and in 1959 one of the large china stores in America had a full window display.

From the 1930s to the 1950s Copeland produced a series of model birds ranging from a large magpie to a small canary. They were hand coloured and in the 1930s a whole painting shop was devoted to them (Colour Plates 122 to 129).

Colour Plate 122. Spode Copeland red-faced love bird (Agapornis pullaria). *Mark 242. Height 6in. (15.2cm).* Photograph W. Cole

Colour Plate 123. Spode Copeland songthrush (Turdus philomelos). *Mark 242 o14 impressed. Height 7in. (17.8cm).* Photograph W. Cole

Colour Plate 124. Spode Copeland canary (Seninus canaria). *Mark 242. Height 5in. (12.7cm).* Photograph W. Cole

Colour Plate 125. Spode Copeland magpie (Pica pica). *Mark 242. Height 16in. (40.6cm).* Photograph W. Cole

Colour Plate 126 (above). Spode Copeland blue tit (Parus caerulus). Mark 242 F18 impressed. Height 4in. (10.2cm). Photograph W. Cole

Colour Plate 127 (right). Spode Copeland golden oriole (Oriolu oriolus). Mark 242 N16 impressed. Height 9in. (22.9cm). Photograph W. Cole

Colour Plate 128. Spode Copeland bullfinch cock (Pyrrhus pyhrua). Mark 242. Height 5in. (12.7cm). Photograph W. Cole

Colour Plate 129. Bone china cock pheasant. Mark 502. 17½in. (44.5cm). Photograph W. Cole

The new Art Deco style, first created in France in 1925 with heavy rather geometric form and bright harsh colours, became popular in Britain by the 1930s. It was hardly surprising that, although Copelands did produce some patterns, those that sold successfully were few and far between, though patterns described as modernistic did sell. 'Polka Dot', advertised in the *Ideal Home* magazine of October 1936, is described as 'linking the vogue of the early 1800s with modern ideas in this Spode Polka Dot service brings a note of charm and freshness to the breakfast Tray '.

It was, however, the shapes introduced during this period which were the most startling. The innovative designs of Eric Olsen, in the new body of onyx and matt glazes of velamour and jade green, were both fresh and appealing. In 1936 Agnes Pinder Davis designed the art deco pattern 'Country Souvenirs' for Copeland, stylised grasses in brown and grey, work she was allowed to sign. Harold Holdway, who designed 'Oklahoma' in 1957, another new style of pattern, saw the backstamp having incorporated within it 'designed by *Holdway*'.

Art and design took a great step forward in the Potteries when the School of Art at Burslem offered scholarships for designers. For the first time the industry tried very hard to train talented men and women in the art of designing for industry. Previously the Art School had trained artists, and thought that they would then be able to design.

Harold Holdway, who became Copelands' Art Director, was the only person the company ever employed who had this training. There is little wonder Thomas Hassall regarded him with grave suspicion when he joined the firm as a young designer. The training was hard. Students not only had to pass academic subjects but be proficient at drawing plant life of all forms, antique drawing (drawing from casts of famous sculptures), to know the history of ornament, the work of the Chinese, and the history of ceramics through the ages. Finally they progressed to the Life class and could paint and draw live models, a fully comprehensive training under the fine artist Gordon Forsyth. This special school, known as the Junior Art School, only lasted until 1939 and the idea has never been revived.

Meanwhile at the factory Ronald Copeland, soon after the death of his father, realised that artists on his staff must have an overall view of many aspects of society and he gave his artists and art directors the opportunity to travel the country to see as many of the works of art as possible. He personally took first Thomas Hassall and, after Hassall's death, Geoffrey Chollerton and Harold Holdway on trips around the country, introducing them to his friends and showing them their fine gardens and antiques, experiences which no formal art training could rival. Often if an order had been placed from important customers Ronald took the artist with him to discuss the designs.

Whilst the Second World War was raging Copelands continued to produce their traditional designs for the overseas market, but throughout the war many learned voices were telling the industry that now was the time to prepare new designs for home and abroad, ready for when the war finished. Few were to heed this advice. The need to keep down prices was a great stumbling block for many potteries who had no resources to spend on new designs.

Modernisation meant that the hand crafts and printing were to be replaced by lithographs of high quality, the difference being very difficult to see to the untutored eye of the public who sought a dinner service perhaps once in a lifetime and added slowly to it over the years. After the war Copelands had a backlog of orders from America which kept the factory in production throughout its modernisation which lasted until the mid-1950s.

When Harold Holdway became Art Director he believed that all artists should be given the credit for the designs that they produced and wherever possible this was done. He started a design studio and when enough new designs had been created he arranged them all on the walls of the design studio and called in representatives from the major customers and his team of artists to discuss them. Some were selected as sample patterns, others were not. The artists at Spode had become designers capable of producing design and decoration suitable for the changing modern requirements and the fashion of the day, typified in the Royal College shape (see Plates 100 and 101), designed not only to have pleasing lines but to be practical when used. Pieces of this shape were advertised as, for example, 'Sauce Boat, long stand to catch the drips', and 'Serving dish, flat dish for easy carving in two sizes'.

Many of the new designs on this shape were the work of student and graduate designers who had been trained at the Royal College of Art and came to join the Spode decorating team, for example a pattern called 'Gothic' (see Plate 101) designed by Michael Kitt and 'Persia' by David Jackson, who were both to become well known in the ceramic industry.

Spode to this day has still the same high standards set over two hundred years ago by Josiah Spode I and II. The market still demands Spode's Italian pattern and fine colourful tableware like 'Christmas Tree' and Spode continues to produce new designs and decoration, responding always to the present market trends.

Chapter 7

ART DIRECTORS, ARTISTS AND GILDERS

1835-1900s

The following details of art directors, artists and gilders have been compiled from the *Art Journal, Staffordshire Advertiser*, family papers from the archives at Trelissick, Cornwall, and from the Special Order Reference Books, pattern books and the small black books in the Spode Archives. Approximate dates have been given when they worked for Copelands, taken from the information available. However, the entries show only some of their work and they may in fact have worked longer than the dates shown. Appendices of artists and pattern numbers in pattern number order show some of the entries for each artist. Hopefully, as pieces of ware are found, they will now be able to be attributed to hitherto unknown artists.

All painters and gilders were under the supervision of the foremen of each decorating shop. The number of painters in each shop would vary, but could be as many as twenty. In the centre of the room was the stillage which was a large three-layered table, full of ware to be painted or decorated and also ware ready to be taken to the kiln for firing. Each painter's and gilder's work was counted at the end of the day by the foreman and noted down in his book. Their pay was carefully calculated. If the ware was not up to standard the foreman would give it back to the painter or gilder to be redone. Painters worked together in one shop and gilders in another. The painters and gilders who had achieved the high accolade of premier craftsmen usually worked in smaller shops, perhaps only four to a shop, but were still subject to the system of having their work counted and checked. Obviously the number of these painting and gilding shops varied throughout the long history of the Spode works. Only one artist had a room or studio of his own and that was Charles Ferdinand Hürten, the floral artist, who agreed special conditions with William Taylor Copeland when he left Sèvres. The other exception to the rule was Samuel Alcock, the artist noted for fine figure painting, who insisted that all work was taken to his home in Penkhull. However, it was the responsibility of the art superintendent to use this skilled work-force to create new bodies, shapes and designs which would appeal to the buying public.

The Special Order Reference Books are dated from 1835. There are no similar books which record Spode I and II products, although many of the pattern books for that period have survived. It is possible that Thomas Garrett started the system when he became a partner in the business and came to live at Stoke. Having been their principal traveller, he would have handled many orders and would have needed an accurate record of sample pieces which were being produced and taken to London and throughout the country. Repeat orders and the names of important customers would also have had to be recorded. The names of painters, artists or gilders who executed them were valuable for future reference. From the entries in the Special Order Reference Books it has been possible to learn the names of many of the painters and gilders from 1835 into the 1900s and the subjects in which they specialised. The books show the cost of painting, gilding and the materials used.

The early period from 1835 to 1850 may be misleading. From 1845 to 1851 the name of Ball is recorded on seventy-six patterns, Greatbatch on forty-eight patterns and Rhodes on 139 patterns. It is not certain whether the recording of these three names means that they individually did the work or that they were the leaders of the groups of artists and artist gilders. Their names have been put at the foot of each relevant entry along with a description of the piece and the cost of the painting, gilding and other relevant details. Ball is sometimes shown as W. Ball, Greatbatch as R. Greatbatch and Rhodes as W. Rhodes. From evidence in the pattern books it appears that Greatbatch gilded some fine work and Rhodes is shown as both gilding and painting. There is no doubt from the following entries that R. Greatbatch did special and highly skilled work for the 1851 Exhibition and may well have been an artist. The entry on 14 January 1851 has no pattern number but is for a china 'Greek Vase decorated with festoons of convolvulus R Greatbatch and Exhibition'. Similarly on 2 July a Dejeuner set signed 'R Greatbatch wreath of orange blossom Exhibition' but no pattern numbers shows that these were special pieces as yet not in production. Greatbatch is shown mainly as a gilder.

All the names listed in the books show craftsmen, be they painters or gilders, producing work of the highest artistic skill. No pieces have as yet been found from this period (1845-1851) with signatures on them. In some cases the entries have a rough sketch at the side showing the intricacy of the gilding involved. The work is on all shapes of ware. Various questions arise. Are the entries shown because of the high cost of the gold involved? Did the names shown do all the patterns recorded under their name? Did they gild and also design them? Finally, why are their names recorded sometimes in the same hand as the entire entry and at other times look like their own signature?

As yet there are no answers to these questions, but it is possible that from the pattern numbers attributed to them (see Appendix 4), and if signed pieces are found, some solutions may be arrived at in the future.

Other names throughout this period do not present the same problem. Barrett certainly painted landscapes; also J. Plant who painted for the Great Exhibition. These entries are clear. From 1858 there is little doubt that the name recorded by the entry is that of the artist or gilder. Men were employed who had special skills, capable of producing some fine and intricate painting and gilding. When William Taylor Copeland persuaded Charles Ferdinand Hürten to come to Stoke his first entry reads 'Sept 8th 1860 Berrisford Vase painted wild flowers by Mons Hürten gilded by Owen'.

Signatures appear on more of the pieces surviving from the 1850s. Customers, perhaps seeing Hürten's signature on fine pieces, were now far more interested in who painted the pieces they were buying at great cost and would perhaps commission services signed by another artist of their choice so they were then able to tell their friends! It has always been assumed that artists were associated with a specific subject, be it floral, landscape, birds and fish in the late 1880s, when specific services were designed for this course at dinner parties. However, the premier artists were capable of painting all subjects with equal skill. Their output depended on the orders that were received and how they were allocated to them by the head of the painting shop. Arthur Perry, when interviewed by Len Whiter in the 1960s, told of how he was one of the few artists who had been taught the art of gilding and he was able not only to paint with ceramic colour but also gold. It is possible, therefore, that the artists and gilders of the early 1840 to 1850 period could have done both.

From 1870 many more examples of signed work can be found and the Special Order Reference Book entries record 'painted by' and 'by' so there is no doubt they are the named artist's work. From this period entries show 'after Hürten', proving that his designs were now copied by skilled artists; these would not be signed.

The role of the art superintendent was crucial to the success of the company starting with Henry Daniel in the early 1800s who set the standard of design and decoration of painting that all future art superintendents were to follow. Thomas Battam was truly a man of his time. He was responsible for the company's exhibits at the 1851 Great Exhibition, Paris in 1855 and London in 1862. He developed the market for Parian ware which was to prove so profitable. He was succeeded by George Eyre for a very short time. Robert Frederick Abraham joined the company from Coalport in the 1870s and took the company's products to the London International Exhibitions in 1871 and 1872, to Paris in 1878 and then had his greatest success in 1889 in Paris when Copelands were awarded the Grand Prix. He was succeeded by his son Francis Xavier Abraham. A fine floral artist, his attention to detail was well known and respected. By the time Thomas Hassall succeeded him in 1910, the work of the art superintendent was changing. Hassall was the first superintendent who became a Director and had a seat on the Copeland Board. He worked more closely with the management. New machinery which increased production necessitated the decorating department to become more cost effective and Hassall had to design the products accordingly. His early death in 1940 left a great void which was difficult to fill. Geoffrey Chollerton had been trained at the Spode works and took over in 1947 and finally in 1958 Harold Holdway became Art Director. Holdway was the first man to hold this position who had had special training as a designer, having attended the new design course in Burslem aimed to produce designers for the industry, run by Gordon Forsyth. Harold Holdway became a director and sat on the Board until his retirement in 1978.

From the early days of Spode I all these names, whether painters, artists, gilders or art directors, played their special part in the company's success, creating new bodies, shapes, designs and decorations which are avidly collected today.

ABLOTT, RICHARD   Active 1860-1865

A landscape artist born in Canada and trained at the Nottingham Road works, Derby. Shown as painting for W.T. Copelands mainly on D pattern numbers on Cambridge shape. His work was influenced by Daniel Lucas (q.v.). Ablott probably left Copelands to go to Coalport and at some period to Davenport. In 1870 a Coalport dessert service painted with Derbyshire views was exhibited at the Midlands Exhibition in Derby by a Mr Carter (Twitchett, *Derby Porcelain,* page 183), and on the *Antiques Roadshow* in January 1995 a Davenport service was shown with painted landscapes signed by Ablott. He is known to have painted on china plaques scenes from the engravings of Edward Finden which he named and signed. In 1887 he was living at 5 Newport Street, Burslem, Staffordshire. To date no signed pieces have been found from the time he was at Copelands.

ABRAHAM, FRANCIS XAVIER   (1861-1932) Active 1882-1900s

Son of Robert Frederick Abraham (q.v.) specialising in figure painting but also known to paint floral studies. He was trained at the Stoke School of Art and in 1883 at the London School of Art in South Kensington. In 1885 he won a travelling scholarship and studied in Belgium. Francis, like his father, was a fine figure painter specialising in Shakespearean subjects. He exhibited two landscape paintings at the Royal Academy in 1887. Abraham signed his work with the monogram F.X.A.

Mary Abraham described her father as meticulous in detail and remembered watching him take any piece of paper and sketch designs on it. He checked all the artists' designs that were brought to him, often bringing them home. She remembered the important days when he travelled from Stoke station, attired in his frockcoat and top hat, to Thomas Goodes in London and how the family gathered on his return, hoping to hear of his success in getting future commissions. She said they were wealthy, and that he was paid £500 a year. Mary was twelve years old when they moved from Shepherd Street to a house in Quarry Street, Stoke, to live amongst 'Doctors not Potters'. Francis Xavier was a true Victorian gentleman. He was art director at W.T. Copeland from 1895 until 1912 when he left to join the Cauldon Pottery. From there he went to S. Hancock and Sons, where it is said his designs were comparable to those of William Moorcroft.

ABRAHAM, ROBERT FREDERICK   (1827-1895) Active 1871-1881

Shown as painting figure subjects and floral studies. First recorded by Jewitt when working at the Coalport manufactory.

> Mr R.F. Abraham, a student from Antwerp and Paris and a successful follower of the school of Etty.

Abraham's work was exhibited in the London Exhibition of 1862. In 1866 he left Coalport to become art director at the Hillside Pottery, Burslem, Staffordshire. Abraham came to W.T. Copeland in the 1870s. Alfred Copeland mentions him in his Diary:

> Abraham from Coalport came in through Fred Painter, the traveller, son of old Painter who was a traveller in ancient days, and known as Copelands elephant. Abraham died this Sept '95 an excellent man, knowing the styles and intricacies of Sevres, Dresden and Chelsea.

Abraham was a figure and floral artist of great skill. Although there are many entries in the Special Order Reference Books under his name, only one pattern number is recorded as actually painted by him, on 13 June 1872: pattern number D 6944 'Gordon china tray and can group of flowers on saucer'. There is no evidence to date that he signed his work at W.T. Copeland.

Abraham was a man of great talent and directed Copelands' art department through the many exhibitions held at home and abroad, producing a range of Copeland ware which was highly praised. He spoke at a Testimonial Meeting for the Attendant of the Stoke and Fenton Art School which was recorded in the *Staffordshire Advertiser* of November 1868, exhorting the students to attend the art school and telling them of the advantages of learning Art in all its forms. His testimonial is best described by Jewitt who wrote:

> the art director of the establishment is Mr R.F. Abraham who was formerly at Coalport with Mr Rose, the softness of touch, purity and delicacy of feeling, the sunny mellowness of tone, chasteness of design, and correctness of drawing produced on the best pieces of his productions, prove him a thorough artist, and render him peculiarly fitted for the post to which he has been called…

Abraham lived at Oak House, Trent Vale, Stoke-on-Trent and had four sons and three daughters.

ABRAHAM, ROBERT JOHN   (1850-1925)

Son of Robert Frederick Abraham (q.v.), painter in oils and watercolours. He trained at the Stoke School of Art, was awarded a National Scholarship and won the gold medal in 1872 for painting from nature. How long he worked at W.T. Copeland is not clear, as there are only a few scattered entries in the

Plate 112. Copeland bone china vase, c.1890s. Painted by Samuel Alcock, jewelling and gilding by Charles Deaville, initialled CJD.
Spode Museum

Special Order Reference Books. From 1877 to 1892 he is listed in Algernon Graves' *Dictionary of Artists* as exhibiting at the Royal Academy and having four paintings hung in the New Water Colour Society exhibitions. His oil painting 'The Burgundy Peasant' or 'The Spinning Wheel', dated 1876 and hung at the Royal Academy in 1877, was shown in 1953 at the Centenary Exhibition of Art in the Potteries.

ADAMS, FREDERICK W.   Active 1895-1914
A floral artist, Adams was trained at the Hanley School of Art where he won prizes. Arthur Perry (q.v.) said of him;

> that when Abraham's [Robert Frederick] introduced Sims Rose colour [origin of name not known but the colour was a very pure rose pink without the usual blueish tint] used on two blooms and a sprig, this became Adams speciality and was a great success being adapted to all shapes and types of ware keeping him busy for years.

This colour was still being used in the 1930s. Adams' work was gilded by the best artist gilder of the day, Harry Boothby (q.v.). There are many fine signed examples of his work in the Spode Museum.

ALCOCK, SAMUEL   (1845-1914) Active 1882-1900s
Figure painter (Colour Plates 89, 130 and 131 and Plate 112). An artist of great skill yet very temperamental, born in Bucknall, Staffordshire, the son of a farmer. The only evidence which has survived in the family archives are the membership cards that he used to attend the Royal Academy and the Print

Colour Plate 130 (above left). Self-portrait of Samuel Alcock. Family Collection

Colour Plate 131 (above right). Copeland bone china dessert plate, Richelieu shape, signed S. Alcock. The Gainsborough head painting by Alcock is thought to be a portrait of his wife whilst Colour Plate 89 is one of his daughters. Mark 241. Diameter 9in. (22.9cm).

Room in the British Museum dated 1871. He attended the South Kensington Art School, London, and from there went to France. Mary Abraham, daughter of Francis Xavier Abraham (q.v.), remembered him, as he married one of her aunts, Mary Alison Abraham (1852-1928), and said:

> He painted people but was so superior and self important that he would not work at the factory, the work was brought to him.

Stories handed down at Copelands say his work was taken to him by a boy pushing it in a hand cart when he lived at Richmond Villas, Penkhull, Stoke-on-Trent. However, the family remember stories saying his work was taken to him by hansom cab, that he had a studio at home and how his nine children played in the garden so that he could work in peace. Alcock made his daughters pose for him, which they hated.

Letters survive in the Spode archives which show how he and Richard Pirie Copeland were often at loggerheads as Alcock, when he received his work for the final firing, would not sign it if he thought it was not up to standard which caused many arguments. He demanded paper and pencils from the company for his sketches and was very difficult when they were delayed. If he thought that he had not been paid on time he refused to do any more work, however important.

Penkull Jan 29th 96

Gentleman

  I gave you suggestions of a new set of dessert plates A 'Watteau' set (male and female figure) A new Classic set, taking a girl's occupation (as nearly as pract for twelve hours) [This would relate to the time he thought they would take to paint.] A new set of Old song Ballads As I am 'standing' for want of material, you will please let me have your decision and plates as soon as possible.

Yours truly
S. Alcock.

Alcock's most noted service was the Midsummer Night's Dream Service which was exhibited in the Paris Exhibition of 1889 and highly praised, each plate depicting a different Shakespearean scene. His work can still be found, often on dessert plates having beautiful jewelled borders done by the finest gilders, and it is usually signed. Alcock painted ladies of fashion, heroines from Watteau subjects, fiction, Gainsborough heads and created work around the songs of the day.

ARROWSMITH, JOHN (JOHNNY)   Active 1880s-1930s

Floral and bird subjects (Plate 113). Arrowsmith is especially known for his painting of exotic birds in the Chelsea style, which belies his natural talent as an artist. Earlier in his career at Copelands he painted flowers and figures on all types of ware from tiles and slabs to dessert services and teaware. He

became well known when he painted the exotic birds on the Mecklenburg services. Examples of his work can still be found, signed J. Arrowsmith. It has not been established where Arrowsmith trained but it is possible that he was an apprentice of Birbeck (q.v). He worked for Copelands for over fifty years.

Plate 113. Copeland bone china large tureen and stand from the Mecklenburg service painted by J. Arrowsmith.

BAGGULEY   **Active 1845-1848**

Crest painter. Shown in 1848 as painting a Victoria shaped comport, pattern number 5246, with the arms of the Inner Temple.

BAKER (?F.)   **Active 1885-1889**

Although recorded as painting floral subjects from 1885 to 1889 and his work being exhibited in the Paris Exhibition of 1889, out of approximately eighteen entries only four are shown with pattern numbers, for example, '1886 China dessert plate, pattern number 1/4892 floral centre by Baker'.

BALL   **Active 1845-1851**

There are over sixty entries for this artist on pattern numbers ranging from 7200 to 8500 showing his ability to paint or gild all subjects with equal skill. It is possible that there were two craftsmen called Ball at this time, one a painter and the other a gilder. There is no doubt that he, or they, were premier artists of the day, and may well have been trained in Henry Daniel's decorating department in the days of Spode II.

One entry of October 1849 shows that he was paid 16s. for a landscape painting on an Egerton shape vase and another artist (not named) was paid

2s.6d. for the flowers. Ball is recorded as Ball and Mr. Ball. The artist Ball has a distinctive style – his leaves and small flowers are all executed with a single stroke of the brush. There is no doubt, however, that he, or they, produced pieces for the Great Exhibition of 1851.

A single entry on 22 December shows: '1850 Dresden shape dessert plate with pierced edge pattern number 8527, Exhibition, flowers in panel and raised gilding'.

BALL, WILLIAM   Active 1860-1880+

Artist gilder, responsible for some of the best gilding and jewelling of the period. First listed in 1860 'Berrisford vase painting of fruit by Hürten [q.v.] but gilding by W. Ball' and in 1870 'Napier shape dessert plate Flowers in centre by Radford [q.v.] Rich Jewel design by Ball'. Unfortunately neither entry shows a pattern number. Ball was the finest artist gilder of his time and it is thought he was also a designer. Arthur Perry (q.v.) remembered him, saying he (Ball) was an old man when he knew him, that he did his own designs and only did jewelling. He is listed as 'Mr.' Ball, a mark of respect at this time.

Plate 114. Tom Barlow, a modeller at Copelands in the 1930s.

BARDELL   Active 1879

He specialised in painting birds and birds' nests, usually on plaques, but it is possible that many of his designs were used on dessert plates.

BARLOW, THOMAS   (1906-1974) Active 1935

He served his apprenticeship at Wedgwoods in Etruria and attended Burslem School of Art, joining Copelands as a modeller in 1935 on the death of Louis Henk. Louis Henk was the principal modeller with his son Max. Thomas and Max worked well together and were responsible for models of all tableware and also for maintaining the quality of the existing shapes. Thomas was drafted into one of the local munitions factories, but after the war he returned to Copelands and stayed until his death in 1974. (Plate 114.)

BARRETT   Active 1845-1850

Capable of painting all subjects with equal skill, and also painted crests. Listed as Barrett, Barrett and Co., and Barratt [sic] Leason and Co. and Glover (q.v.) and Barrett. The significance of these alternative names is not known, but the combination suggests that Barrett led a group of decorators. He is shown to have painted only on highly decorated china dessert

Colour Plate 132 (above left). Copeland bone china dessert plate hand painted by two artists, the centre attributed to L. Besche. Floral artist not known. Mark 235. Diameter 9in. (22.9cm).

Colour Plate 133 (above right). Copeland 16in. (40.6cm) plaque, mark 202. Initials LS (Lucien Besche).

Colour Plate 134 (right). Copeland 6in. (15.2cm) tile, unmarked. Design for October attributed to Lucien Besche.

services and teasets. There are over forty entries attributed to him with pattern numbers and it is hoped that more of his work will be found in the future. Another Barrett is listed in 1893 as painting game centres.

BATTAM, THOMAS   (1810-1864) Active 1835-1860s

Born in London, Battam was trained in his father's decorating business there. He became Copeland's Art Superintendent in 1835 at the age of twenty-five. The *Art-Union Journal* of November 1846 described him as:

an artist of classical taste, whose great natural abilities have been cultivated by assiduous study, and whose inventive genius is too powerful to be confined within the dull limits of ordinary routine.

His discovery and marketing of Parian played one of the most important parts in the history of the Spode works. Battam maintained the standard of design and quality of new ware, creating innovative designs which, when exhibited in the great exhibitions of the day, kept the Copeland name in the forefront of the ceramic industry.

He is known to have played a part in encouraging the potters to support the Great Exhibition in 1851, speaking at meetings in the six towns on the subject.

Battam became a friend and mentor to the young Alfred Copeland who wrote:

Now in trade when I came on the scene Battam had done great things for W.T. Copelands… In 1855 Battam did well and in 1862 the exhibition we did well.

The most important entry about Battam in Alfred's Diary of 1895 was:

After a while Battam had a shine [became annoyed] and he went, but a year or two afterwards I got him back…

In the intervening period Alfred missed him sorely as he had then to do all the work for the coming exhibitions. Battam possibly lived at Trent Vale before moving to Fenton. In 1855 on 8 September the *Staffordshire Advertiser* showed the coming sale of Battam's residence, Heron Cottage, Great Fenton, about one mile from Stoke Station. This was a particularly fine house having stabling for four horses and being surrounded by gardens and pleasure grounds. The hall was 27ft. (8.2m) long and the principal room 33ft. (10m) long, and it had nine bedrooms.

Battam's decision to leave Copelands was far reaching. He went to London to manage the formation of the art department at the Crystal Palace, by then re-erected at Sydenham. The exhibition which he arranged there traced the making of pottery from its inception, showing the work of British and Continental manufacturers. Battam then took a prominent part in the formation of the Crystal Palace Art Union in 1858, possibly with his brother Frederick.

It is interesting to note that in 1857 Alderman Copeland appointed William Henry Goss (q.v.) as chief artist for Copelands. He had been Goss's patron, paying for his art education, and was much impressed with the young man's designs. However, time showed how temperamental Goss was! The addition of Goss's jewel ware to the Copeland range of products would not have been to Battam's taste. The exact date Battam returned to Copelands is so far not known but it is thought that he returned in 1858 when Goss left. His exhibition expertise was invaluable to Copelands. He was one of the Jurors for the Pottery Class at the 1862 exhibition and he had become a Fellow of the Society of Arts. He remained with Copelands until his early death at Notting Hill, London, on 28 October 1864.

BESCHE, LUCIEN   **(d.1902) Active 1872–1879**

Figure painter, especially cupids (Colour Plate 132). Besche was trained in France and came to Mintons in 1871, possibly because of the turmoil in France at that time. He joined Copelands a year later in 1872 and is shown in the Special Order Reference Books as painting Watteau subjects and figures, mainly on dessert plates and vases, although his work has also been seen on large plaques (Colour Plates 133 and 134). Unfortunately none of the entries shows a pattern number but they are descriptive of his creative style: '1873 Mortimer shaped vase – large vase with perforated panels, Birds and Flies by Weaver [q.v.] paid £10 guineas Figures by Besche paid £3/2/6d gilding by Owen'; 'March 1873 Cecil shaped Vase large vase Flowers four days to paint, figures by Besche paid £8.15.10, Muller [q.v.] 5 shillings'. The entries show he painted after the style of Rischgitz (q.v.), scenes from Aesop's Fables and Don Quixote. In 1876 he is recorded as painting a Goldsmiths shaped vase with figures on each side with raised gilt and scrolls by Ball (q.v.).

Besche and Hürten (q.v.) became great friends and Besche married one of Hürten's daughters. It is thought that one of their children was employed at Copelands but in what capacity is not known. Besche lived in Regent Street, Stoke-on-Trent, very near to the Spode works, and owned another house in Milton Place, Stoke, which he rented to Hürten. In 1884 he rented a studio from a Miss Harvey on Trentham Road, Stoke. There is little doubt that Besche was not employed by Copelands in the traditional way but was commissioned by them, demanding a high price for his work.

He was interested in the life of the theatre and designed scenes for comic opera and also illustrated books. Besche was an artist of rare creative talent, being able to paint not only on the ceramic surface but also in oils on canvas with equal skill. He exhibited at the Royal Academy from 1883 to 1885. Copelands sent many examples of his work to the 1873 Universal Exhibition in Vienna. Besche was a volatile and charismatic character, working only when the spirit moved him. He signed his work L.B. or L. Besche.

BIRBECK, FRANCIS   **(b.1822) Active Copelands 1882**

Son of Joseph, born at Coalport. Brother to William (q.v.). Employed as a gilder, but soon left Copelands.

BIRBECK, JOSEPH   **(b.1820) Active Copelands 1882**

Also son of Joseph and brother of William and thought to have been apprenticed at Coalport. A versatile artist painting fine landscapes after Turner.

203

Colour Plate 135. Copeland bone china dessert plate of St. George's shape hand painted by William Birbeck. Named 'Brunnen' on the reverse. Mark 235 and impressed for 1877.
Copeland China Collection, Cornwall

He was at one time an overseer at Coalport, but finally went to Doultons from 1904 to 1920, where he became one of their premier artists specialising in fish and game subjects. His hobby was collecting birds' eggs, fossils and butterflies.

BIRBECK, WILLIAM   (1826–1886) Active 1860–1886

William was born in Broseley, the son of Joseph Birbeck (b.1789) who worked for the Chamberlain Worcester manufactory. Joseph specialised in painting roses and fruit and in the 1820s he took his family to work at Coalport where in 1844 he became foreman of painters. William and his artist brothers joined their father and it is thought they served their apprenticeship at Coalport. When the management changed in the 1840s they left to join Copelands. William, however, first went to France in the 1850s and it is thought he painted at Sèvres. He went to Copelands in the 1860s where he stayed until his death.

He was one of the finest artists employed at this time, painting Watteau subjects, landscapes (Colour Plate 135) and birds. George Perry senior (a mould maker at Copelands) and Birbeck were firm friends and Perry junior (q.v.) became one of Birbeck's apprentices. Unfortunately after a year Birbeck died. Perry said of him that he was the nicest painter he had ever seen.

Birbeck's work commanded a high price. For a full centre landscape on dessert plates he was paid £4.4s.0d. a centre to £9.10s.10d. for twelve plates in 1879. Many examples of his work are still to be found and they are often signed. By the 1880s Abraham (q.v.) had decided to give Yale (q.v.) much of the landscape work but Birbeck then painted Chelsea bird designs with equal skill. He painted mainly on china but some of his work can be found on tiles and slabs. William lived in James Street, Stoke-on-Trent and was well respected by all who knew him.

He had one son, John Holland, born in 1852, who trained at Copelands and is shown in the special order books c.1869 as Birbeck j. No doubt the young Birbeck could not see a future in the Potteries and left to go to Devon, working for the Watcombe pottery. He had two sons, Harry and Robert, who followed in the Birbeck tradition of fine ceramic painting. Their work is signed.

BIRD
Active 1846-1849
Painted crests. Also entered as Bird and Co.

BOOTHBY, HARRY   Active 1930+
(Plate 115.) Artist gilder, a kind gentleman producing fine artistic gilding. He sat at the same bench as Fred Hulme (q.v. and see Plate 122). Boothby lived in Fenton and was a lifelong friend of Arthur Perry (q.v.). He and Perry bought defective white pieces from the factory and painted and gilded them at home, then took them into a friendly kiln fireman who for a pint would fire them. The Perry family have some fine examples of their work.

Plate 115. Harry Boothby, gilder at W.T. Copeland & Sons c.1900. Note the arm rest all artists and gilders used to create their work.

BOULTON, W.   **Active 1878**

Shown as painting on tiles and slabs. Painted figure subjects and heads described as 'painted heads' representing The Seasons, Midsummer Night's Dream. He also painted heads after Rich, 'a Head of Shakespeare'. On 9 July 1880 'a china plaque painted figure subject Miss Penelope Boothby after Joshua Reynolds'. Boulton is known to have signed his work.

BOURNE   **Active 1858-1864**

A floral painter of great merit The entry in 1864 'Pattern number D 3626 Painted by Bourne after Hürten [q.v.]' shows his ability faithfully to reproduce the work of other great artists.

BOURNE   **Active 1886-1891**

Eighteen entries show this artist painted landscapes on china dessert services and teawares, only occasionally flowers. There is no evidence to show that the two Bournes were of the same family.

BRADLEY or BRADLEY, J.   **Active 1846-1859**

Crest and arms painter mainly, but also painted musical emblems. Nothing else known.

Plate 116. Charles Brayford Brough, artist, c.1900s.
Family Photograph

BRAYFORD, CHARLES   **Active 1878-1887+**

Mentioned by Jewitt, 'Brayford whose productions are of a high order of merit'. Listed as Brayford, C. Brayford and young Brayford, he specialised in painting plates in rich gold, raised and sanded. His birds were unique, but he is also shown as painting flowers. He painted on all types of ware from fine dessert services to tiles and slabs.

BROUGH, CHARLES BRAYFORD

(1855-1922) Active 1880-1903

An artist capable of painting all subjects with equal skill (Plate 116), Brough was born at Shelton New Road, Stoke, son of Benjamin, a publican, and Elizabeth. He married at the age of nineteen and had five children. The family moved from Stoke to Rhyl, North Wales in 1896, where it is said Brough was there only part of the time – a bit of a wanderer! Family records reveal that he was six feet tall with a waxed moustache. He was a keen cyclist and Captain of the North Staffordshire Wheelers, and he became a Wesleyan local preacher.

Brough became one of Copelands' premier artists. There are thirty-three entries for him in the Special Order Reference books but only one with a pattern number: 'April 1889 a Coventry shape comport pattern number C 309 decorated with raised gold flowers and gold edge'.

Some entries show him painting in gold in the style of Brayford (q.v.). His work is signed C. Brough. He painted pieces for the Paris Exhibition of 1889 which won him praise in the *Staffordshire Advertiser*. He kept a cutting from this paper recording the private visit of the Princess of Wales to the Copeland Spode works, which states;

> The Royal Visit to Staffordshire. Mr C. Brough who is a successful artist of the Sevres School, was engaged upon a copy of the Windsor Vase, now in the possession of the Queen, a luxurious ornament, and typical of the artistic reproductions of the firm in this elegant porcelain. Mr Brough, it may be mentioned was the painter of the valuable plaques which the Queen presented to the Czar as a wedding present.

Arthur Perry (q.v.) was his first apprentice and said that Brough pushed him on, which was good for him. In 1903 he left Copelands to become one of Doulton's premier artists and where again he painted for the Royal Family and Indian princes. He won a Bronze Medal at the Universal Exhibition at St. Louis in 1904. His obituary shows he left Doulton to join Poulson Bros. Pottery as manager of their decorating department in the West Riding of Yorkshire.

BROUGH, JOSEPH   Active 1873-1900s
Son of Charles (q.v.) and known to have been an apprentice at Copelands painting most subjects.

BRUCE, ELLEN   Active 1844-1900s
Freehand paintress, she trained at Copelands and became foreman of the female paintresses. When the Princess of Wales visited the Spode works in 1897 the reporter from the *Staffordshire Advertiser* wrote:

> Mrs Bruce who after 53 years of service with the firm still skillfully handles the camel's hair pencil, and was engaged in applying a cornflower decoration to some plates.

CARTLIDGE, GEORGE   Active 1930+
An engraver of great skill, engraving crests, coats of arms, lettering and subjects which required precision. He lived in Trent Vale near to the Spode works. He was first made head of the engraving department, then decorating manager and finally was put in charge of all the departments decorating prestige ware.

In 1944 the coppers for the 'Blue Italian' pattern, having been repaired and copied so often, had lost much of the fineness of the original engraving. Cartlidge was asked if he could engrave a new copper for the roller printing machine. When this was used for printing it was so good that there was a debate as to whether customers accustomed to the older printed ware would buy the new one, which was a more detailed print and also different in colour. However, Mr Gresham decided to market the 'new' Italian which was a great success.

CARTLIDGE, JOHN   (d.1869) Active 1850-1858

Flower painter His obituary written by his friend in the *Staffordshire Advertiser* on 3 April 1869 has been included as it could well have been written of many of the unknown artists of the time:

For many years he was a servant of the late Alderman Copeland and at the Exhibition of 1851 he shone conspicuously. At this period the firm gained for themselves high honour but nothing in those days nor indeed up to a recent date was heard of a workman's ability, or indeed how much he did to build up his employers reputation; but we are happy to be in a position to state, that now working men are considered more than human machines. With no apparent ambition (or at least the ambition of ordinary men) he made himself a position in the ranks of art, and maintained his stand for long against foreign competitors, the grace variety and beauty of his outline was equaled only by the richness of his colouring marvellous in its natural sweetness and freedom. The late E Baker of Worcester and formerly of the Potteries, who also made himself to the writer's knowledge, was a warm admirer of his countryman. I name this by the way merely as an instance of good sense and equally good feeling, so widely different from a few inferior men, who could never see anything particular to admire (but did to copy) in the studies of Mr Cartlidge. He never seemed to have the idea to make capital out of his great abilities, as some have done, and wisely not even in his hours of leisure and pastime; he never seemed to have time, only to make general studies; indeed he must not have had the remotest notion of money making. He was remarkable for his courtly demeanor, unassuming, firm in friendship in manners courteous, combined with an air of refinement, his real hobby was Music, in which, had he studied he would doubtless have excelled. I have no other motive in penning this brief sketch than simply as a friend to pay a tribute which l consider due to his memory.

CHOLLERTON, GEOFFREY   c.1911-1960

Trained at the Hanley School of Art and became an art teacher at the Stoke School of Art. He joined W.T. Copeland and Sons Ltd. and in 1947 became Art Director He was a floral artist of great talent and highly regarded by Ronald Copeland. In 1953 his work on Copeland bone china was exhibited at the Centenary Art Exhibition in the Potteries, showing his skill in painting camellias and orchids.

CLOWES   Active 1845-1851

Entered as Clowes, H. Clowes and Clowes and Co. A floral artist of great skill recorded as painting pattern No. 7236.

CONNELLY, ANTHONY   Active 1950s

Connelly trained at the Stoke and Fenton School of Art where he won a bronze medal in 1889. He worked mainly at Mintons under Mussill. Connelly was a Bohemian character patronised by the Grand Duke Michael who was living at Keele Hall, Staffordshire, in the early 1900s. In the summer Connelly worked as a labourer and is known to have been in charge of a gang of men

Colour Plate 136. Copeland bone china jewelled vase, c.1900s. Signed on the bottom CJD (Charles James Deaville). Height 9in. (22.9cm).

Colour Plate 136A. Base of the jewelled vase in Colour Plate 136, showing the CJD signature.

who built a road at Cheddleton village in North Staffordshire. In the 1930s he was living at the Salvation Army Hostel and often sold watercolour sketches in the local pubs. When seventy years of age he answered a Copeland advertisement for men painters. A floral artist of great talent, his skill won the respect of the decorating department. Connelly's watercolour study of lilies was exhibited at the Centenary Exhibition of Art in the Potteries in 1953.

DEAN   **Active 1878-1881**
Painted flowers and birds. There are twenty-two entries showing Dean painted flowers and birds, being paid for a 'Japanese shaped dessert plate 90 shillings decorated with birds and flies'. Unfortunately not one entry gives a pattern number.

DEAVILLE, CHARLES   **(d.4 January 1939) Active 1889-1907**
Artist gilder, one of the few who was allowed to initial their work (C.J.D.). There is no doubt he worked for Copelands before and after the entries shown. By the 1930s he and Harry Hammersley (q.v.) shared the same room. He was the finest artist gilder Copelands ever employed, working only with the premier artists of his time such as Hürten and Alcock (qq.v.). (Colour Plates 136 and 136A.)

He worked for Copelands for over sixty years, taking part in all the outside activities which the firm provided, such as the Copeland flower show, where he won many of the prizes. Charlie was a keen member of the Boys' Brigade, becoming Captain of the Stoke division. He had the honour of representing the work-force at the funeral of Mrs. R.P. Copeland (Henrietta, Richard Pirie's wife). She was often to be seen at the factory and was well known to the work-force as a formidable lady! Charlie designed many of the fine borders on Copeland plates which were the secret of Copelands' success throughout the late 1890s and early 1900s.

Charlie was a happily married man whose son Leslie became one of Copelands' finest engravers.

DEGG (W. ?)   Active 1890-1898
Artist gilder producing fine jewelling work for the premier artists of that time. He had a son, Jimmy, who was also a gilder at Copelands.

DUDLEY, H.   Active 1887-1897
Artist gilder known for the fineness of his jewelling work.

EATON ? RICHARD   Active 1890-1900s
Mainly a floral artist. Recorded as painting flowers and birds on dessert services and vases.

EDGE   Active 1845-1849
Figure painter. Painted many of the Greek and Etruscan designs of Thomas Battam (q.v.).

Plate 117. Joe Fenn, artist, c.1900.

FENN, JOSEPH   Active 1930+
One of the last Victorian artists at W.T. Copeland & Sons and capable of painting all subjects with equal skill (Plate 117). Fenn probably trained at one of the local arts schools and is known to have worked at George Jones' Crescent Pottery in Stoke and to have signed his work both at Copelands and George Jones. Fenn died when painting at his bench at the Spode works. He was very popular with his colleagues and and was greatly missed.

FUNGALSTAD   Active 1890-1891
He spent a short time at Copelands and is known to have painted rose studies. Arthur Perry (q.v.) remembered him, but thought that his roses were not as good as Sadler's (q.v.).

FURNIVAL, Frederick   Active c.1905-1906
Landscape and floral artist at Copelands c.1905-1906. He lived at Sunnyside House, Scholar Green, Odd Road, Cheshire, and is shown

as painting pattern numbers R2374-5 and R2954-4. After he left Copelands he moved to Watford in Hertfordshire and worked for the Carlton Studios in Great Queens Street, Kingsway. He became a book illustrator for the *World Wide* magazine and *Tit Bits* record companies. In about 1923 he created the Kensitas cigarette advertisement featuring the butler Jenkyns, based on the butler at Ramsdell Hall. Furnival is said to have also painted portraits and exhibited at the Royal Academy. His hobbies included playing the piano, He was cremated at Golders Green.

GLOVER   **Active 1845-1851**

Floral artist, shown as Glover, Glover and Co., Glover Swetnam and Co., Glover Pedley and Co., Glover Ferrington and Co. and Glover Barrett and Co. It is thought that Swetnam, Pedley and Ferrington were all gilders, but Barrett was an artist and they painted a service together. As with Barrett (q.v.), the combinations of names suggests that Glover was in charge of a group of decorators. Glover's work was on tea services and dessert services, but he also painted vases and scent jars etc. on pattern numbers ranging from 4719 to 8034. Entry 20-2-1851 was a 'Pompeian shaped double handled vase blue dip richly gilt for exhibition' (Great Exhibition of 1851). Many of the pieces had crests and mottoes with sprigs of flowers and floral groups.

GOLTERMAN   **Active 1870-1879**

Floral studies mainly, also grasses, flies and bird studies, shown to have been painted only on china vases and dessert services. Wild flowers were his specialty. The entries for the Vienna Exhibition of 1873 gave only numbers, for example, '82- 1872 China Gordon Can and Tray no 16, and no 17 Wild roses and flowers Exhibition'. Some of his work was gilded by Muller (q.v.), Owen and Bell. Few pattern numbers are given.

GOODWIN, JOHN EDWARD   **Active 1887-1890s**

Artist gilder, jewelling borders for the work of the artists Hürten, Alcock and Yale (qq.v.). Fine work done on egg-shell porcelain, vases and dessert services. Only two pattern numbers are listed: 1/6034 a table plate with wreath ribbon and 1/5997 table plate with gold scroll panels.

'Ted' Goodwin and Charlie Deaville (q.v.) were not only colleagues but also great friends. One of the stories handed down about them is that they saw the job of Head Gilder at Wedgwoods advertised and after great discussion decided that one of them would apply for the vacancy, the decision hanging on the toss of a coin. Charlie Deaville won and opted to stay at Copelands; 'Ted' applied for the job and was successful, joining the Wedgwood design team in 1892 and becoming Art Director 1902-45.

GOSS, WILLIAM HENRY   **(1833-1906) Active late 1850s**

Studied at the School of Design, Somerset House, London, sponsored by

Colour Plate 137. Pair of Copeland bone china vases signed by H. Hammersley. Mark 241. Height 10in. (25.4cm). Copeland China Collection, Cornwall

William Taylor Copeland. In 1857 Goss was appointed Chief Artist at Copelands. He specialised in jewelled porcelain with innovative designs. He is known especially for his creation of the service known as the Shah's Service, which has superb heraldic designs (see Colour Plates 119 and 120 and Plate 110). This service had a special type of jewelling: small coloured pieces of glass were set into the china body to simulate precious stones. Goss was a temperamental man who left Copelands in 1858 to set up his own business in Stoke-on-Trent.

GREATBATCH   Active 1845-1860

Listed as Greatbatch, R. Greatbatch (only listed after 1848) and Greatbatch and Co. There are 112 entries for these craftsmen. From the entries Greatbatch was apparently the artist and R. Greatbatch the artist gilder. They painted and gilded designs of floral studies, birds, and landscapes with equal skill and their work was exhibited at the Great Exhibition of 1851. The floral groups have a distinctive style, but unfortunately there are no examples with signatures so the work can only be attributed to them. Greatbatch and Co. can be interpreted as either Greatbatch overseeing the work of other artists on a pattern he designed or 'the company' may have been his apprentices.

GREGOIRE, CHARLES   Active 1860-1866

Floral artist (Colour Plate 62). It would appear that he was employed to paint solely on Parian ware, especially roses, which, although not signed, are attributed to him in the Special Order Reference Books.

HAMMERSLEY, HARRY   (d.1934) Active 1889-1930

Floral artist (Colour Plate 137). One of few artists employed at Copelands able not only to paint floral studies on the ceramic surface and fine watercolour studies, but also able to design best-selling patterns. The few entries in the records do not reflect the skill of this talented artist. Hammersley was a contemporary of Arthur Perry (q.v.) and it is thought he received all his artistic training at Copelands, He lived and worked through many important changes in Copeland's art department but was never given the status he so richly deserved, being always a piecework painter and never a member of the staff. Hammersley followed the Spode tradition of designing a different floral study on each piece, a practice which demanded great skill in design. His pattern 'Gainsborough', c.1930s, designed for the American market, became a best seller. The floral studies were transfer printed under glaze and painted by girls. When the service was viewed as a whole it was difficult to believe anyone could have created such a variety of arrangements.

Colour Plate 138. Copeland fine earthenware plaque painted and signed by J. Hassall. Photograph Robert Copeland

In 1931 Prince George, the Duke of Kent, visited Spode Copeland and the tour of the factory included a visit to the artists' room where he saw Hammersley engaged upon elaborate drawings similar to those which had been inspected in the museum.   (*Pottery Gazette,* August 1931).

Hammersley signed his work H.H.

Harold Holdway (q.v.), who was to become Art Director, wrote in his memoirs:

> When I studied the work of Harry Hammersley and watched his skillful fingers deftly composing groups of flowers and other subjects with such ease, l asked myself how I could ever hope to compete with such ability and acquire such knowledge.

Holdway tells of the help and advice he received and describes Hammersley as a slight, short man with greying hair, a fine conversationalist, extremely generous and mild in character, happily married and living in Penkhull, Stoke-on-Trent, and writes:

> I think particular praise should be given to him for his version of the fruit and flower service which he painted so skillfully. The examples of his work in the Spode Museum are an honour to his memory.

HANDLEY, A.   Active 1881-1882
Shown painting figures and copying Old Masters on to tiles and plaques, but also specialised in painting cupids, bathing figures and heads. He signed his work.

HARTSHORN   Active 1869
Shown as painting groups of flowers.

HASSALL, JOSEPH   Active 1871-1897+
An excellent floral (Colour Plate 138) and bird artist, he trained at Stoke and Fenton Art School. From there he won a year's free tuition to the Science and Art Department in London in 1868, returning to Copelands where he worked for thirty years. Hassall had two sons, both trained at Copelands. Thomas (q.v.) became Art Director and his younger brother Joseph worked in the engraving department, becoming foreman by the 1930s. Joss, as he was known, was an unusual character, but because of the quality of his painting he was allowed his eccentricities. According to Arthur Perry (q.v.), when he spoke to Len Whiter in 1968:

> Tom's father was Joss who was a painter, a miniature Falstaff Great friend of Brushy Beardsmore, whose wife kept a fish shop, and if he met Brushy on his way to work he'd just go off with him for two or three days and help sell his brushes (which Brushy made) from his horse and cart and get drunk with him.

*Plate 118. Thomas
Hassall, Art Director.*
Photograph Harold
Holdway

Joss must have been a good artist, however, as an entry of 5 October 1880 shows that he was paid 24s. for a set of seventeen tiles painted with laburnum and birds.

HASSALL, THOMAS (1878-1940)

(Plate 118.) Hassall worked only for Copelands all his life. He went to Hanley School of Art and, like his father Joseph (q.v.), was a floral painter. In 1892 at the age of fourteen he came to the Spode works, being first apprenticed to Charles Brough (q.v.) and then to Thomas Sadler (q.v.), and at the early age of twenty-three became head of one of the painting departments. In 1910 he was made Art Superintendent. In 1931 he designed a coffee service for the Prince and Princess of Wales and in 1935 was appointed a director of the company, the first art director in the history of Spode to be given this appointment. His death in 1940 at the age of sixty-two was sudden and a great shock to workers and management alike. He was sorely missed.

HEWITT, JOHN P. (1855-1930) Active 1878-1882

Trained at the Minton studio in London under W.J. Coleman and worked for the Copeland, Wedgwood and Doulton factories. Hewitt became well known for painting figure subjects and heads at Copelands. In 1882 he painted a charger for Wedgwood of Petruchio (a character from *The Taming of the Shrew*) in the style of T. Allen, so it is possible that he left Copelands at this time and went to Wedgwood. (He later worked as a representative for Harrison and Son, the ceramic colour manufacturers.) His style of painting and design was fashionable as there are later references for both Arrowsmith and Lea (qq.v.) painting pieces 'after Hewitt'.

A man of genial temperament, he was particularly fond of skating, holding the bronze medal for roller skating in the international style and acting as judge at many local roller skating competitions.

Colour Plate 140. Small bone china cup and saucer, c.1870 by C.F. Hürten, initialled CFH under the cup handle, and decorated with British butterflies. Impressed 1884. Mark 252a. Private collection

Colour Plate 139. Portrait of Charles Ferdinand Hürten painted by his son-in-law, Lucien Besche. Photograph Robert Copeland

Colour Plate 141. Copeland bone china vase painted and signed C.F.H. No mark.
Photograph Douglas Chadbone. Private Collection

Colour Plate 142. Copeland bone china vase painted and signed C.F.Hürten. Height 13½in. (34.3cm).
Photograph Mark Diamond. Private Collection

Plate 119. *Harold Holdway in his design studio working on the design for the Royal Artillery commemorative plate (see Colour Plate 106). The source of his inspiration is the Royal Artillery banner in the background.*

Plate 120. *Pieces taken from a Copeland bone china tea and coffee service designed by Harold Holdway, Hamburg shape, Y6638. The rhododendrons used in the designs were carefully packed and sent by train from Trelissick to the factory by Ronald Copeland.*

HEAPY, WALTER   Active 1930s+

Gilder, trained at Copelands – a huge man weighing over eighteen stone. His bench mate was William Ball (q.v.); both men were excellent precision gilders.

HOLDWAY, HAROLD   (b.10 June 1913) Active 1933-1978

(Plates 119 and 120.) Educated at Cauldon Road Elementary School in Shelton, Stoke-on-Trent until 1926 when he won a two year art scholarship to the Burslem School of Art, Junior Art Department. He later won a bursary to continue his art education at the senior school and became an art teacher at Stoke School of Art. Holdway's first job was with George Jones' Crescent Potteries, Stoke-on-Trent, until 1933 when, due to a change in management, he left and, after a short time at a lithography firm, joined W.T. Copeland on 24 February 1934 as a designer and assistant to Thomas Hassall (q.v.), the Art

Plate 121. Fred Hulme, a gilder at W.T. Copeland & Sons c.1900.

Plate 122. Fred Hulme and Harry Boothby in the gilding department, 1930s.

Director. After Hassall's death in 1940 Holdway was appointed chief designer and head of the decorating department. In the evenings he taught design at the Stoke School of Art until 1943 when he was called up to join the Fleet Air Arm. On his return from active service he rejoined Copelands in his former capacity. In 1956 he was appointed Art Director.

Holdway believed very strongly that all artists and designers in his department should get the credit for their designs. In 1966, when the Carborundum group of companies took over W.T. Copeland and Sons Ltd., he was given the opportunity to design the new Design Studio, in which he trained his staff by example. In 1976 he became a member of the Spode-Copeland Board and in 1977, when the Royal Worcester Spode Limited Company was formed, a board member of the group until his retirement on 16 June 1978. His designs of rhododendrons, birds and lilies on bone china plates was lent by W.T. Copeland & Sons Ltd. for exhibition at the Centenary Art Exhibition in the Potteries in 1953.

HULME, FREDERICK   (b.1864) Active 1930+
(Plates 121 and 122.) Known to have been aged seventy in 1934, Hulme lived in Shelton and walked to Copelands each day. He did very fine gilding and sometimes put his initials, F.H., on the back of a piece in red. This was not a signature but a factory identification mark. Many more initials like this may

Colour Plate 143. Copeland bone china oval and framed plaque. After a painting by Sir Laurence Alma-Tadema, O.M., R.A. and signed by H.C. Lea. Copeland China Collection, Cornwall

Colour Plate 144 (left). Copeland bone china dessert plate of Crete shape painted by H.C. Lea. Commissioned by David Collamore & Co., New York, 1900. Pattern R146 impressed. Private Collection

Colour Plate 144a (above). Close-up of the H.C. Lea signature on the Crete shaped dessert plate.

Colour Plate 145. Copeland bone china service made for Phillips of London, thought to be a special commission. Each plate is hand painted and signed by Harry Lea. Dated 1895. Copeland mark 274. Private Collection

come to light in the future and they could be the gilder's mark as even as late as the 1930s gilders were not allowed to sign their work.

HÜRTEN, CHARLES FERDINAND (1820-1901) Active 1858-1890s
(Colour Plates 139 to 142.) A floral artist, Hürten studied at the Municipal School of Art in Cologne, then went to Paris. In 1858 Alderman Copeland persuaded him to come to Stoke-on-Trent by offering him a salary of £320 a year and his own studio. Hürten accepted and stayed with Copelands until the late 1890s when he went to London, it is thought to live with his daughter and to illustrate books. He died in 1901.

Hürten was the greatest floral artist of his time, having the ability to create unique floral studies on all types and sizes of ceramic ware.

> Mr Hürten was a most industrious and prolific artist. His productions were a notable feature of the Copelands exhibits at the London International Exhibition in 1862, the Paris Exposition of 1878 and the Exhibitions of Vienna, Berlin, Philadelphia, Melbourne, Sydney and Chicago, and it is not to much to say that there is scarcely a Royal Palace or National Museum in Europe which does not contain specimens of Mr. Hürten's craft.
>
> (Obituary *Evening Sentinel,* Monday 7 January 1901)

The reports of these exhibitions praise his work and there is little doubt that Copeland's success at them was due to his unique talent.

In 1880-1881 Hürten lived in Milton Place, Stoke-on-Trent, owned by his son-in-law Lucien Besche (q.v.), but by 1892 had moved to Shepherd Street, Stoke, both within easy walking distance of the Spode works. He had an expensive lifestyle – it is said that he ordered food hampers from Fortnum and Mason which arrived by train at Stoke Station. Hürten was popular with his colleagues, often to be seen in consultation with the kiln fireman ensuring this his work was placed in the most suitable spot in the kiln to ensure that it would fire perfectly.

Hürten's work was displayed in the showroom at the Spode works through-out his time at Copelands and is now to be seen in the Spode Museum. He had many private commissions, one of which was to design panels for the Duchess of Devonshire's grand drawing room at Chatsworth. His work, signed either C.F.H. or C.F. Hürten, is avidly collected today.

KEELING   Active 1879-1885
Painted plants and figure subjects after Hewitt (q.v.).

LEA, HARRY   Active 1880-1900s
(Colour Plates 143 to 145.) The son of a traveller for Copeland's, known as a true Victorian gentleman, rather superior but a very pleasant character. He painted all subjects with equal skill and was allowed to sign his work, usually H.C. Lea. Listed as painting hawking subjects, marine landscapes and flowers, particularly roses. Nine dessert plates decorated with a poppy design (Colour

Plate 144) were found in America, pattern number R 146, impressed mark for 1900, specially commissioned for David Collamore & Co., New York and bearing their backstamp. Only one of the plates was signed H.C. Lea (Colour Plate 144a). They are a fine example of his work.

LUCAS, DANIEL Junior   Active 1862-1863

The son of Daniel Lucas (1788-1867) who worked first for the Davenport pottery, then went to Derby where he became their foremost landscape artist. In 1848 he left Derby to go to Birmingham to paint japanned ware on a free-lance basis. He is listed as being a member of the North Staffordshire Society of Artists in 1841.

Daniel was the youngest of his three sons. John went to work at the Rockingham pottery, William was employed at Mintons as a gilder, but Daniel followed in his father's footsteps, becoming a fine landscape artist.

Daniel Lucas Junior first worked for Coalport and is shown on the weekly wages sheet as earning £2.5s.0d. It is thought that he painted for Copelands on a free-lance basis as the entries in the Special Order Book show that he painted rustic subjects and in 1862 a tray with the painting 'Passing the Brook' after the Belgian artist, M. Verboeckhoven, depicting sheep and cattle in a pastoral setting. In 1868 there was an exhibition in the Mechanics Institute, Hanley, where it was reported that Mr Lucas had sent examples of his new process of transferring and printing gold. By 1879 he lived at 30 Sutherland Terrace, Longton, where he had a studio and workshop.

Many of the fine landscapes on Copeland ware dated to the late 1850s have been attributed to Daniel Lucas Junior, He is known to have painted exhibition pieces for the Great Exhibition of 1851 and the Paris Exhibition of 1868. Only three entries in the small black books record his name: pattern numbers D2338, D2132 and D2070. Recently a breakfast set for one has been found, pattern number D2609 c.1862 from the *Rivers of France* service listed in the Special Order Reference Books (Colour Plate 146). It consists of a teapot, sugar and cream and one cup and saucer. The teapot holds two and a half cups of tea. All the scenes are taken from *Rivers of France* and named on the bottom of each piece, and each fine landscape is named on the back in gold. This is undoubtedly the work of Lucas, being painted at exactly the same period that he is recorded in the books. The fine landscape painting has the depth and mystique of his work. All pieces attributed to him lead the eye through the painting which has fine architectural buildings depicted within it. The chased gilding is of the highest quality and the service must have been specially commissioned for a wealthy aristocratic family. There are two entries for this service listed: 13 January 1863 'Middle-sized Festoon pierced basket – three painted landscapes as Rivers of France centerpiece'; 4 March 'Comport Theeds season figure – Landscapes as Rivers of France'. These must have been further special orders to add to the original service.

No other landscape artist in the history of Copelands has achieved his skill. Another service known as *The Rivers of England* service may have been done at the same time by this artist, but so far no pieces have been found.

To date no signed pieces of his work have been found.

LYCETT, EDWARD   Active 1850s

Born in Newcastle under Lyme on 27 April 1833 and shown in 1851 as an enamel painter. One entry in the Special Order Reference books shows a Lycett gilding pattern number 6286, a Royal shape dessert plate.

He emigrated to New York in 1860. Family records claim he became the first American ceramic painter of note and taught the art of painting china. In addition he operated his own china painting business. One of his noteworthy commissions was painting a set of china for President Lincoln for the White House. He devised a unique method of applying gold to china which has never been duplicated, the secret of which he never revealed. His work can be seen in Dearborn, Michigan and in other museums. His china is still on display in the White House, Washington.

MANSFIELD   Active 1849-1860

One of the premier artist gilders of this period, shown to have worked on all types of ware from candlesticks to vases and dessert services on Louis, Regimental, Royal and Queen Anne shapes and on pattern numbers ranging from 5877-8614. In September 1860 Mansfield J. is shown as gilding a Berrisford Vase painted by Hürten (q.v.), and his final entry is in July 1884, a Queen Anne shape table plate pattern number 1/3817.

MARSHALL, ROBERT (BOB)   Active 1930s

One of the last fine gilders to work for Copelands, he was still employed by them up to the Second World War. He is described as a neat and quiet man, having a small moustache and being of a retiring nature.

MICKLEWRIGHT, FREDERICK (1868-1941) Active late 1920s-1930s

(Plate 123.) Micklewright came to the Potteries from Dudley and worked at Aynsleys for a long time. He is known to have gone to Dumfries to manage a pottery there which was not a success, and then returned to the Potteries, where in the 1930s he became one of Copelands' premier artists. One of the last true pottery artists, he is remembered with affection as being a quiet, dignified Victorian gentleman with a little white beard and wearing a white wing collar, sitting at his bench painting mainly landscapes, totally oblivious of the noise and horseplay of the young apprentices who worked nearby. He signed his work, an example of which is shown in the Goode's Special Order Book of 1 March 1929, pattern number C 1387, Eton College centre, and C 1387, Iona Abbey, and in 1931 pattern number C2564 on a Royal Embossed shape dessert plate, 'the centre Holyrood Castle painted by Micklewright [q.v.]'. Later in his career he painted landscapes of famous places which were taken to the engraving department, engraved and then printed on the ware and hand coloured. There are some fine examples of his work in the Spode Museum.

Micklewright was an unworldly gentleman who loved to paint. When work was scarce he sat and painted at home and if a visitor came and admired his work he would very happily give it to them, totally oblivious of the financial state of his household.

MILLWARD, W.   **Active 1882-1890s**

Artist gilder known to have had his work exhibited at the Paris Exhibition of 1889, a Chelsea shaped dessert plate with a rich jewel design. He was a contemporary of both Goodwin and Deaville (qq.v.) and possibly at this time the senior artist gilder of the team.

MULLER   **Active 1870-1873+**

An artist gilder working mainly on fine china dessert services and vases, shown as jewelling pieces for the London International Exhibitions of 1871 and 1872. These pieces were not given a pattern number, only a number, for example, 'Cup and saucer No 46 rose sprays jewelled gilded and chased; Vase on claw feet, Winthrop shape jewel borders by Muller'. There are twenty-eight entries of his work during this period which also show that Etruscan figure decoration and gilded pieces were sent for exhibition. There is an entry in the Minton wages book of 4 January 1877 for gilding a pair of pâte sur pâte vases painted by Solon and also on a pair of vases painted by Mussill. Perhaps Muller had by then left Copelands to work for Mintons.

Plate 123. Frederick Micklewright, landscape artist at W.T. Copeland & Sons c.1900.

Colour Plate 146. Copeland bone china early morning teaset with all pieces painted by D. Lucas junior. Part of 'The Rivers of France' service, pattern D2609. Left to right: sugar pot, scenes 'St Denis' and (reverse) 'Bridge of St. Cloud & Sevres'; tea or coffee pot, scenes 'Mantes' and (reverse) 'Pont de L'Acre' – this hold 2½ cups of tea, chocolate or coffee; milk jug, scenes 'St. Cloud' and (reverse) 'Vernon'.

Colour Plate 147. Spode Copeland bone china tray painted with a scene of Scarborough after Turner by A. Perry. Mark 242. Length 9½in. (24.1cm). Spode Museum

Colour Plate 148. Spode Copeland bone china seaux painted and signed by A. Perry with views of Norham Castle and Scarborough after Turner. Mark 242. Length 11in. (27.9cm). Spode Museum

Colour Plate 149. Spode Copeland bone china Cottage shape cup and saucer, pattern R1127, commissioned by Tiffany's of New York. The landscapes are painted and signed by A. Perry.

Plate 124. Presentation to Arthur Perry at the Spode works by Spencer Copeland (centre), 1960s. Left Harold Holdway, Art Director, right Leonard Whiter, Home Sales Manager.

OLSEN, ERLING B. (1903-1992) Active 1930s

Designer born in Drammen in Norway. Eric, as he was affectionately known at Copelands, studied at the Oslo school of Art, St. Martin's School of Art, London and the faience studio at Sèvres. He first joined Wedgwoods, where his work was very popular, but in 1932 came to Copelands, being offered a studio of his own and the opportunity to experiment with glazes and new shapes. His animals and Toby jugs are very collectable. In 1942 Eric was called up and went to join the Norwegian Quartermaster General where he became a camouflage expert. After the war he became chief designer for Haeger Potteries, Illinois.

PEACH Active mid–1880s-1890s

Floral artist, shown only on the 1/ over series of pattern numbers as painting flowers, either sprig designs or large groups. He painted mainly on dessert services and occasionally is shown as painting tea services, but there is no record that he painted on vases. His work is found on pattern numbers in the 1/500 range, but to date no signed pieces have been found.

A prolific ceramic artist thought to have been a native of Derby, he was possibly trained at the Derby works and is known to have painted for the Paris 1889 exhibition. He married Elizabeth Tarns, a paintress at Copelands, They returned to Derby and he advised the whole Tarns family to move to Derby saying, 'there were always Italian skies in Derby unlike smoky Stoke'.

PERRY, ARTHUR (1871-1973)

(Colour Plates 147 to 149 and Plate 124) His father George was a mould and figure maker at Copelands. The Perry family were great friends of the Birbecks. Arthur was trained at the Hanley School of Art and was an apprentice at Copelands under first William Birbeck (q.v.) and, on his death, Charles Brough (q.v.). Perry was one of the few ceramic artists who had the opportunity to learn the art of gilding. He was proud to boast that he had never been short of work, having the ability to paint any subject with consummate skill, such as heraldic designs, landscapes, fish, game and flowers.

In the late 1880s he left Copelands, seeing at that time no future, and went to Coalport. There are many examples of his signed work on both Copeland and Coalport ware. After a time he returned to Copelands, where he is remembered with great affection as a man with a lively wit and razor sharp mind, always ready to help the young apprentices.

However, he and Thomas Hassall (q.v.), the art director, disagreed and at the age of fifty-five he left Copelands for the last time. No doubt they would not pay him the rates of pay he thought he deserved. Perry went to Doultons as their premier fish and game painter, where he stayed until he retired. In 1965 he was interviewed on the radio programme *Woman's Hour,* describing ceramic painting. He said it took many hours of diligent study, great dexterity of hand and keenness of the eye, and that many good artists left as their pay was so poor.

Perry was not only an exceptional artist but also had the ability to design for copper plate engravings. His best example was in 1929 when he took the paintings of twenty-four hunting scenes by Lionel Edwards, A.R.C.A., and created designs from them which became a best-selling pattern. He retired aged seventy-six because his eyesight was failing, but continued his hobbies of gardening, walking and swimming. When he retired he lived with his daughter in Eccleshall, Staffordshire.

PLANT Active 1845-1851

Landscape artist, shown as painting pattern numbers from 5594 to 8557, particularly landscapes. It is possible that many of the fine landscapes painted in the late Copeland and Garrett period were done by him, but no signed examples have been found; for example, 'December 1846 Victoria shape china dessert plate pattern number 7547 landscape centre named view in gold letters' and another entry without pattern number of Goodwood House is attributed to him. Many of the examples have monograms and names written in gold lettering on them.

Plate 125. Copeland bone china sample plate signed by B. Potts, an artist gilder, 1860.
Copeland China Collection, Cornwall

POTTS, ?B.   **Active 1872-1897**

An artist gilder who throughout this time is shown as gilding the work of the premier artists on vases, baskets and jardinières, but not on tea services or dessert services. He worked with Alcock, Hürten, Brough and Besche (qq.v.), but no pattern or ornamental shape numbers are given. There is one plate known which is signed by him, now in the Copeland China Collection at Trelissick, Cornwall (Plate 125).

RADFORD   **Active 1869-1889**

There are thirty-five entries under his name, six of which are under J. Radford, in this case possibly Radford Junior as six of them are under this name after 1877. Radford painted on all surfaces from tiles to fine china vases, always shown as painting flowers and fruit, such as begonias and blackberries. His work was mainly gilded by Ball (q.v.). Two entries show he painted 'after' Hürten (q.v.) and there are three showing his work was exhibited in the London international exhibitions of 1871 and 1872. Some pattern numbers are shown as, for example, February 1871 'pattern number D 7857, cup and saucer with an ivory ground painted with festoons of flowers for the Exhibition'; an entry for the 4th Dragoon Regiment reading 'Paris shape dessert plate Pattern number D 8916'; finally tiles decorated with painted wreath of ferns for Cubitt and Co., London (the firm owned by Thomas Cubitt which built many of the buildings in the Belgravia district of London).

RANDALL   **Active 1869-1871**

An artist painting birds on pattern numbers D 7936 and D 7201. He may have been the artisan reporter sent to the Paris Exhibition in 1879.

RHODES   Active 1845-1851

This craftsman or men are listed as Rhodes and Mr. Rhodes. There are 139 entries under the name, eighteen for Mr. Rhodes. When comparing the entries from the Special Order Reference Books and the pattern books, no true picture emerges as to the exact role of these craftsmen, as some entries say 'gilded by' and others 'painted by'. The work shown can be divided into three categories: beautiful floral studies on china dessert plates of all shapes; sprigged and swagged festoons of flowers on teawares; and, finally, a series which could be transfer printed and hand painted.

Although no definite conclusion can be reached it is possible that Rhodes was a superb floral artist. Mr. Rhodes was an artist gilder, listed as early as 1845, and shown also as painting crests of the many families who ordered dessert and tea services.

RISCHGITZ, EDOUARD   (1828-1908) Active 1871-1872

Born in Ghent, he came to the Potteries in the 1860s to work for Mintons. He is shown as working for Copelands in 1871, painting landscapes and Aesop's Fable subjects on Crown body earthenware. His work is signed and very distinctive, with great attention to detail – the buildings in true proportion, the people and animals superbly drawn. He was an artist who could paint in any medium and had paintings exhibited at the Royal Academy. It is possible that he left continental Europe to escape the Franco-Prussian War, knowing he would find work in the Potteries.

When Rischgitz actually left the Potteries to go to London and set up a studio is not known. It is said that he became art master to Queen Victoria's children. Rischgitz had two talented daughters, Mary and Alice, who painted floral subjects with great skill. Their work was hung in many art galleries around the country,

RIVERS, LEONARD
(1863-1939) Active early 1900s

(Plates 126 to 128.) Flower painter of great talent who worked for Mintons from the 1880s. He is shown as painting fish and game subjects for Copelands in 1901. It is possible that he was asked by William Fowler Mountford Copeland (Richard Pirie Copeland's eldest son) to paint the many new species of daffodils that

Plate 126. Leonard Rivers, artist. Rivers spent only a short time at Copelands. Family Photograph

Plate 127. Copeland bone china dessert plate, Richelieu shape, painted and signed by L. Rivers. Mark 242.
Photograph Robert Copeland. Private Collection

Plate 128. Copeland bone china dessert plate painted and signed by L. Rivers. Mark 242.
Photograph Robert Copeland. Private Collection

Copeland was propagating at Kibblestone Hall in the early 1900s. A member of the Copeland family has a fine dessert plate painted with a daffodil study signed by Rivers (Plate 127).

ROBINSON   **Active 1845–1850**
Shown as Robinson, Mr. Robinson, Robinson Junior and Robinson and Co. painting crests, mottoes in gold and pretty floral patterns in the style of Sèvres on all types and bodies of ware.

SADLER, THOMAS   **Active 1892–1906+**
Floral artist known for his rose studies (Plate 129) and floral arrangements in hanging baskets He signed his work either T. Sadler or in monogram TS. He had no formal education, learning his craft at Copelands, and as far as is known he never attended art school. Robert Wallace (q.v.), a gilder who became head of the decorating department, encouraged the young artist, recognising his talent. His work was in constant demand in America. His rose painting is unique, often framed with the fine gilding of Degg (q.v.), Wilson, or Tomlinson. Examples of his work can be seen at the Spode Museum.

SALT, W.H.   **Active 1871–1903**
Artist gilder, shown in 1873 as having worked on a Berrisford shaped vase painted by Besche (q.v.). Salt was also recorded as burnishing and chasing the gilded decoration but some of the gilding on the vase was done by Potts (q.v.).

Salt worked on the dessert service which was painted by Weaver (q.v.) for the London Exhibition of 1871.

SIMPSON

This name is recorded from 1845-1864, then again from 1881-1902. It is possible that the early entries are those of the father and son, and after 1881 his son as Simpson Junior is on some of the entries. Pattern number D 2075 shows fine floral painting. One entry of a cream boat and cover was commissioned by Lady Peel. Most of their work is wreaths of flowers, roses and groups of flowers, none of which is signed, but pattern numbers 7169, 7720, D1723, D1873 are shown as their work.

SIMPSON, ANNE   c.1859

Known to have attended the Hanley School of Art where she won a silver medal, painting floral subjects, but whether she ever painted at Copelands is not known, although an Anne Simpson is recorded as painting floral subjects in 1849. The only female paintress recorded other than Ellen Bruce.

SLATER, FRANK   (d.1939) Active 1900s

Crest painter who for a short time succeeded William Fenton (a crest painter of whom nothing is as yet known), shown as painting on tiles.

Plate 129. Copeland bone china Coupe shape plate signed T. Sadler. Mark 235. Photograph Jack Shaw. Private Collection

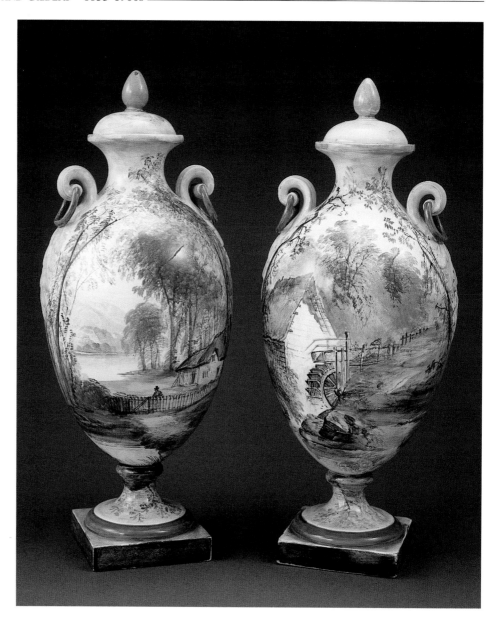

Colour Plate 150. Pair of fine earthenware vases, both sides of each vase painted and signed by W. Yale, c.1880s. Rare pieces.
Copeland China Collection

SWAN

Floral artists recorded from 1858-1872 as Swan, Swan Senior, Swan Junior, Swan's boys and Swan and Co. It would seem that father and son worked together at Copelands throughout this time, painting delicate floral studies and small groups of flowers on the D pattern number series from 1308 to 1720. One example has been found of Swan's work (see title-page) but no signatures have been recorded.

SWETMAN   Active 1845-1851

Crest painter shown as Swetman and T. Swetman and as painting and gilding from pattern numbers 5613-8546, also as painting crests and badges for Regimental orders. One entry is of a special interest pattern – number 6554, a China pen tray, was ordered for Lord Calthorpe.

Colour Plate 151. Fine earthenware picture of a copy of the painting by Richard Ansdell R.A. and Thomas Creswick R.A., The Summer Way to Cross the Ford. *Painted and signed by William Yale. Late 1890s after he had left Copelands and had his own studio at Liverpool Road, Stoke-on-Trent.*

THOMPSON, ALBERT   Active 1850s-1903

A precision gilder who came from Coalport. He is remembered at Copelands as being a fine old gentleman with short white cropped hair. By the 1900s his eyesight was failing and he wore two pairs of spectacles, but was still capable of really fine skilled work . He went to the pub every day for his tot of whisky and was a really popular character in the works. A photograph of him is displayed in the Spode Museum.

WALLACE, ROBERT   Active 1864-1900+

Wallace became an apprentice at Copelands on 7 January 1864. He became an artist gilder. His fine jewelling on pieces of the Midsummer Night's Dream service painted by Samuel Alcock (q.v.) was exhibited at the Paris exhibition of 1889. Wallace is known to have spent all his working life at Copelands, becoming Decorating Manager in the 1900s. He helped many of the artists and gilders, encouraging them to study at the local art schools, and was an example to them all.

235

WEAVER, Charles   **Active 1869-1877**

One of the premier artists of this time, painting for the London exhibitions of 1871 and 1872, specialising in birds in a very distinctive style. They are true to nature and have the appearance of flight, difficult to achieve on the ceramic surface (Plate 130). His work was greatly influenced by the Chinese and Japanese art style. Often his designs have flies and grasses incorporated in them, making the bird studies appear to be in a natural habitat. Much of his work was jewelled and superbly gilded. No other artist at Copelands painted birds with his skill. Very few of the entries in the Special Order Reference Books have pattern numbers against them. His work was gilded by Owen and Salt (q.v.). When Jewitt listed the artists employed at Copelands in 1877 in *The Ceramic Art of Great Britain* he wrote:

> Weaver, now dead (but worthily succeeded by his son) whose birds are equal to those of any other painter.

WEAVER, CHARLES (Junior)   **Active 1886-1900s**

Son of Weaver who finished his apprenticeship at Copelands in 1886. He never achieved the same artistic skill as his famous father but was a versatile artist, shown as painting not only birds and Japanese subjects but also cattle and landscape subjects. He retired early due to ill health.

WHALLEY   **Active late 1880s-1900s**

A flower painter and one of the premier artists of this period. Whalley was an artist of great ability painting mainly on prestige dessert services and teawares. His floral studies used the combination of wild flowers and grasses, but he also painted roses, and designed hanging baskets of flowers which became popular. His work was gilded by the finest gilders, for example Millward and Goodwin (qq.v.), and is usually seen on the 1/over series of pattern numbers from 1/5943. The latest entry is a tea service of a rose pattern number R 2056 painted in 1904.

WORRALL, JAMES (JIMMY)   **Active early 1900s**

Most famous for painting roses on all types and shapes of ware, mainly on the R pattern number series from R1000 to R3000. He signed his work J. Worrall, but his signature is often difficult to find, being hidden in, for example, the leaf of a rose. Worrall was trained at Copelands and much of his work was done for American china houses such as Tiffany's of New York, but the time of highly painted rich services had gone and, as there was no work, he left to join a lithograph firm.

YALE, WILLIAM (BILLY)   **Active 1869-1895**

(Frontispiece, Colour Plates 88, 150 and 151.) Yale trained as an artist at one of the local art schools where he won many gold medals, of which he was very proud. He was a small, portly gentleman. Whether he served an apprenticeship at Copelands is not known but it is more than possible. It is said that when Birbeck

(q.v.) was getting older Yale took over the landscape orders from him and that Birbeck then painted exotic bird paintings. Yale is first shown as painting 'China vases painted with swallows in landscape' and another described as 'birds' for the London exhibition of 1872. Also in this early part of his artistic career he painted marine views and winter scenes. These paintings are much finer than the later style he adopted which became so popular by the early 1880s. These entries show he was painting rough body plaques, umbrella stands and tiles, often in one colour such as cobalt blue, sepia and crimson. They have the name of the view on the reverse with Yale's signature. No doubt they were in great demand but have little artistic skill. By 1889, however, the entries show that Yale painted views of Venice on Coventry shaped dessert plates, pattern number 1/5948. They had a burnished gold drop border and were commissioned by Tiffany and Reed Co. For the Paris Exhibition of 1889 he painted pattern number 1/5945, painted views, also eggshell cups and saucers with two views on the cup and three on the saucer. It would seem that when asked to paint far more artistic studies Yale was still capable of painting them. Most of his work seen today is on plaques, but hopefully some of his finer work may be found. It is thought that Yale left Copelands around 1895, and set up his own studio in London Road, Stoke-on-Trent, where he displayed his work and his medals in the window. In 1889 he lived at Birch Villa, James Street, Stoke-on-Trent.

Plate 130. Pair of Copeland bone china vases with Dog of Fo finials painted and signed by Charles Weaver.
Copeland China Collection

237

Plans

OF THE SPODE WORKS FROM 1911 TO 1969

POTTERY COLOUR CODE.

⭕	CHINA BISCUIT OVEN.	◼	CHINA PLACING.
⭕	GLOST OVEN.	◼	MUSEUM. SHOWROOM. & OFFICES.
⭕	EARTHENWARE BISCUIT OVEN.	◼	MOULD CHAMBERS.
⭕	FRIT KILN.	◼	WAREHOUSES.
⭕	HARDENING ON KILN.	◼	PRINTING.
⭕	ENAMEL KILN.	◼	PAINTING.
◼	OBSOLETE BUILDING.	◼	CHINA MAKING.
◼	CHINA WHITE GLOST WARE HOUSE.	◼	E/W. MAKING.
◼	ENGRAVERS.	◼	MAINTENANCE & MACHINERY.
◼	GROUND LAYING.	◼	E/W SORTING W/H.
◼	CHINA DIPPING.	◼	CHINA FINISHED W/H
◼	MOULD MAKERS & MODELLERS.	◼	DIPPING E/W.
◼	R&D. LABORATORY.	◼	SAGGAR HOUSE.
◼	FIRE STATION.	◼	CANTEEN.
◼	BLACK BANK.	◼	BODY MATERIALS PREPARATION.
◼	TOILETS.	◼	CLAY & SLIPMAKING
◼	COLOUR SHOP.	◼	E/W PLACING.
◼	STRAW STORE.	◼	CHINA BISCUIT. W/H.
		◼	GENERAL UTILITY BUILDINGS. STORES TOILETS. ETC.

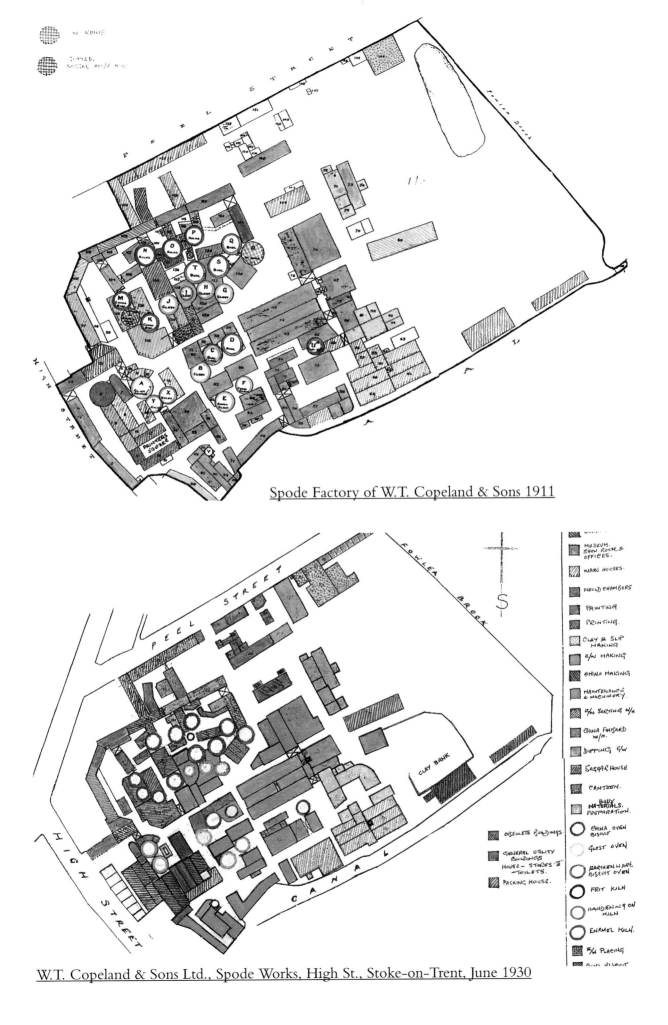

Spode Factory of W.T. Copeland & Sons 1911

W.T. Copeland & Sons Ltd., Spode Works, High St., Stoke-on-Trent, June 1930

KEY TO SPODE WORKS PLAN 1937
SHOWING THE USE OF THE BUILDINGS
AND NAMING THE FOREMEN AND WOMEN IN CHARGE

1.	GROUND FLOOR	Packing	
2, 3.	FIRST FLOOR	Under-glaze printed wares	
	SECOND FLOOR	Under-glaze printed wares	
		Producing patterns "Tower'	
		and 'Italian' under Mr. H.	
		Cheshire	
4.	FIRST FLOOR	Mr. Hewitt's office;later used	
		by Mr. Gresham and Mr.	
		Ronald Copeland's secretary,	
		Miss E. Clowes	
5-7.		Under-glaze painting department	
8.		The New Building; housing the	
		gas-fired glost earthenware	
		tunnel oven and	
9.		the glost sorting warehouse	
		under Miss Annie Davidson	
10.		Under-glaze painting	
		department	
11.		Printing under-glaze biscuit	
		ware department	
12-14.		Stillaging for drying of the	
		printed ware prior to	
		hardening-on	
15-16.		Under-glaze painting shops	
		under Mrs. Avis Murray who	
		also counted the work	
17-18.		Under-glaze printing under Mr.	
		Fred.Roberts	
19.	GROUND FLOOR	Directors' kitchen head cook	
		Mrs. Rebecca Pullen	
	FIRST FLOOR	The Master's Office	
	SECOND FLOOR	Store room, colour room and	
		files	
20.	FIRST FLOOR	The laboratory	
21.	FIRST FLOOR	The Boardroom	
22.		The clay manager's office. Mr.	
		John Whalley	
28.		Under-glaze painting	
31.		Potting shops for earthenware	
		under Mr. John Whalley	
32.		Earthenware biscuit warehouse	
35.	GROUND FLOOR	Cup making	
	FIRST FLOOR	Earthenware biscuit warehouse	
		under Mr. Joe Lee. Also colour	
		mixing for printers	
36.		Earthenware making	
		departments	
37.	FIRST FLOOR	The laboratory on the first floor	
38-42.		Earthenware making	
		department	
47.		Slip house	
49-53.		Obsolete slip kilns	
55.		Milling,grinding etc. areas for	
		preparing the	
56.		materials for manufacturing	
		purposes	

70.		The boiler house – for heating	
		and lighting providing power	
		for the generators	
73.		The electric power house	
74.		The clay bank. Here Clay-	
		making materials were	
		'weathered' out of doors	
75-76.		To be demolished	
77.		The saggar makers, run by	
		the Burton family. On the	
		upper floor were the mould	
		makers	
79.		Maintenance departments,	
		blacksmiths	
80-86.		Fitters etc.	
88, 92.		Canteen, dining and	
		recreational facilities	
95-96.		The sawpit. Poorest quality	
		works store	
97.		The timber store.	
98.		General stores	
99-105.		Weighbridge and stores	
106.	GROUND FLOOR	Modelling department under	
		Mr. L. Henk, Mr.M. Henk and	
		Mr.T.Barlow. Also in this area	
		was the joiners' shop. The	
		senior joiner was Mr. George	
		Edwards and tool filing was	
		under Mr. A. Ridge	
106.	FIRST FLOOR	Mould chamber	
106a.		Acid gilding department under	
		Mr. G. Wood on the ground	
		floor and Mr. Stratherne, the	
		works engineer's office	
107.		'The Villa' wooden structure.	
		Enamel painting department.	
		Used solely for the painting of	
		the 'Indian Tree' pattern,	
		number 959	
107a.		The end section of the Villa	
		was the studio of Mr. Eric	
		Olsen, modeller, designer and	
		sculptor	
110.	GROUND FLOOR	Mould makers	
	FIRST FLOOR	Mould chamber	
111.		Earthenware making	
		department under	
112.		Mr. John Whalley,	
113.		clay manager	
114-116.		Mould makers	
119.	GROUND FLOOR	Ground laying under Mr. Harry	
		Hundley	
	MIDDLE FLOOR	China printing in colour and	
		gold	
	TOP FLOOR	New apprentice paintresses	
		under Mrs. Challinor	

121.	MIDDLE FLOOR	Warehouse for printed ware awaiting painting
	TOP FLOOR	Mrs. Ball's shop. The senior ladies' painting shop. Here the best quality women's work was produced
122.	GROUND FLOOR	Banding and lining
	MIDDLE FLOOR	Handicraft free hand painting
	TOP FLOOR	Female painting apprentices' department under Miss Trimble
124.		Red shop
	GROUND FLOOR	Earthenware placing
	FIRST FLOOR	Pluck and dust enamel printing. Here special fan ventilation was installed
142.	GROUND FLOOR	Earthenware finished warehouse under Mr. J. Harvey and Mr. W. Eccles
	FIRST FLOOR	China white glost house under Mr. Jack Goodyear
144.	GROUND FLOOR	China finished ware selection under Mr. Jim Pullen and Mr. Jack Dabbs
	MIDDLE FLOOR	China white glost ware
	TOP FLOOR	Gilders and painters
145.		Wooden building. The china decorated finished warehouse
146.		Burnishing shops under Miss Rosamund
147.		Toilets
148.		As 142
149.	GROUND FLOOR	The earthenware enamel warehouse
	FIRST FLOOR	The china printing shop
149a.	GROUND FLOOR	Receive for the ware to be fired
	FIRST FLOOR	The enamel painting shop known as 'The Bob Shop'
150.	FIRST FLOOR	Apprentice painters and journeymen
151	GROUND FLOOR	China dipping
	FIRST FLOOR	China biscuit warehouse
152.		The colour shop under Mrs. Hammond. The colours were mixed and distributed throughout the departments
153.	GROUND FLOOR	The pattern book safe and the records office under Mr. Sam Williams
154.		Continuation of the museum.
155.	GROUND FLOOR	As 153
	FIRST FLOOR	The studios of Mr. Harry Hammersley, Copeland's floral artist, and Mr. Charles Deaville, head gilder
156.	GROUND FLOOR	China potting
	FIRST FLOOR	Mould chamber
157.	GROUND FLOOR	The works museum
	FIRST FLOOR	The works showroom
158.		A large four storeyed building. First and second floor china making standard wares. Third floor Mould chamber under Mr. Will Johnson. Fourth floor all engraving under Mr. Joseph Hassall

158a.	FIRST FLOOR	Turning
	SECOND FLOOR	Mr. Harold Holdway's studio
	THIRD FLOOR	Mr. Thomas Hassall's office and studio
	FOURTH FLOOR	Housing the block moulds
159.		The clay cellar for china clay processing, pugging, wedging etc.
160.		The wages office
161		China making with scolloping and handling on the ground floor
162.	GROUND FLOOR	China placers
	FIRST FLOOR	The china biscuit warehouse china casting, dish making
163.		
	FIRST FLOOR	Mr. E. Steele modelling birds and figures
	TOP FLOOR	The earthenware under-glaze decorations warehouse under Mr. Albert Bowden
165.		The office block
166.		with the executive
167.		offices on the ground floor
175.		The engineering fitting shop under Mr. Bert Lockett
176.		The electricians' department under Mr. Ernest Thornton

CHINA BISCUIT FIRING OVENS
B = Pump   C = Middle   D = New-un   E = Exchange
Head Fireman Mr. Jim Evans

EARTHENWARE BISCUIT OVENS
J = Back   K = Dukes   L = Middle   M = Entry
Head Fireman Mr. Ashton Maskery

ENAMEL ON-GLAZE FIRING KILNS
A and B were bottle kilns which were obsolete and awaiting demolition.
H & C ROTOLEC (electric circular kilns used for ordinary firing and ground firing) on site number 123.
Head Enamel Fireman Mr. Frank Simpson

F B H Kilns were used for china glost firing

E = Frit kiln for glaze making

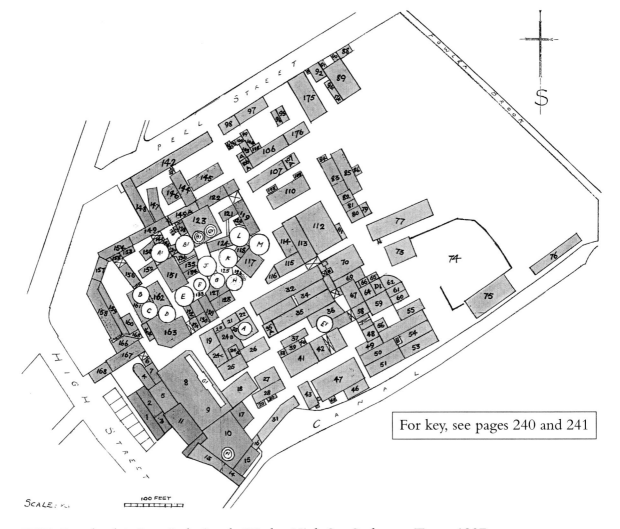

For key, see pages 240 and 241

SCALE:

100 FEET

W.T. Copeland & Sons Ltd., Spode Works, High St., Stoke-on-Trent, 1937

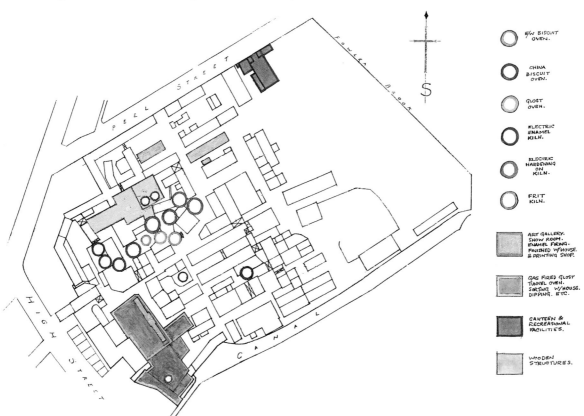

E/W BISCUIT OVEN.

CHINA BISCUIT OVEN.

GLOST OVEN.

ELECTRIC ENAMEL KILN.

ELECTRIC HARDENING ON KILN.

FRIT KILN.

ART GALLERY.
SHOW ROOM.
ENAMEL FIRING.
FINISHED W/HOUSE.
& PRINTING SHOP.

GAS FIRED GLOST TUNNEL OVEN.
SORTING W/HOUSE.
DIPPING. ETC.

CANTEEN &
RECREATIONAL
FACILITIES.

WOODEN
STRUCTURES.

W.T. Copeland & Sons Ltd., High St., Stoke-on-Trent, 20th August 1939

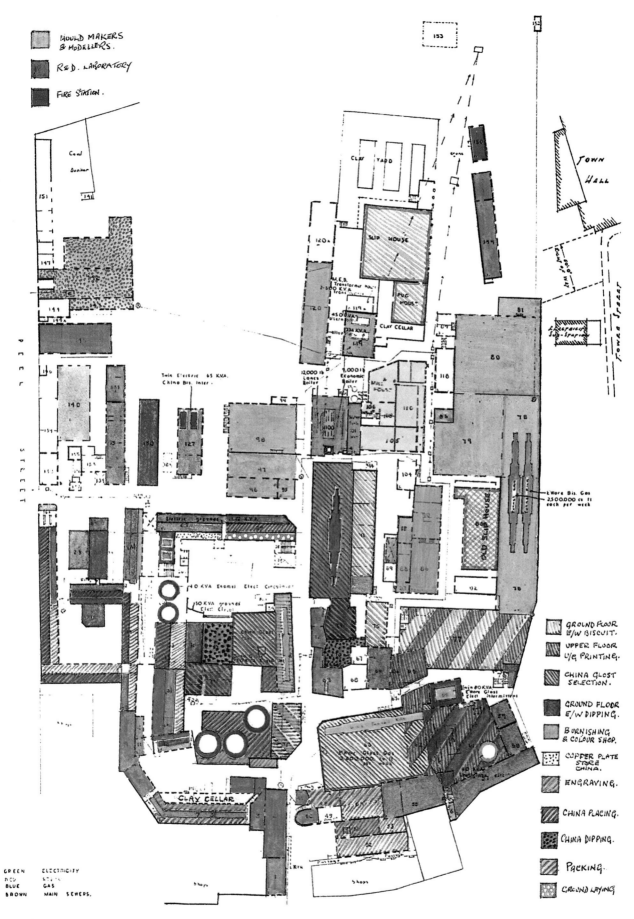

Appendix 1

SPECIAL COMMISSIONS

Copelands had the expertise to cater for special markets, supplying regiments, hotels, shipping lines, gentlemen's clubs and railway companies with earthenware and bone china services which had patterns incorporating badges and crests, and also ware commissioned by or for Royalty. They were the acknowledged leading manufacturers of large ceramic slabs and plaques. The most notable examples are listed in this appendix.

1857 The Shah's Service (Plate 131)
This was first seen by Mr M.I.W. Willis-Fear in the 1960s at the Golestan Palace in Tehran, then the property of the Shah of Persia, hence its name. Some pieces of the service are recorded in the Special Order Books on 25 September 1857.

In 1970 part of the service was displayed at the bicentenary celebrations at the Royal Academy, London. Mr. Leonard Whiter, then Copelands' Home Sales Manager, went to Tehran to collect and pack the pieces and after the exhibition returned them personally to the Shah. This was the first time that the service had been seen in England.

It was designed by W.H. Goss, Copelands' chief designer (see Chapter 7). The table centres were supported by three gilded lions, one bearing a shield decorated in proper heraldic colours with the arms of Queen Victoria and Prince Albert and the other two shields had the embossed profile heads of the Queen and Prince Albert in raised gold. The other comport bore the arms of Napoleon III and the Empress Eugénie, and their heads similarly decorated The service is thought to be the first known examples of Goss's heraldic design. All pieces of the service had jewelled decoration and landscapes. The name of the artist who painted the service is not recorded but it is attributed to Daniel Lucas junior. It is not known who first commissioned this superb service but it is thought that it was given to Napoleon III by Queen Victoria when he visited England.

1863 The Prince of Wales Service (Colour Plate 151)
Commissioned by the Prince on his marriage to H.R.H. Princess Alexandra of Denmark in March 1863 in St. George's Chapel, Windsor, the service consisted of 198 pieces: a large centrepiece, eight comports, two cream bowls, two ice pails, twelve sweetmeat comports, seventy-two cups and saucers and fifty plates. This commission took three years to complete (see Chapter 3).

Plate 131. Copeland china oblong comport from the Shah's service. Scene not named. Length 13⅛in. (33cm).

Plate 132. Copeland bone china dessert plate from the Star of India service thought to have been presented to Queen Victoria by her Brigade of Guards

1863 The City Banquet Set (Colour Plate 152)

After the marriage of the Prince and Princess of Wales, the City of London held on 8 June a Banquet and Ball in honour of the Royal couple, when the Prince was made a Freeman of the City. The jewelled set consisted of a pillar candlestick, ringstand, chamber ewer and bowl, rose knob toilet box, another ewer and bowl with sponge drainer, covered soap and brush dishes and a ribbon-handled tray. It is recorded in the Special Order Book as: 'China, pink scollop, jewel border, painted leaf of bay leaves. Blue medallions with letter in raised and chased gold'. The cost of the decoration was listed as £32.6s.2d.

The Guildhall Library have records showing that Mr. Thomas Crase was responsible for the toiletries needed in the retiring rooms and that he designed them. Copelands were paid £52 for this set, some of which is now displayed in the Spode Museum. (Research by Robert Copeland.)

1891 The Star of India Service (Plate 132)

Thought to have been presented to Queen Victoria by the Brigade of Guards, this small service of eighteen plates and four comports was commissioned by Thomas Goode, pattern number C898. The pattern consists of an elaborate border of turquoise blue with York and Tudor roses linked with two thin chains in proper colours. In the centre the monogram V.R.I. is surmounted within crimson and gold upon the jewelled device of the Star of India. The five pointed star has the motto 'Heavens light our guide' and the whole is surmounted with the gilded rays of the sun. The initials V.R.I. (Victoria Regina et Imperatrix) are from the title Queen Victoria adopted when on May Day 1876 she was declared Empress of India. (Research by Robert Copeland.)

The Mecklenburg Service (See Plate 113)

The Chelsea factory made this service in 1793. It was commissioned by King George III and Queen Charlotte as a present for Duke Adolphus Frederick IV of Mecklenburg-Strelitz, where it remained until the early 1920s when it was bought by Sir Joseph Duveen. He returned it to the Royal Family in 1948 and it is displayed at Buckingham Palace.

Copelands made four copies of the service. The first was exhibited at the Paris Exhibition of 1889 and bought by the King of Greece. In 1892 Sir Henry Lochard ordered one for the British High Commissioner in Cape Town. The citizens of Norwich presented one to George, Duke of York, on his marriage in 1893, and again in 1932 Norwich presented a service to King George V and Queen Mary. All were painted by J. Arrowsmith (see Chapter 7).

1901 The 'Ophir' Dessert Service

Made for the liner H.M.S. *Ophir* for a world cruise with the Duke and Duchess of York aboard, the service was commissioned by Thomas Goode, pattern number C1247, and decorated with a gold print of the 'pheasant's eye'

Colour Plate 151. Copeland bone china cup and saucer commissioned by the King of Norway as a present to Queen Alexandra, c.1867. The painter is C.F. Hürten, but the gilder is unknown.

Colour Plate 152. Copeland bone china dressing table set made for the use of Princess Alexandra in her boudoir at the City of London Banquet, 8 June 1863.

design. In the centre the York rose is enclosed within the blue garter ribbon with a crown and anchor. Pieces of the service are at Windsor Castle. (Research by Robert Copeland.)

Services for the Royal Yacht (Plates 133 and 134)

The first service bearing a crown over an anchor with the initials P.R., one on either side of anchor, was supplied by Spode and although the Prince Regent was not renowned for any nautical inclinations it has always been assumed that this first service was in use on the Royal Yacht. There were eight royal yachts used by the Royal Family during the twenty year period of the Regency and the reign of George IV.

The Arms Book No. 1 in the Spode archives records pattern number 8120, a design with scroll type motifs in blue and gold on the border with a simple blue garter and in the centre 'Her Majesty's Yacht' in gold; a crown surmounts the garter. Arms Book No. 3 has an entry for the Royal Yacht *Osborne* which is decorated with the Prince of Wales plumes in the centre, pattern number 8195 supplied in July 1884. In July 1901 Thomas Goode commissioned pattern number C1003; the border is a rim depth of a rich Sèvres green on which are circular reserve panels, six on the plates, four on the coffee saucers and three on the coffee cups. Alternative panels display the Royal cipher, with

Plate 133. Spode. Left: cream or sauce tureen from the service made for the Prince Regent. Right: plate from a service made for H.M. King George IV.

the motto 'Honi Soit Qui Mal Y Pense' inscribed on the blue garter, and an anchor. As the monarch changed the pattern remained the same but the ciphers of the reigning monarch were used dating up to 1954. (Research by Robert Copeland.)

Regimental Services (Colour Plates 153-156)
There are three Arms Books in the Spode archives which record the badges of the many famous regiments which ordered services of earthenware and bone china from Spode and Copeland. The decoration ranged from simple border patterns incorporating the badge of the regiment, for everyday use, to highly decorated services used in the officers' mess. One of the most popular patterns was number 6622, having a gold band on the rim with a blue band underneath and the badge of the regiment.

Slabs and large plaques
Copelands were the recognised leading manufacturer for slabs and large plaques. Perhaps the most important commission for decorated panels came

from Mr. Walter Macfarlane of Glasgow for tiles to decorate the walls of certain rooms in his house at 22 Park Circus. Llewellyn Jewitt gave a graphic account in the *Art-Journal* of 1875:

Messrs Copeland & Sons New Internal Mural Tile Decoration

In several of the apartments of this mansion – the billiard and bathrooms, for instance – Mr.Macfarlane desired to introduce some new feature which should, if possible inaugurate what might with propriety be called a nineteenth-century style of decoration. He therefore wisely consulted Messrs. Copeland, who, acting on his idea, prepared a series of designs in which, while the classic laws of Art were faithfully adhered to are, both in subject and in treatment, strictly characteristic of the present day. The general design is a terra-cotta dado of full Indian red tone of colour, walls of pale celadon tint, and a frieze painted in monochrome, in continuous subjects apposite to the uses of the various rooms which are thus covered with tiles, in one grand design, from floor to ceiling. The walls between the dado and the frieze are covered, as just stated, with celadon tiles placed diagonally, with the joints made just sufficiently apparent to give a geometrical break to the surface, and so remove what otherwise might be a sameness in appearance; while those of the frieze (which are of a pale yellow ground-colour well adapted for throwing out the figures, and which, when the room is lit up, disappears, and gives the effect of a luminous sky to the pictures) are placed horizontally and their edges fitted with such mathematical precision

Plate 134. *Copeland bone china dessert plate and coffee cup and saucer made for George V for use on the Royal Yacht.*

Colour Plate 153. Example taken from the Arms Pattern Book 2. Q was the code for the family whose crest is in the centre of the plate, as yet unidentified. Pattern D6730. Floral panels painted by Hürten.

Colour Plate 155 (below left). Badge of the 37th Volunteers, pattern D576 1868. Arms Book 2. Spode Archives

Colour Plate 156 (below). Pattern book entry for the 2nd Madras E.L. Infantry dated 5 November 1852. Arms Book 2. Spode Archives

Colour Plate 154. Pattern book entry for the 28th Regiment, pattern 9981 dated 28 December 1858. Arms Book 2. Spode Archives

and nicety that their joints are invisible. The whole of the tiles have a dead, or purely fresco surface, and are most perfect for the purpose for which they are intended; and from their peculiar hardness and other characteristics – the result of much anxious thought and experiment – are perfectly impervious to the action of damp, and cannot fail to be permanent.

The frieze (three feet in height) of the billiard-room represents, in four separate groupings on the four sides of the apartment, the sports of the British race; one side being devoted to 'Health', in which youthful games conducing to that essential from infancy, with its doll and other playthings, to boyhood and youthhood, with hoop, cricket, skating, curling, snowballing, and so on; another to 'Strength', with its central allegorical figure and groups representing pole-leaping, shot-throwing, wrestling, football, hockey, boxing, &c.; a third to 'Courage', a central allegorical figure supported by genii, the one proclaiming, and the other crowning, deeds of heroism in the army, in saving lives from shipwreck, fire, and other casualties, and the wild sports of our Eastern empire and North American colonies; and the fourth to 'Fortitude', in which the central group surrounding the allegorical figure is composed of lifelike portraits of such men as Livingstone, Burton, McClintock, Layard, and others; the remaining portions showing athletes contesting in a foot-race, and crews in a boat-race. The friezes of this room, painted in monochrome, are the work of Mr. R.J. Abraham (son of the Art-Director of the Works), who recently won the Art-Union prize, and is a gold-medalist, and Mr. Besche, a skilful artist, whose works are in high repute.

The frieze of the heating-room of the Turkish baths, which is lined in a precisely similar style to the other, is entirely composed of tropical plants and flowers, arranged in a masterly and effective manner, and painted, even to the most minute detail, with consummate skill and with true artistic feeling. This frieze, which is painted in sepia with its fullest and best effect, is entirely the work of Mr. Hurten, and is a worthy example of his pencil both in arrangement and in treatment. The whole of the plants represented are, without an exception, studies from nature, sketched and arranged for this special purpose from the plants themselves in the magnificent conservatories of the Duke of Devonshire at Chatsworth; and they are in each individual instance reproduced with pre-Raphaelite accuracy and precision.

The friezes are masterpieces of Art as well as of manipulative skill. They reflect the highest credit on Messrs. Copeland and their Art-Director, Mr. Abraham, by whom they have been produced, and who have thus inaugurated a new, and what we pronounce to be a successful style, of internal decoration – one that is sure to be followed in many a mansion and home of taste in our country and abroad. Mr. Macfarlane will have reason to be proud of his acquisition, and has the satisfaction of feeling, that with the aid of Messrs. Copeland and their skilled staff of artists, he has originated a novel feature in Art-decoration, and carried it to an enviably successful issue. Messrs. Copeland are renowned for the excellence of their work and for the true artistic feeling and skill which characterises everything that passes from their hands, and their present productions will, if that be possible, add to their celebrity.

Appendix 2

WARE COMMISSIONED BY RAILWAY COMPANIES, HOTELS AND
REFRESHMENT ROOMS, SHIPPING LINES, GENTLEMEN'S CLUBS
AND HOSPITALS
taken from the Arms Books 1-3 in the Spode Archives 1847-1912

Pattern No.	Date	Railway Company
7772 & B786	1848	Eastern Counties
		Cambridge Refreshment Rooms
D129	1855	Great Western Hotel, Reading
D 3753	1864	The Great Eastern
D8914 & D 9237	1873	The Great Western
2/159	1876	Manchester, Sheffield & Lincolnshire
2/735	1877	London North Western railway commissioned ware for their refreshment rooms at Holyhead, Stafford, Bangor, Nuneaton, North Walls, Dublin, Victoria Station and Manchester. No pattern number given for ware supplied to the Great Central Railways dining cars

Pattern No.	Date	Shipping Line
D 4893	1874	White Cross Line
no pattern number	1880	Greenock Steam Co
no pattern number	1883	New Haven & Honfleur steam packet
119608	1899	White Star Line
R 416	1901	White Star Line
R4311&2	1911	White Star Line

The Badge Books show that Copelands were also commissioned to supply ware for the Orkney & Shetland Steam Navigation Company and the Red Funnel line. They also had orders from many yacht clubs including:

8195	1884	Royal Yacht Osborne
D 3370	1885	Royal London Yacht club

Pattern No.	Date	Hotels
D 3832	1866	Clarendon Hotel, Watford
D5112	1867	The Old Blue Boar Inn, Leicester
D 4456	1867	The Imperial Hotel, Southampton
D 5268	1868	The George Hotel, Glasgow
D 6034	1869	Bristol City Hotel

D 1490	1870	The Shelbourne Hotel, Dublin
D 1490	1870	The Pitts Hotel, Dublin
D7299	1870	The Royal Marine Hotel, Kingston
D6074	1870	The George Hotel, Dublin
D966	1870	The Balmoral Hotel, Edinburgh
D4795	1871	Manor House Hotel, Leamington Spa
8195	1873	The Royal Hotel, Lowestoft
7886	1877	Royal Pier Hotel, Ryde
D 2629	1878	The Marine Hotel, Worthing
1/2541	1881	Imperial Hotel, Torquay
D3315	1881	The Burlington Oyster Bar, Dublin
D 8818	1881	The Hynes Oyster Bar, Dublin
D3370	1884	Royal Hotel Esplanade, Guernsey

Pattern No.	Date	Gentlemen's Clubs
7749 & 7742	1847	Windham Club
7772	1847	Union Club
7962	1849	Brooks Club
9036	1855	Westminster Club
D 749 & 789	1858	The Reform Club
8195	1863	Union Club, Sydney
8195	1863	Shanghai Club
7608	1863	National Club
D2389	1863	Queensland Club
D 3774	1864	The New University Club
D5348	1868	Hong Kong Club
D 749& 4460	1873	The Reform Club
D6987	1873	The Adelaide Club
2/159	1875	The Royal & Military Club
8195	1879	The Conservative Club London house
D749	1884	The Royal United Service Club

Pattern No.	Date	Hospitals
D2746	1863	Craig Royal Hospital, Ballarat
D 9814	1874	The General Royal Infirmary, Leeds
1/1024	1877	Markwells Royal Hospital, Brighton

W.T. Copeland & Sons also produced ware for the House of Commons in 1864, the Corporation of London in 1876 and the Parliament of Queensland in 1914.

Appendix 3

DETAILS TAKEN FROM THE SPECIAL ORDER REFERENCE BOOKS
1833-1900s – SPODE ARCHIVES

Pattern	Artist or Gilder	Description of Decoration	Pattern	Artist or Gilder	Description of Decoration
2036	Ball	Landscape centre	5800	Pedley H	Birds on each side
2285	Smith	Matching	5810	Mansfield	
2379	Owen	Gilt by Owen	5836	Robinson	Plant in centre
4197	Barrett		5836	Robinson	Badge
4577	Barrett H	Badge	5877	Mansfield	
4577	Clowes H	Badge	6164	Greatbach	Painted by
4719	Glover		6202	Greatbach	Fruit in border instead of figures
5015	Barrett H	Richly gilt			
5061	Robinson		6206	Lycett	Gilding on the ground
5073	Robinson		6237	Barrett	
5193	Mansfield		6279	Plant	
5242	Mansfield		6279	Robinson	
5246	Bagguley	Arms of INNER TEMPLE	6286	Lycett	
5251	Robinson	Badge instead of group	6377	Rhodes	
5292	Rhodes		6425	Rhodes	
5336	Greatbach		6456	Bagguley	
5349	Robinson		6462	Greatbatch	
5349	Wood	Badge	6517	Glover	Also single candlestick
5349	Wood	Knob and handle gilt	6532	Robinson	89th painted in gold
5349	Mansfield	Inscribed in gold	6579	Dudley	All Painted
5349	Wood R	With Gold Arms	6579	Rhodes	Painting 1/3d Ground laying 1/6d
5349	Bradley	Badge of 6th in gold			
5464	Mansfield		6609	Rhodes	
5484	Greatbach R	Badge of 3rd Bengal Native Infantry	6662	Rhodes	
			6622	Plant	ASTRA CASTRA NUMEN LUMEN
5580	Barrett H	Eagle crest			
5594	Plant	With MARIANA DE REBAZA in gold	6622	Wood	Griffins head Crest on rim
			6622	Wood	Garter, Motto, Initials
5613	Swetman	Badge of the 28th Regiment	6622	Bagguley	Lion and Motto on rim Painting 8d
5617	Ball	Crest and Motto			
5617	Barrett		6672	Wood	Arms AT SPEC NON FRACTA
5622	Glover	Elephant Head and Motto			
5627	Greatbach	With Mr Burns Arms	6622	Glover	Crest in gold cypher
5690	Rhodes		6622	Bird	With WENTWORTH CLAY crest
5726	Mansfield				
5761	Greatbatch		6622	Bradley	Wellesley crest
5766	Bagguley		6622	Wood	Blue lines with Griffin and head
5794	Mansfield	Gold star	6622	Bradley	NIL TEMERE TENTH NIL TIMIDE
5800	Mansfield Joseph	Border of 5800 A.M. FULLER BORN Dec 3 1849			Leopards Head
			6622	Wood	With Crest
5800	Ball	Raised gold compartments and birds	6635	Ball	
			6694	Glover	
5800	Ball	Wreath of flowers			

Pattern	Artist or Gilder	Description of Decoration
6703	Rhodes	
6720	Edge	Blue with Gilt handles
6737	Greatbatch	
6747	Barrett H	Bruces groups colouring
6748	Barrett	
6749	Mansfield	
6763	Rhodes	
6810	Rhodes	
6830	Robinson	Gold borders in Serpentine form
6841	Rhodes	Flowers and flies
6841	Wood	Arms on rim
6865	Rhodes	
6869	Rhode	
6924	Ball	
6949	Greatbach	Coat of Arms
6950	Rhodes	
7009	Rhodes	
7011	Robinson	
7011	Rhodes	
7020	Rhodes	
7027	Rhodes	Gold crest and cypher
7027	Rhodes	Lion and Cypher in gold
7056	Rhodes	
7078	Rhodes	
7092	Ball	Richly gilt
7108	Ball	Monogram in centre
7112	Glover	
7132	Ball	Flowers in panel
7169	Rhodes	Print and enamel
7182	Ball	
7184	Rhodes	Badge in blue and gold
7194	Barrett H	Crest in Armour
7197	Greatbach R	Flowers of 7197
7199	Rhodes	
7207	Greatbatch	
7240	Thompson	No figure
7245	Greatbach	
7245	Ball	Pencil colours and gilding
7251	Glover	No group
7262	Steel	Lions crest printed in gold
7262	Plant	
7271	Ball	Badge on rim
7279	Plant	Wreath of flowers
7279	Rhodes	Lions Crest
7279	Bagguley	
7280	Rhodes	
7283-4	Rhodes	
7285	Barrett	
7290	Bagguley	
7291	Plant	

Pattern	Artist or Gilder	Description of Decoration
7295	Rhodes	
7296	Greatbatch	
7304	Barrett	
7316	Bagguley	
7317	Boffey	Blue patches and gilding
7323	Rhodes	
7337	Rhodes	For London Warehouse
7339	Rhodes	Border of 7279 and badge
7342	Greatbach	Bruce's printed groups
7346	Rhodes	
7348	Barrett H	Floral centre painting 9d
7351	Ball	Panel and badge
7352	Bagguley	
7352	Barrett H	Water Mill
7357	Ledder	Badge
7380	Rhodes	With gold crest
7380	Wood	Sprig of 341 gold edge
7389	Greatbatch	
7390	Barrett	
7393	Ball	
7394	Ball	Roses and blue ribbon
7394	Glover	Roses and ribbon
7395	Ball	
7398	Greatbach	Groups of roses and forget me knots
7399	Evans	Badge of 17th Regiment
7399	Rhodes	Badge in panel
7400	Rhodes	Wreath of flowers painting 6/5d
7401	Greatbach	Panels with two crests
7402	Rhodes	Aquatic border
7404	Ball	
7405	Plant	
7407	Plant	Painting 6/-
7408	Plant	
7414	Rhodes	
7417	Rhodes	Aquatic pattern
7418	Greatbach	Dresden borders
7418	Greatbach	Printed dresden border
7418	Robinson	
7419	Glover	
7419	Ball	
7421	Ball	Flowers in centre
7430	Rhodes	
7432-4	Rhodes	
7438	Glover	
7441	Rhodes	Chinese flowers in different styles
7444	Rhodes	Arms in blue on rim
7444	Rhodes	With Badge printed EURYDICE

Pattern	Artist or Gilder	Description of Decoration	Pattern	Artist or Gilder	Description of Decoration
7444	Rhodes	Badge ROYAL HOTEL LOWESTOFT	7583	Rhodes	
7444	Rhodes	Badge in Brown	7591	Barrett	
7445-6	Rhodes		7591	Ball	
7454	Rhodes	Badge only	7591	Greatbatch	
7454	Nicholls	Rafaellesque pattern	7593	Greatbach	
7456	Bassett	Painting 4/3d gilding 5/6d	7593	Robinson	
7461	Ball	Lace and vine border	7596	Barrett	
7464	Greatbatch		7602	Barrett	
7467	Barrett H	Badge of 90th light infantry	7605	Rhodes	
7467	Wood	Elephant ribbon and motto on badge	7607	Rhodes	
7469	Rhodes		7608	Rhodes	
7472	Wood	Handles solid gilt	7614	Glover	
7475	Barrett H	Harp and shamrock in centre	7631	Greatbatch	
7480	Rhodes		7642	Ball	
7481	Rhodes	Blue Garter Lion NIL DESPERANDUM	7645	Greatbatch	
7482	Rhodes		7649	Rhodes	
7483	Greatbach	Watteau subjects in centre	7652	Rhodes	
7483	Ball	Watteau in centre border gilt and chased	7655	Greatbatch	
7484	Ball W	Flowers and Birds	7664	Barrett	
7485	Ball	Crest, Richly gilt Bird in centre	7665	Rhodes	
7485	Ball	Rose & thistle panels and Watteau centre	7667	Greatbatch	
7485	Plant		7680-1	Rhodes	
7487	Ball	Foreign mark and Hieroglyphs	7688-9	Rhodes	
7491	Evans	Elks head crest in centre	7696	Glover	
7492	Rhodes	All with Persian Characters	7699	Barrett	
7502	Rhodes	Crest 7 NONEM EXTENDRE FACTIS	7712	Rhodes	
7503	Glover		7720	Ball	
7506	Glover	But sprig in centre	7724-6	Ball	
7507	Greatbatch		7730	Greatbatch	
7513	Barrett		7733	Ball	
7523	Rhodes		7734	Rhodes	
7532	Greatbatch		7737	Barrett	
7532	Ball		7737	Robinson	
7532	Plant		7739	Rhodes	
7533-4	Rhodes		7741	Barrett	
7541	Rhodes		7761	Greatbatch	
7547	Plant		7773	Rhodes	
7554	Greatbatch		7781	Rhodes	
7555	Rhodes		7789	Rhodes	
7559	Barrett		7798	Greatbatch	
7561	Ball		7810	Ball	
7563	Glover		7813	Glover	
7565	Greatbatch		7816	Ball	
7569	Ball		7820	Ball	
7572	Rhodes		7822-3	Ball	
			7825	Barrett	
			7830	Ball	
			7839	Ball	
			7842	Ball	
			7843-5	Ball	
			7846-7	Rhodes	

Pattern	Artist or Gilder	Description of Decoration	Pattern	Artist or Gilder	Description of Decoration
7850	Ball		8118	Robinson	Lion rampant and gold letters
7853	Rhodes		8118	Barrett	
7855	Barrett		8119	Rhodes	
7857	Mansfield		8132	Rhodes	
7865-7	Ball		8134	Rhodes	Crest in blue centre
7869	Rhodes		8139	Thompson	Gilt border
7872	Rhodes		8140	Ball	
7886	Rhodes		8143	Greatbatch	
7887	Greatbatch		8157	Barrett H	Fruit in centre
7887	Ball		8157	Steel	White and gold
7888	Rhodes		8157	Greatbatch	
7890	Ball		8159	Barrett	
7892-3	Greatbatch		8166	Ball	Painted group in wreaths richly gilt
7894	Rhodes				
7897	Greatbatch		8189	Mart G	Star of 8266 on cup
7902	Rhodes		8197	Mansfield	
7905	Ball		8205	Rhodes W	Painted group
7908	Plant		8205	Greatbatch	
7912	Rhodes		8225	Greatbatch	
7913	Greatbatch		8231	Ball	Wreaths of flowers
7932	Ball		8231	Greatbatch	
7936-7	Ball		8236	Ball	
7955	Ball		8241	Greatbatch	
7965	Rhodes		8244	Steel John	Narrow lines each side of gold
8001	Rhodes	Groups in pencil chrome	8255	Rhodes	Blue lines with star in centre
8003	Ball	Watteau subject and gilt	8270	Rhodes	
8014	Ball	Groups and sprigs	8292	Rhodes	Flowers in panel & centre richly gilt
8014	Ball	Gold spriggs in place of groups			
8014	Greatbatch		8297	Rhodes	Landscape in centre
8015	Ball	Wreath of flowers and dentil edge	8301	Barrett H	Lion crest in centre
			8303	Barrett	
8016	Barrett H	3 goldpanels fruit & flowers	8338	Mansfield	
8026	Rhodes	Pink done by women	8350	Ball	
8028	Greatbatch		8353	Rhodes	
8035	Ball	Wreath of ribbon centre Gold letters	8390	Ball	With THOMAS in wreath
			8390	Greatbatch	
8045	Rhodes	Roses printed in black and tinted	8414	Ball	Landscape with name in gold letters
8069	Rhodes				
8080	Ball	Bead and dresden borders	8430	Mansfield	
8082	Greatbatch		8431	Barrett	
8084	Rhodes	Black ground and gold curls	8432	Greatbatch	
8084	Rhodes	Richly gilt	8434	Barrett	
8084	Hartshorn		8463	Greatbach	LORD BATEMANS CLUB
8086	Rhodes	Gold edge to scollops	8488	Rhodes	
8086	Rhodes	Badge of AMERICAN BOWLEY SCHOONER	8494	Ball	Lace border blue and gold
			8502	Greatbatch	
8086-8175	Rhodes		8503	Ball	
8090	Rhodes		8527	Ball	3 gold compartments with wreaths of flowers
8099	Ball	Raised gold border	8532	Ball	Gold panel with flowers and birds
8117	Rhodes				

257

Pattern	Artist or Gilder	Description of Decoration	Pattern	Artist or Gilder	Description of Decoration
8549	Greatbach	R crest in centre NON SlBI SEB ALIS	1/3164	Weaver	Landscape
8553	Rhodes		1/3169	Brayford	
8557	Plant	Style of 5193 Blue done by women	1/3290	Birbeck Francis	Rich cashmere design cost 4/-
			1/3636	Brayford Charles	Raised gold bird centre
8558	Greatbach R	With star in centre	1/3817	Mansfield Joseph	Burnished gold
8561	Cloves H	Light sutherland green ground	1/3823	Hall	Gilt by Hall
8614	Mansfield	Raised gold of 8208 Scroll	1/4039	Yale William	Painted flower centre
8662	Ball		1/4087	Alcock	
8716	Robinson	Gilt work round the panels	1/4592	Baker	Full centre well gilt and jewelled
8718	Ball	Alhambra blue ground and raised gilding	1/4692	Birbeck W	Birds in panel and centre
8768	Rhodes	Embossing with blue and gilt	1/4935	Hall T	Gilt by T. Hall
8832	Ball	Festoons of flowers richly gilt	1/5108	Hurten Charles F	Rich raised and sanded gold
9072	Bourne	Heath pattern	1/5463	Hyatt	Gilt on royal blue ground
9952	Cartlidge	Flowers and birds	1/5581	Bourne	Landscape in centre
B700	Barrett		1/5597	Peach	Centre
C309	Brough		1/5709	Peach	Painted flowers in three panels
1/88	Peach	Painted and raised flowers after Brayford	1/5901	Birbeck W	Chelsea Birds
			1/5945	Yale William	Painted Views
1/222	Golterman	Sea plant	1/5948	Yale William	Views
1/222	Golterman	Violets	1/5997	Goodwin Edward	Gold scroll panels
1/282	Wallace R	Gilt by Wallace	1/6034	Goodwin Edward	Printed and painted wreath ribbon
1/1323	Radford				
1/1774	Birbeck W	Full Centre landscape paid 4/4/0	1/6217	Peach	3 panels of flowers
			1/6229	Howell	Monogram centre 6 panels on rim gold sprigs
1/1774	Birbeck.W	Full landscape			
1/1984	Birbeck W	Painted full centre landscape	1/7056	Brough Charles	Painted flowers
1/2020	Yale William	Full Landscape centre 3.18.0d	1/7148	Brough Charles	Violets
1/2028	Birbeck	Painted bird	1/7187	Brough Charles	Sprays and Humming birds
1/2195	Birbeck	Painted bird Painting 4/4/0d	1/7221	Arrowsmith John	Painted trophies in 5 panels
1/2880	Birbeck W	Bird Centres cost 84/-	1/7398	Brough Charles	Spray or yellow chrysanthemums
1/2909	Birbeck				
1/2910	Yale William	Landscape in Indian blue	1/7415	Baker	Flowers and white enamel
1/3047	Birbeck W	Painted full landscape	1/7451	Arrowsmith John	Flowers after Walley
1/3114	Weaver	Birds & three nests with flowers	1/7484	Howell S	Raised and chased gold border
1/3119	Yale William	Full centre landscape	1/7874	Hulme Frederick	Sanded solid gilt
1/3120	Yale William	Full landscape centre	1/7912	Barrett H	Game
1/3123	Brayford Charles	Fruits	1/8078	Stevenson	Gilt by Stevenson
1/3126	Yale William	Full centre landscape	1/8228	Yale William	Full centre landscape
1/3127	Yale William	Full landscape	1/8535	Lea H	Fish centre
1/3127	Yale William	Full landscape centre	1/8585	Sadler Thomas	Festoons of roses and forget-me-nots
1/3129	Yale William	Painted full centre Sheep etc			
1/3131	Brayford Charles	Sanded Birds Nests	2/1546	Hurten Charles F	Painted full centre
			2/3967	Poole	Gilt by Poole

Appendix 4

PATTERN NUMBERS, ARTISTS AND GILDERS
COMPILED FROM THE BLACK BOOKS c.1890-1910 – SPODE ARCHIVES
(Please note that some patterns were painted by more than one artist, as shown)

Pattern No.	Artist or gilder	Subject
1/1688	Birbeck	View of the Thames
1/2029	Yale William	Full size landscape
1/2030	Yale William	Full size landscape
1/2111	Weaver Charles	Birds on landscape crimson ground
1/2174	Weaver Charles	Bird in background
1/2195	Birbeck	Bird in background
1/2905	Brayford	Orchids & birds
1/3296	Brayford	Painted japanese style
1/3550	Weaver	
1/3560	Brayford	
1/3578	Radford	4 panels pencilled in Royal blue
1/3653	Cartlidge	3large 3small panels with Roses
1/3655	Brayford	Raised enamel flies and leaves see Brayford
1/3656	Brayford	Birds and Stems See Brayford for pattern
1/3809	Weaver Charles	Painted animals by Weaver fish with gold edge
1/3848	Weaver Charles	coloured and gilt by Weaver
1/3858	Weaver Charles	3 panels with trophies game centre by Weaver
1/3901	Alcock	
1/4042	Brayford	Birds flies and grass and gilt
1/4043	Brayford	Ferns with bulrush in centre
1/4045	Brayford	Raised birds with spray
1/4057	Brayford	Raised with leaves on grass
1/4058	Brayford	links of leaves on ivory ground
1/4064	Brayford	Raised and gilded and knots of flowers
1/4042	Brayford	
1/4925	Yale William	Painted landscape in square, Stag
1/5227	Yale William	Fish centre
1/5338	Yale William	Centre landscape royal blue ground
1/5347	Hassall J.	Centre

Pattern No.	Artist or gilder	Subject
1/5353	Hassall J.	centre with raised key border
1/5358	Hassall J.	group painted in centre
1/5359/62	Hassall J.	painted by Hassall
1/5364	Peach	centre by Peach
1/5365	Hassall J.	Birds & sprays on three small & large panels
1/5369	Bourne	landscape gilding by S. Arrowsmith
1/5376	Peach	centre by Peach on Coventry & ribbon shape
1/5386/7	Peach	
1/5386/7	Perry Arthur	landscape
1/5390	Yale William	Rose du Barry ground centre by Yale
1/5391	Hassall J.	Group of flowers on crimson ground
1/5399	Yale William	landscape
1/5435	Peach	painted by
1/5476	Arrowsmith Samuel	Flowers by Bourne gilt by Arrowsmith
1/5526	Peach	Painted gilt & raised
1/5536	Bourne	landscape
1/5545	Peach	centre
1/5546	Peach	game centre
1/5547	Bourne	landscape
1/5550/1	Bourne	landscape
1/5552	Peach	centre
1/5562	Peach	raised and gilt in light & dark gold with flies
1/5570	Peach	
1/5570	Perry Arthur	Ivory ground painted by Perry
1/5588	Hassall J.	painted by Hassall
1/5595	Peach	group of flowers in white
1/5632	Peach	centre
1/5655	Gould	Cobalt blue painted by Gould
1/5690	Gold	painted gilt by Gould
1/5714	Brough	Ivory ground, painted by Brough
1/5782	Yale	
1/5792	Peach	

Pattern No.	Artist or gilder	Subject	Pattern No.	Artist or gilder	Subject
1/5792	Perry Arthur	painted centre	1/6191	Funglestand	Wreath of flowers and forget me knots
1/5795	Yale William	View of Venice			
1/5825	Peach		1/6192	Hassall	
1/5825	Perry Arthur	Imperial Yellow ground painted wreath	1/6193	Hammersley Harry	painted roses
			1/6201/2	Funglestand	
1/5831	Whalley		1/6207	Funglestand	Roses
1/5862	Yale William	View of Chatelain	1/6211	Whalley	
1/5868	Peach		1/6212	Whalley	
1/5868	Perry Arthur	Landscape centre	1/6213	Whalley	
1/5893	Peach	painted by	1/6214	Whalley	
1/5898	Peach	panelled centres pansies	1/6217	Peach	
1/5905/6/7	Whalley	painted	1/6239	Yale William	Cobalt Blue with landscape
1/5934	Whalley	Painted and gilt			
1/5943	Whalley	painted	1/6241	Whalley	
1/5945/6/7	Whalley	painted and gilt	1/6281	Whalley	
1/5948	Yale		1/6283	Whalley	
1/5950	Peach	painted	1/6294	Whalley	
1/5952	Peach	Rose in centre	1/6295	Whalley	Grass and flies
1/5953/4/5	Peach	sprig in centre	1/6297	Whalley	Violet and Heath
1/5956	Yale William	landscape	1/6302	Whalley	
1/5959	Whalley	Celeste ground painted and gilt	1/6304	Whalley	
			1/6307	Whalley	
1/5968	Yale William	landscape	1/6308	Whalley	
1/5982	Peach		1/6309	Whalley	
1/5982	Perry Arthur	painted	1/6345	Whalley	
1/6007	Bourne	painted centre	1/6347	Whalley	Hanging basket & flowers
1/6009	Peach	painted centre			
1/6017	Yale William	painted centre	1/6401	Whalley	
1/6074	Yale William	painted centre	1/6441	Funglestand	Roses
1/6077	Yale William	Painted centre	1/6492	Arrowsmith	
1/6078	Yale William	painted centre	1/6495	Hassall	
1/6079	Yale William	painted centre	1/6500	Funglestand	Roses gilt by F.Davies
1/6080	Yale William	painted centre	1/6501	Funglestand	Gilt by Myatt
1/6082	Deaville Charles	Gilt and flat gold burnished	1/6524	Heaton	Painting on Yellow groundlay
1/6094	Yale		1/6576	Hassall	
1/6112	Yale William	Marine centre	1/6577/8	Hassall J.	Geranium sprigs
1/6113	Whalley	Groups and flies	1/6579	Hassall	
1/6114	Yale William	Centre	1/6581	Hassall J.	painted vine
1/6119	Whalley	painted by Whalley	1/6588	Hassall J.	Ferns and flowers
1/6124	Yale William	Roses and background and gilt in burnished gold	1/6593	Bourne	
			1/6601	Hassall	
			1/6602	Arrowsmith J.	Cobalt blue gilt in burnished gold
1/6127	Yale William	Fish centre			
1/6136/40	Hammersley Harry	painted	1/6608	Whalley	raised roses sanded and gilded
1/6141	Whalley	painted by			
1/6148	Whalley	painted by	1/6613	Arrowsmith J.	painted by gilt in sanded gold
1/6155	Whalley	painted by			
1/6156	Whalley	painted by	1/6613	Deaville Charles	Tinted in mixed colours and painted
1/6165	Bourne	by Bourne and Whalley			
			1/6637	Bourne	
1/6190	Whalley		1/6640	Hassall	

Pattern No.	Artist or gilder	Subject	Pattern No.	Artist or gilder	Subject
1/6642	Arrowsmith		1/6794	Funglestand	Painted raised and gilt
1/6650	Hassall J.	Painted by Hassall	1/6798	Hassall J.	Raised and gilt centre by Hassall
1/6651	Dewsbury	painted Dewsbury and gilt	1/6810	Bruce	painted in alternate panels
1/6652	Arrowsmith J.	painted by Arrowsmith in gilt and burnished	1/6811/12/	Bruce	Cornflower and sprigs
1/6655	Dewsbury	painted by	1/6823	Bourne	Centre by Bourne flowers by Whalley
1/6656	Bourne		1/6823	Whalley	Painted and raised and gilt in light & dark gold
1/6657	Alcock	Gilt in burnished gold			
1/6658	Dewsbury	painted by Dewsbury	1/6824	Funglestand	Centre by Funglestand
1/6659	Dewsbury	Painted Dresden style	1/6828	Hassall	
1/6660	Dewsbury	flowers ribbon and birds in panels	1/6836	Funglestand	
			1/6837/8	Eaton R	Pencilled in turquoise
1/6663	Whalley	Raised and gilt in sanded gold	1/6839	Eaton R	Pencilled in cobalt Blue
1/6664	Alcock	painted centre jewelled border	1/6845	Hassall	
			1/6849	Whalley	
1/6669	Hassall J.	Painted panels on cup & saucer	1/6864	Whalley	Painted by Sadler
			1/6866/69	Whalley	Painted sprigs and gilt
1/6671/2	Hassall		1/6890	Brough	
1/6678	Bourne	Landscapes on cup & saucer	1/6892	Bruce	
			1/7050	Hassall	
1/6680	Bourne	Raised rococo and gilt	1/7054	Alcock	Classic figure salmon ground and jewelled
1/6682	Heaton	Fruit and flower Solid gold in panels	1/7055	Brough	Ivory ground painted centre
1/6683	Heaton	Group of flowers and grass and flies	1/7108/09/	Hammersley Harry	painted and spotted in white
1/6694	Hassall		1/7122	Hammersley Harry	Basket work painted wreath
1/6700	Hassall				
1/6716	Heaton		1/7146	Arrowsmith	
1/6745	Bruce	Painted sprigs	1/7150	Hammersley Harry	Cobalt blue ground to painting
1/6750	Dewsbury	pencilled in turquoise and gilt	1/7245	Heaton	Heaton and women
1/6751/2/3	Whalley		1/7255	Besche Lucien	Painted by Besche in pencil
1/6756	Hassall J.	Pencilled in ivory			
1/6761	Peach		1/7265	Bruce	
1/6770	Dewsbury	Gilt centre & panels by Dewsbury	1/7274	Bruce	painted sprigs
			1/7282	Dudley	Gilding Boughs lads centre
1/6771/2	Eaton R	pencilled in Water green and painted centre			
			1/7286	Hammersley	
1/6773	Hassall J.	Blush pink ground lay	1/7296	Bruce	Sprigs and wreaths
1/6774	Hassall		1/7320	Alcock	New seasons centre jewelled border
1/6775	Funglestand	painted by Funglestand			
1/6776/7	Hassall J.	painted by Hassall	1/7439	Palmer	Initially drab and gilt
1/6778	Hassall J.	painted by Hassall	1/7451	Hammersley Harry	gilded by Bevington
1/6779	Arrowsmith		1/7455	Brough	Gilt by Lewis
1/6780	Peach		1/7459	Wycherley	
1/6783	Dewsbury	Raised and gilt painted by Dewsbury	1/7482	Wycherley	
1/6790	Arrowsmith J.	Background tinted in various colours painted	1/7459	Weaver Charles	Apple green ground burnished gold by Brough
1/6791	Eaton R	Pink Drab Ground painted by Eaton			

Pattern No.	Artist or gilder	Subject	Pattern No.	Artist or gilder	Subject
1/7482	Weaver Charles	Sprays in red gilt	R2041	Brough	
1/7640	Heapy	Coloured by women gilt by Heapy	R2221	Sadler Thomas	Basket with flowers gilt by Degg
1/7813	Peach		R2310	Wallace	Roses in panels
1/7813	Perry Arthur	Game birds	R2330	Wallace	Centre fish subjects gilt by T Taylor
1/7825	Deaville Charles	Gilded by			
1/7826	Palmer	Gilded by	R2331	Sadler Thomas	Gilt by Mr Tomlinson
1/8147	Wycherley		R2331	Worrall James	Painted centre
1/8147	Weaver Charles	painted by boys gilded	R2356	Nerwich	Salmon spots by J Hilton
1/8579	Eaton R	Flowers in centre lilies on border	R2374	Funglestand	
1/8928	Yale William	Landscape centre	R2375	Funglestand	
1/9629	Palmer	Gold band edge T Palmer gilder	R2374	Furnival	landscapes in crimson and gilt
R0077	Sadler Thomas	painted fruit and flowers	R2375	Furnival	landscapes Gilt by W. Ball
R0097	Deaville Charles	gilded by	R2409	Nerwich	gilt by J Wycherley
R0161	Rivers Leonard	Game centre	R2414	Brough	gilt by S Arrowsmith
R0199	Wycherley		R2613	Sadler Thomas	Roses gilt by P Hollingsworth
R0226	Rivers Leonard	Game centre with gilding	R2671	Sadler Thomas	Roses gilt by Tomlinson
R0227	Rivers Leonard	Fish centre	R2779	Nerwich	panelled plate
R0252	Sadler Thomas	flowers	R2782	Wallace	
R0259	Eaton R	Fruit with gilding by Hulme	R2782	Whalley	Full centre gilt by J Palmer
R0286	Sadler Thomas	flowers			
R0592	Hammersley Harry	flowers traced by men	R2785	Worrall James	Roses gilt by J Palmer
R0667	Alcock	figure in centre jewelled and gilt	R2805	Worrall James	Ribbon roses gilt by J Leese
R0774	Brayford	flowers in centre	R2832	Sadler Thomas	Roses gilt by W Timmis
R0774	Brough				
R0975	Heapy		R2833	Nerwich	Wreath of roses Gilt by G Wood
R1049	Arrowsmith				
R1079	Hall	raised spots and gilt by Hall	R2984	Furnival	painted by Furnival
			R2985	Furnival	Basket of flowers
R1127	Boothby F.	panelled and burnished gilt	R2994	Worrall James	painted Roses
			R3009	Lea Harry	Sprigs of flowers
R1371	Sadler Thomas	Flowers	R3112	Boothby F.	Ivory ground, gilt by F Boothby
R1554	Brough				
R1720	Worrall James	painted roses	R3170	Nerwich	Cobalt blue ground painted by Nerwich
R1779	Sadler Thomas	painted by Sadler on ivory ground	R3171	Worrall James	Ivory ground painted by Worrall
R1889	Sadler Thomas	painted by Sadler gold by J Wycherley	R3174	Nerwich	raised and chased gilt by B Marshall
R1927	Worrall James	Painted by Worrall gilt by Heapy	R3190	Wallace	Painted sprigs by Wallace gold by Gould
R1945	Brough	Rose wreaths by Brough Gilt by J Lowe	R3236	Wallace	Roses and Ferns by J.Wallace
R1950	Wallace		R3357	Adams	painted by Adams, Hammersley in pencil
R1950	Whalley	Rose festoons			
R1975	Heapy				
R1983	Adams	Fruit painted by Adams			
R2000	Sadler Thomas	painted by Sadler			

Appendix 5

DATES, SHAPES AND PATTERN NUMBERS OF COPELAND & GARRETT
AND W.T. COPELAND AND SONS 1845-1908
RESEARCH TAKEN FROM THE SPECIAL ORDER BOOKS
AND BLACK BOOKS

Date	Shape	Pattern No.	Date	Shape	Pattern No.	Date	Shape	Pattern No.
11.10.45	Acanthus	6949	1.01.84	Belinda	1/3809	28.05.47	Bute	7541
30.08.48	Acanthus	6697	17.01.86	Belinda	1/4925	15.07.01	Bute	R0592
20.12.48	Acanthus	6694	25.06.88	Belinda	1/5545	14.06.47	Cabinet	7617
17.10.49	Albert	8225	16.01.91	Belinda	1/6679	16.03.49	Cabinet	8034
22.10.49	Albert	8231	10.09.01	Boston	R0199	15.06.50	Cambridge	D1709
5.12.49	Albert	8270	16.10.01	Boston	R0252	15.06.60	Cambridge	D1717
22.02.50	Albert	8255	2.09.05	Boston	R 2356	15.06.60	Cambridge	D1719
5.03.50	Albert	8350	2.12.45	Bourbon	7341	15.06.60	Cambridge	D1710
8.03.50	Albert	5800	10.02.46	Bourbon	7400	15.06.60	Cambridge	D1718
25.07.50	Albert	7197	16.03.46	Bourbon	7419	15.06.60	Cambridge	D1711-4
29.07.50	Albert	8494	19.03.46	Bourbon	7399	15.06.60	Cambridge	D1715,
31.07.50	Albert	8431	23.03.46	Bourbon	7456			D1863
31.07.50	Albert	8432	30.03.46	Bourbon	7402	15.06.60	Cambridge	D1716
23.08.50	Albert	8463	24.04.46	Bourbon	7418	21.06.60	Cambridge	D1720
2.02.51	Albert	8555	28.04.46	Bourbon	7430	26.11.60	Cambridge	D1722
20.02.51	Albert	8561	19.07.46	Bourbon	6622	2.06.93	Carlyle	1/7826
6.10.45	Amherst	6988	30.09.46	Bourbon	7357	20.11.88	Charlotte	1/5662/3/4
4.09.45	Antique	7340	23.10.46	Bourbon	4069	1. 12.89	Charlotte	1/5690
5.11.45	Antique	7325	22.12.46	Bourbon	7816	1.12.89	Charlotte	1/5691
8.09.48	Antique	7523	13.01.47	Bourbon	5349	1.01.90	Charlotte	1/6141
16.06.46	Artichoke	7461	20.01.47	Bourbon	7565	11.02.90	Charlotte	1/6201/2
22.06.46	Artichoke	7464	24.02.47	Bourbon	7607	18.02.90	Charlotte	1/6207
16.02.73	Bamboo Embossed	D227	15.03.47	Bourbon	7577	18.02.90	Charlotte	1/6211
28.04.47	Barrel	7536	31.03.47	Bourbon	7570	18.02.90	Charlotte	1/6214
30.10.48	Barrel	7469	4.04.47	Bourbon	7591	1.04.90	Charlotte	1/6304
13.01.49	Barrel	8084	14.05.47	Bourbon	7608	19.09.90	Charlotte	1/6495
2.04.49	Barrel	7240	1.06.47	Bourbon	7572	5.12.90	Charlotte	1/6576
20.04.49	Barrel	1595	26.06.48	Bourbon	6425	6.12.90	Charlotte	1/6593
19.07.50	Barrel	8084	31.07.48	Bourbon	7467	6.12.90	Charlotte	1/6588
30.08.47	Beavais	7445	30.09.48	Bourbon	7418	6.12.90	Charlotte	1/6601
23.03.48	Beavais	7712	5.10.48	Bourbon	7108	6.12.90	Charlotte	1/6580
19.07.81	Belinda	1/2905	30.12.48	Bourbon	7987	6.12.90	Charlotte	1/6579
4.11.81	Belinda	1/2775	25.01.49	Bourbon	8716	6.01.91	Charlotte	1/6637
18.04.82	Belinda	1/2910	16.05.49	Bourbon	7532	6.01.91	Charlotte	1/6640
18.04.82	Belinda	1/3047	22.04.50	Bourbon	8082	6.01.91	Charlotte	1/6642
18.04.82	Belinda	1/2909	1.02.91	Bow flute	1/6771/2	16.01.91	Charlotte	1/6669
18.04.82	Belinda	1/2880	11.02.91	Bow flute	1/6759	16.01.91	Charlotte	1/6671/2
8.02.83	Belinda	1/3169	17.01.90	Burne	1/6165	16.01.91	Charlotte	1/6694

Date	Shape	Pattern No.	Date	Shape	Pattern No.	Date	Shape	Pattern No.
26.01.91	Charlotte	1/6700	19.06.89	Chelsea	1/5945/6/7	8.07.88	Coventry	1/5364
28.01.91	Charlotte	1/6720	2.07.89	Chelsea	1/6009	8.07.88	Coventry	1/5376
11.03.91	Charlotte	1/6811/12/	28.08.89	Chelsea	1/6217	8.07.88	Coventry	1/5391
11 .03.91	Charlotte	1/6844	17.09.89	Chelsea	1/6082	8.07.88	Coventry	1/5399
11.03.91	Charlotte	1/6810	25.11.89	Chelsea	1/6119	8.07.88	Coventry	1/5358
18.03.91	Charlotte	1/6892	11.02.90	Chelsea	1/6190	8.07.88	Coventry	1/5365
22.07.91	Charlotte	1/7009	11.02.90	Chelsea	1/6191	8.07.88	Coventry	1/5353
22.07.91	Charlotte	1/7021	18.02.90	Chelsea	1/6212	8.07.88	Coventry	1/5369
30.09.91	Charlotte	1/7108/09/	7.03.90	Chelsea	1/6241	4.01.89	Coventry	1/5714
1.03.92	Charlotte	1/7265	7.03.90	Chelsea	1/6239	16.02.89	Coventry	1/5795
12.04. 92	Charlotte	1/7274	1.04.90	Chelsea	1/6302	28.03.89	Coventry	1/5792
13.10.92	Charlotte	1/7439	1.04.90	Chelsea	1/6297	16.04.89	Coventry	1/5948
2.06.93	Charlotte	1/7825	14.04.90	Chelsea	1/6309	16.04.89	Coventry	1/5945
14.05.88	Charlotte flute	1/5526	29.06.90	Chelsea	1/6441	27.04.89	Coventry	C309
1.11.88	Charlotte flute	1/5655	5.12.90	Chelsea	1/6577/8	24.05.89	Coventry	1/5893
2.05.89	Charlotte flute	1/5825	6.12.90	Chelsea	1/6608	28.05.89	Coventry	1/5868
25.11.89	Charlotte flute	1/6077	6.12.90	Chelsea	1/6585	28.05.89	Coventry	1/5905/6/7
14.11.75	Chelsea Flute	1/1323	11.02.91	Chelsea	1/6761	7.06.89	Coventry	1/5943
8.02.83	Chelsea	13131	11.02.91	Chelsea	1/6756	19.06.89	Coventry	1/5934
8.02.83	Chelsea	1/3129	2.03.91	Chelsea	1/6780	19.06.89	Coventry	1/5948
8.02.83	Chelsea	1/3119	11.03.91	Chelsea	1/6828	2.07.89	Coventry	1/5862
8.02.83	Chelsea	1/3114	11.03.91	Chelsea	1/6837/8	2.07.89	Coventry	1/5959
16.01.84	Chelsea flute	1/3550	11.03.91	Chelsea	1/6845	2.07.89	Coventry	1/6007
18.01.84	Chelsea flute	1/3560	30.09.91	Chelsea	1/7055	2.07.89	Coventry	1/5968
2.04.84	Chelsea	1/3655	30.09.91	Chelsea	1/7095	2.07.89	Coventry	1/5982
1.01.84	Chelsea	1/3578	30.09.91	Chelsea	1/7050	17.09.89	Coventry	1/6017
2.04.84	Chelsea	1/3653	8.12.91	Chelsea	1/7122	25.11.89	Coventry	1/6136/40
2.04.84	Chelsea	1/3656	1.03.92	Chelsea	1/7255	25.11.89	Coventry	1/6080
14.10.84	Chelsea	1/3901	29.11.01	Chelsea	R0667	25.11.89	Coventry	1/6114
23.10.84	Chelsea	1/3636	16.06.60	Clarendon	D1722	25.11.89	Coventry	1/6124
6.02.85	Chelsea	1/4045	16.06.60	Clarendon	D1725	25.11.89	Coventry	1/6127
17.04.85	Chelsea	1/4039	16.06.60	Clarendon	D1726	1.01.90	Coventry	1/6155
8.06.86	Chelsea	1/4592	16.06.60	Clarendon	D1727-8	14.04.90	Coventry	1/6308
23.05.87	Chelsea	1/590	16.06.60	Clarendon	D1723	6.12.90	Coventry	1/6583/4
2.10.87	Chelsea	1/5227	27.10.45	Cord edge	7330	6.12.90	Coventry	1/6599
12.06.88	Chelsea	1/5550/1	1.01.88	Coventry	1/5338	6.01.91	Coventry	1/6651
18.06.88	Chelsea	1/5552	1.01.88	Coventry	1/5347	11.02.91	Coventry	1/6751/2/3
25.06.88	Chelsea	1/5547	1.01.88	Coventry	1/5476	11.02.91	Coventry	1/6774
8.07.88	Chelsea	1/5386/7	12.03.88	Coventry	1/5435	2.03.91	Coventry	1/6778
8.07.88	Chelsea	1/5390	4.05.88	Coventry	1/7415	11.03.91	Coventry	1/6849
2.11.88	Chelsea	1/4935	14.05.88	Coventry	1/5536	11.03.91	Coventry	1/6824
16.02.89	Chelsea	1/5782	14.05.88	Coventry	1/5542	11.03.91	Coventry	1/6823
16.02.89	Chelsea	1/5788	23.06.88	Coventry	1/5562	30.09.91	Coventry	1/7054
6.05.89	Chelsea	1/5938	25.06.88	Coventry	1/5546	1.06.94	Coventry	1/8928
6.05.89	Chelsea	1/5831	7.07.88	Coventry	1/5632	15.01.95	Coventry	1/8228
28.05.89	Chelsea	1/5898	8.07.88	Coventry	1/5359/62	30.09.45	Craigle	4809

Date	Shape	Pattern No.	Date	Shape	Pattern No.	Date	Shape	Pattern No.
28.02.48	Craigle	5594	29.12.45	Gothic	4902	7.04.46	Lowther	7483
18.01.02	Crete	R0774	8.05.46	Gothic	7435	3.07.46	Lowther	7341
26.05.01	Denmark	R0097	24.07.46	Gothic	7091	7.07.46	Lowther	5766
12.07.04	Denmark	R1945	18.09.46	Gothic	7507	13.07.46	Lowther	5836
12.09.04	Denmark	R1983	7.01.47	Gothic	7593	22.07.46	Lowther	7485
18.03.91	Dove	1/6866/69	19.03.47	Gothic	7591	17.09.46	Lowther	7475
26.02.50	Dover	8832	23.06.47	Gothic Pierced	5521	1.03.47	Lowther	7591
17.04.50	Dover	8434	9.09.47	Gothic	7649	10.05.47	Lowther	7483
1.01.51	Dover	8557	4.02.48	Gothic	7182	11.06.47	Lowther	7483
20.02.51	Dover	8552	27.09.48	Gothic	7913	12.11.47	Lowther	7655
6.11.45	Dresden	1741	16.01.91	Habsburgh	1/6658	11.05.48	Lowther	7830
2.12.45	Dresden	7207	16.01.91	Habsburgh	1/6659	9.09.48	Lowther Embossed	7892,
26.02.46	Dresden	5193	16.01.91	Habsburgh	1/6660			7893
27.11.46	Dresden	6554	16.01.91	Habsburgh	1/6682	20.04.49	Lowther	7532
12.08.47	Dresden Embossed	7667	16.01.91	Habsburgh	1/6683	25.05.49	Lowther Embossed	8098
9.12.47	Dresden	7730	28.01.91	Habsburgh	1/6716	27.08.49	Lowther	7132
10.01.48	Dresden	7733	11.02.91	Habsburgh	1/6748/49	11.12.49	Lowther	8301
22.02.49	Dresden	6279	11.02.91	Habsburgh	1/6750	15.12.49	Lowther	7631
22.11.50	Dresden	8527	11.02.91	Habsburgh	1/6770	2.03.50	Lowther	7485
11.02.90	Dresden	1/6192	26.03.79	Japanese	1/1774	20.03.50	Lowther	7897
26.08.50	Exeter	D1272	26.03.79	Japanese not		16.04.86	Lowther	1/4692
22.02.59	Exeter	D1033		pierced	1/1774	11.03.91	Lowther	1/6864
4.01.04	Exeter	R1720	24.02.80	Japanese Plain	1/2020	14.10.91	Lowther Embossed	1/7451
28.07.05	Exeter	R2330	18.02.80	Japanese Plain	1/2195	14.10.92	Lowther	1/7451
2.09.05	Exeter	R2414	30.07.80	Japan Embossed	1/1984	2.07.89	Madrid Pierced	1/5956
9.04.46	Flower Embossed	7194	2.05.83	Japan	1/3123	18.12.48	Moresque Embossed	7965
9.04.46	Flower Embossed	4881	12.11.81	London	D7911	22.10.68	Napoleon	D6272
18.02.48	French Embossed		15.05.48	Louis	7820	15.06.69	Napoleon	D6368
24.10.45	Gadroon	7331	24.05.48	Louis	7813	22.07.73	Napoleon	D7308
12.04.92	Gadroon	1/7282	27.06.48	Louis	7845	3.09.88	Napoleon	D8711
6.12.92	Gadroon	1/7482	28.06.48	Louis	7846	17.01.90	Nemo Pierced	1/6156
17.10.98	Gadroon	1/9484	30.10.48	Louis	7942	6.12.90	Nemo pierced	1/6602
27.09.01	Gadroon	R0227	5.10.49	Louis	8197	6.12.90	Nemo pierced	1/6613
27.09.01	Gadroon	R0226	27.12.49	Louis	8297	6.01.91	Nemo Pierced	1/6652
25.10.05	Gadroon	R2613	15.01.50	Louis	8414	16.01.91	Nemo Pierced	1/6663
29.06.88	Gladstone	1/5570	24.06.48	Louis Embossed	7850	11.02.91	Nemo Pierced	1/6776/7
16.01.91	Gladstone	1/6678	20.12.48	Louis Embossed	6164	11.02.91	Nemo Pierced	1/6775
12.08.04	Gladstone	R2000	1.03.92	Louis XV	1/7245	11.03.91	Nemo pierced	1/6836
1.07.71	Gordon Tray	D8198	12.04.92	Louis XV	1/7286	8.12.91	Nemo pierced	1/7146
24.05.72	Gordon Tray	D6944	14.10.92	Louis XV	1/7455	24.02.47	New	7583
24.05.72	Gordon Tray	D6718	14.10.92	Louis XV	1/7459	12.06.47	New	5349
28.05.72	Gordon Tray	D6944	8.05.93	Louis	1/76400	16.06.47	New	7584
13.06.72	Gordon Tray	D6944	1.06.94	Louis XV	1/8147	12.05.47	New Dresden	7609
27.12.72	Gordon Tray	D6944	14.02.96	Louis	1/8579	25.05.49	New Dresden	7262
19.09.45	Gothic	7296	5.11.45	Lowther Embossed	6840	21.08.45	New Pembroke	7387,
17.10.45	Gothic	7240	9.12.45	Lowther	7559			7388

Date	Shape	Pattern No.	Date	Shape	Pattern No.	Date	Shape	Pattern No.
21.08.45	New Pembroke	7285	23.03.46	Pembroke	7339	25.11.89	Primula	1/6074
21.08.45	New Pembroke	7283,	8.05.46	Pembroke	7436	20.03.90	Primula Dinner	
		7284	11.07.46	Pembroke	7444		ware	1/6281
29.09.45	New Pembroke	7305,	22.07.46	Pembroke	7459	20.03.90	Primula	1/6283
		7306	10.10.46	Pembroke	7506	14.04.90	Primula	1/6307
29.09.45	New Pembroke	7304	12.10.46	Pembroke	7492	14.06.90	Primula	1/6401
16.02.46	New Pembroke	7380	21.10.46	Pembroke	7503	6.12.90	Primula	1/6586
8.06.50	New Windsor	D1308	14.12.46	Pembroke	7513	6.12.90	Primula	1/6581
13.10.48	Octagon	7112	14.12.46	Pembroke	7516	6.01.91	Primula	1/6650
14.01.50	Octagon	6841	3.04.48	Pembroke	7798	6.01.91	Primula	1/6655
19.01.61	Osbourne	D2077	15.09.48	Pembroke	7884	11.02.91	Primula	1/6745
19.01.61	Osbourne	D2075	20. 10.48	Pembroke	7380	11.02.91	Primula	1/6773
13.07.49	Oval	7847	13.06.49	Pembroke	8120	2.03.91	Primula	1/6779
21.02.46	Plain Lowther	7394	5.02.85	Pierced madrid	1/4042	2.03.91	Primula	1/6790
25.04.60	Parian Ware	D1660,	6.02.85	Pierced Madrid	1/4064	4.03.91	Primula	1/6798
		D1662	15.10.02	Pierced Paris	R1127	4.03.91	Primula	1/6794
25.04.60	Parian Ware	D1681	12.05.04	Pierced paris	R1779	18.03.91	Primula	1/6890
30.09.72	Paris	D8918	20.08.50	Pierced Windsor	D1411	8.12.91	Primula	1/7150
20.06.73	Paris	D9430	6.02.85	Pierced Windsor	1/4043	25.10.05	Primula	R2671
24.07.74	Paris	D5114	24.03.46	Pineapple	7352	23.02.83	Queen Anne	1/3147
5.01.74	Paris Embossed	D9539	5.06.88	Plain	1/5581	7.01.84	Queen Anne	1/3817
18.05.76	Paris	1/1011	1.07.80	Plain Japanese	1/2029	17.09.84	Queen Anne	1/3848
21.06.77	Paris Plain	D7775	1.07.80	Plain japanese	1/2030	9.02.85	Queen Anne	1/4057
20.03.90	Paris	1/6294	25.09.80	Plain japanese	1/2111	9.02.85	Queen Anne	1/4058
20.03.90	Paris	1/6295	8.12.80	plain Japanese	1/2174	25.11.89	Queen Anne	1/6078
16.01.91	Paris	1/6664	20.12.80	plain Japanese	1/2195	18.02.90	Queen Anne	1/6213
8.07.92	Paris	1/7320	8.02.83	Plain Japanese	1/3127	29.04.90	Queen Anne	1/6345
27.11.01	Paris	R0286	8.02.83	Plain Japanese	1/3126	2.09.05	Queen Anne	R2374
17.10.02	Paris		4.06.83	Plain Japanese	1/3296	6.02.46	Regimental	B700
12.07.04	Paris	R1889	25.02.46	Plain Lowther	7390	24.06.49	Regimental	6924
1.07.05	Paris	R2221	8.09.48	Plain Lowther	7199	8.07.50	Regimental	8338
2.09.05	Paris	R2375	9.10.45	Plain Lowther	7245	28.05.89	Regimental	1/5896
25.08.06	Paris	R2805	24.11.82	Plain Paris	1/3290	1.01.99	Regimental	1/9629
21.08.45	Peel	7291	22.09.84	Plain paris	1/3858	25.08.02	Regimental	R1049
25.08.45	Peel	7392, 7393	7.07.88	Plain paris	1/5595	12.09.02	Regimental	R1074
23.09.45	Peel	7240	3.04.89	Plain Paris	1/6229	12.07.04	Regimental	R1927
23.10.45	Peel	7207	3.10.91	Plain Paris	1/7221	12.09.04	Regimental	R1975
25.10.45	Peel	7245	23.04.46	Plain Royal	5580	28.07.05	Regimental	R2331
8.06.47	Peel	7593	23.08.48	Plain Victoria	7245	28.07.05	Regimental	R2310
17.07.47	Peel	7563	2.05.49	Plain Victoria	7251	3.08.06	Regimental	R2779
23.07.47	Peel	7533	6.10.45	Plain Victoria	7328	3.09.06	Regimental	R2782
13.06.49	Peel	8139	5.12.45	Plain Victoria	7352	12.12.06	Regimental	R3009
19.01.46	Pembroke	7359	23.11.47	Plain Victoria	7720	27.02.07	Regimental	R3083
12.02.47	Pembroke	7555	25.05.49	Plain Victoria	7236	1.07.07	Regimental	R3112
29.09.45	Pembroke	7305	30.09.50	Plain Victoria	8532	1.07.07	Regimental	R3170
20.01.46	Pembroke	7346	25.11.89	Primula	1/6113	22.07.07	Regimental	R3171

Date	Shape	Pattern No.	Date	Shape	Pattern No.	Date	Shape	Pattern No.
22.07.07	Regimental	R3174	22.10.01	Scoop	R0259	19.05.49	Trentham	8117
17.09.92	Richlieu	1/7407	5.07.02	Scoop	R0975	13.06.49	Trentham	8140
2.06.93	Richlieu	1/7824	13.10.03	Scoop	R1554	15.06.49	Trentham	8143
2.06.93	Richlieu	1/7813	28.07.05	Scoop	R2331	27.06.49	Trentham	8159
2.06.93	Richlieu	1/7730	2.09.05	Scoop	R2409	19.12.49	Trentham	8045
7.10.93	Richlieu	1/7912	25.08.06	Scoop	R2832	10.11.48	Trentham Embossed	7936, 7937
19.07.01	Richlieu	R0161	25.08.06	Scoop	R2833			
1.11.06	Richlieu	R2985	1.11.06	Scoop	R2984	9.12.48	Trentham Embossed	7955
30.08.47	Royal	7631	12.12.06	Scoop	R2994	25.10.73	Trinket	D9357
29.11.47	Royal	6286	27.02.07	Scoop		28.10.73	Trinket	D9357
22.02.48	Royal	5617	1.06.07	Scoop	R3190	6.11.45	Turk	7351
19.05.48	Royal	5015	30.09.07	Scoop	R3236	19.12.46	Turk	7491
24.05.48	Royal	8016	13.05.08	Scoop	R3357	6.03.46	Tuscan	7407, 7408
8.03.49	Royal	7857	13.04.48	Scroll Embossed	7890	4.04.46	Tuscan	7407, 7405
27.12.49	Royal	8292	28.06.48	Scroll Embossed	7844	20.07.49	Tuscan	6237
12.07.04	Royal	R1950	6.01.49	Scroll Embossed	8001	9.04.46	Victoria	7421
25.05.49	Royal Albert	7236	30.10.45	Silver	7169	26.10.46	Victoria	7478
18.11.45	Royal Embossed	5622	12.09.46	Silver	7446	29.10.46	Victoria	7323
12.12.45	Royal Embossed	7348	16.06.47	Silver	7020	31.12.46	Victoria	7547
19.06.89	Royal Embossed	1/5950	10.12.48	Silver	5193	24.04.47	Victoria	7642
19.06.89	Royal embossed	1/5952	21.02.49	Silver	7855	29.07.47	Victoria	7614
2.07.89	Royal embossed	1/5953/4/5	6.07.50	Stafford Embossed	8475	12.05.48	Victoria	7825
			12.09.02	Stafford	R1079	15.05.48	Victoria	7823
25.11.89	Royal embossed	1/6094	30.09.73	Stanley	D9636	23.05.48	Victoria	5251
11.02.90	Royal embossed	1/6193	30.09.73	Stanley	D9593	14.02.49	Victoria	5617
19.09.90	Royal embossed	1/6492	1.01.51	Stoke	5877	31.07.49	Victoria	5246
19.09.90	Royal embossed	1/6501	16.12.47	Sutherland	7680	17.08.49	Victoria	6377
3.11.90	Royal embossed	1/6563	23.06.48	Sutherland	7681	13.12.49	Victoria	8014
6.01.91	Royal embossed	1/6656	25.07.48	Sutherland	7688	20.03.50	Victoria	8337
16.01.91	Royal embossed	1/6680	30.12.48	Sutherland	6462	1.01.90	Victoria plain	1/6148
6.12.90	Royal Wellington	1/6613	6.01.49	Sutherland	7696	6.07.88	Walpole	1/5588
6.01.91	Royal Wellington	1/6657	6.01.49	Sutherland	7698	29.04.90	Walpole	1/6347
2.03.91	Royal Wellington	1/6783	30.03.49	Sutherland	8069	31.01.49	Watteau Embossed	2036
2.03.91	Royal Wellington	1/6791	11.05.49	Sutherland	8014	23.12.47	Wellington	5627
11.03.91	Royal Wellington embossed	1/6823	17.03.03	Sutherland	R1371	8.12.48	Wellington	5193
			11.03.91	Tiverton embossed	1/6839	9.02.49	Wellington	5336
14.07.78	St Georges	1/1688	12.09.04	Tiverton embossed	R2041	19.09.90	Wellington	1/6500
5.04.80	St Georges	2/1546	17.09.91	Toilet	1/7148	6.10.90	Wellington	1/6524
8.02.93	St.Georges	1/3127	6.11.45	Toy	7303	27.11.89	Wellington Embossed	1/6079
16.07.88	Sardine	1/4249	31.08.48	Toy	7036, 7137			
18.02.90	Scale	1/6217	30.08.50	Toy	2009	1.02.93	Wig shape	1/7581
24.04.91	Scale	1/7056	28.01.48	Trentham	7743	14.05.60	Windsor	D1559
12.04.92	Scale	1/7296	21.06.48	Trentham	7842	4.07.60	Windsor	D2124
3.08.06	Scale	R2785	27.09.48	Trentham	7912	25.11.89	Windsor pierced	1/6112
26.01.01	Scoop	R0077	3.03.49	Trentham	5073			

Appendix 6

Pattern No.	Artist	Subject	Pattern No.	Artist	Subject
D0227	Weaver	Panels birds and flies	D2829	Hürten	Painted flowers, with raised and chased gold border
D1033	Bruce	Painted sprigs and gold lines, little roses by Bruce	D2925	Hürten	Monogram
D1061	Cartlidge	Rose border and gilt painted by Cartlidge	D3371	Bourne	Plants centre, 3 panels, 2 with flowers and 1 with badge
D1081	Swan	Groups of flowers	D3625	Simpson, T.	Groups of flowers Simpson Thomas
D1146	Cartlidge	Heaths	D3626	Bourne	Painted plant 'after Hürten', printed outline filled in by Bourne
D1234	Bourne	Bourne geraniums and gold line			
D1272	Bourne	Rose ground, heaths, comport	D3626	Bourne	Plant 'after Hürten', printed border by Bourne
D1308	Swan	Flowers by Swan, turquoise and rose grounds	D3703	Bourne	Fruit different coloured borders
D1411	Swan	Gilt and groups by Swan	D3708	Bourne	Plant in centre after Hürten
D1660	Gregoire	Panel with raised gold birds one side, flowers reverse	D3819	Robins	Painted rose gold wreath style of Robins
D1681	Gregoire	Panel with cameo on gold ground, wreaths of flowers	D5114	Golterman	Wreath of roses
			D6272	Birbeck	Landscape in centre
D1687	Cooper	Painted sprigs on different coloured grounds	D6341	Bruce	Pink flowers medallions
			D6352	Hartshorn	Painted groups of flowers
D1709	Swan Jnr	Large plants Swan Junior	D6368	Hürten	Hürten's curtain pattern
D1710	Swan	Pink ground, gold cord, strawberries	D6718	Hürten	Heaths flies and ferns
D1711	Swan	Landscape, pink ground, gold cord and sprigs, three groups	D6759	Harris	Painted birds, flies and grass
			D6944	Weaver	Ferns
D1715	Abraham, R.	D1863 pink, D1862 green. Landscapes in centre	D6944	Weaver	Ferns and flies
			D6944	Moorcroft	Painted heath and ferns
D1717	Swan Jnr	Small groups, turquoise cords	D6944	Golterman	Groups of wild flowers
D1718	Swan	Three groups of flowers	D6944	Moorcroft	Painted heath and ferns
D1719	Swan	Fruit centre	D6944	Abraham, R.	Wreaths on cup groups on saucers
D1720	Swan Jnr	Large plants	D7201	Randall	Randall's birds in white
D1722	Swan Jnr	Pink and gilt border, small group centre	D7308	Hassall	Plants
			D7618	Radford	Wreaths for Lord Clifton
D1723	Simpson	Group centre pale blue margin	D7640	Radford	Mistletoe sprigs
D1725	Swan Jnr	Turquoise border small plant centre	D7857	Radford	Ivory ground festoons of flowers
D1726	Swan Jnr	Pink border plant centre	D7905	Robins	See Exhibition book 1871
D1728	Cooper	Turquoise grounds and sprigs			
D1799	Cooper	Festoons of flowers on different coloured borders	D7936	Randall	Painted birds
			D7941	Bell	Tinting in celadon and gilt by Bell, chasing by Salt
D1800	Cooper	Fuschia ground flowers and gold wreaths			
D1862	Abraham, R.	Green. Landscapes in centre	D8198	Golterman	Painted D8191-98
D1863	Abraham, R.	Pink. Landscapes in centre	D8397	Potts	Ornamenting by J. Potts
D1871	Bourne	Wreath of violets	D8498	Weaver	Painted swallows
D1873	Simpson	Rose buds and group in centre	D8782	Radford	Flowering iris plant
D1990	Swan Jnr	Roses Swan Junior	D8918	Radford	Done for the 4th Dragoons QUI SEPATT with sketch
D2075	Simpson	Garden green ground, plants by Simpson Junior			
			D9357	Cooper	Hawthorns and blossoms
D2077	Abraham, R.	Landscape	D9357	Hassall	White roses
D2078	Abraham, R.	Landscape	D9369	Bell	Decoration by Bell
D2100	Gregoire	Flowers	D9430	Radford	Honey suckle six panels, gilt by Bell
D2122	Hürten	Hürten's plants	D9539	Radford	Flowers in panels
D2124	Hürten	Hürten's groups	D9593	Radford	Creeping plant
D2567	Hürten	Three painted panels HOPE initials raised chased gold and flowers	D9636	Radford	Begonias
D2600	Yale	Painted by Yale	D9702	Radford	Raised by Potts, gilt by Bell

Appendix 7

Pattern No.	Artist	Description of Design	Pattern No.	Artist	Description of Design
1 /3560	Brough	Raised Cranes		Goltermann	painted groups of flowers
C/612	Peach	Wild roses		Goltermann	Raised gold oak leaves
C/50	Wallace	Jewel design	C/151	Brough	Fish and seaweed
C/153	Hurten	Jewelled ornament and festoons of roses		Hurten	Festoons of roses 18 days painting 22/10/0
C/577	Yale	Cobalt blue landscapes		Hurten	Heathers
C/315	Brough	Large bird and foliage	C/402	Hurten	Full flower centre
1/3243	Ball	Raised gold border	C/169	Brough	Gold bird and foliage pattern number 1/4042
C/143	Millward	Jewelled design			
C/172	Brough	Raised gold birds Chrysanthemum border	C/475	Alcock	Figure subject after Angelica Kauffman
C/306	Brough	Bird of paradise		Yale	Small landscape jewelled border
C/307	Brough	Stork and foliage			
	Alcock	Group figure A Midsummer Night's Dream	C/155	Wallace	Jewelled and pearls after Ball
			C/537	Hurten	Heaths
1/5575	Baker	Wild flowers C/317 and with Blackberries	C/538	Brayford	Stork and foliage gold
			C/567	Yale	landscapes
!/5948	Yale	Views of Venice C/720		Alcock	Group of Cupids after Boucher
C/308	Brough	Raised gold flowers in ruby panels		Brayford	Raised peacocks in listed gold
C/309	Brough	Painted gold flowers		Wallace	Jewel design
C/401	Wallace	Bird in centre		Hurten	Roses each side
C/568	Millward	Rich jewel design	C/175	Hurten	Painted Fruit
	Hurten	Crysanthemums, roses on reverse		Birbeck	Cashmere design in each panel
	Hurten	panel of painted flowers	C/156	Millward	Gold and jewelled decoration
C/148	Yale	Bird subject each branch	C/297	Howell	Persian border Coloured and gilt by Howell
C/556	Yale	Landscape	C/574	Howell	Scrolls and gilt
	Hurten	Orange blossom, fruit as Prince of Wales		Yale	Rose du Barry Ground, Windsor castle View
C/149	Arrowsmith	Tapestry decoration, much gilding	C/431	Hurten	Azaleas
			C/437	Hurten	Chrysanthemums
	Hurten	Flowers painting cost 62/-		Yale	Painted landscapes of Swiss views by Yale
C/620	Hurten	Flowers in 4 panels			
	Goltermann	Gold ground 3 panels of flowers	C/812	Yale	Landscape in centre
			C/168	Brough	Raised gold birds

Appendix 8

STAFFORDSHIRE POTTERIES

PRICES CURRENT OF EARTHENWARE, 1814
REVISED AND ENLARGED DECEMBER 1ST, 1843, AND JANUARY 26TH,
1846, IN PUBLIC MEETINGS OF MANUFACTURERS.

Whatever rate of Discount is taken from this List of Prices, Five Pounds per Cent. is expressly considered in the same for the item of Breakage.

TABLE WARE

	Inches	Cream colored		Edged		Printed	
		s.	d.	s.	d.	s.	d.
Table Plates	10	1	9	2	0	4	0
Supper ditto	9	1	9	2	0	4	0
Twifler ditto	8	1	4	1	6	3	6
Muffin ditto	7	1	2	1	4	3	0
Ditto	6.	1	0	1	2	2	6
Ditto	5	0	10	1	0	2	0
Ditto	4	0	8	0	10	1	9
Ditto	3	0	6	0	8	1	6
Flat Oval Dishes	7	1	6	2	0	0	4
Ditto	8	1	9	2	3	0	5
Ditto	9	2	0	2	6	0	6
Ditto	10	2	6	3	0	0	9
Ditto	11	3	0	4	0	1	0
Ditto	12	3	6	5	6	1	3
Ditto	13	4	6	7	0	1	6
Ditto	14	5	6	9	0	1	9
Ditto	15	7	0	11	0	2	3
Ditto	16	9	0	14	0	2	9
Ditto	17	11	0	17	0	3	3
Ditto	18	14	0	20	0	4	0
Ditto	19	17	0	24	0	4	6
Ditto	20	20	0	28	0	5	0
Oval Baking Dishes	6	1	3	2	3	0	5
Ditto	7	1	6	2	6	0	6
Ditto	8	2	0	3	0	0	9
Ditto	9	2	6	4	0	1	0
Ditto	10	3	6	5	0	1	3
Ditto	11	4	6	7	0	1	6
Ditto	12	6	0	9	0	1	9
Ditto	13	8	0	11	0	2	0
Ditto	14	10	0	13	0	3	0
Round Bakers, Turtles, and Nappies	6	1	6	2	6	0	6
Ditto ditto ditto	7	2	0	3	0	0	9
Ditto ditto ditto	8	2	6	4	0	1	0
Ditto ditto ditto	9	3	6	5	0	1	3
Ditto ditto ditto	10	4	6	7	0	1	6

TABLE WARE cont.

			Cream colored		Edged		Printed	
	Inches		s.	d.	s.	d.	s.	d.
Ditto ditto ditto	11		6	0	9	0	1	9
Ditto ditto ditto	12		8	0	11	0	2	0
Ditto ditto ditto	13		10	0	13	0	3	0
Ditto ditto ditto	14		12	0	15	0	4	0
Gravy Dishes	16 in.	each	2	6	3	6	5	6
Ditto	18 in.	"	3	6	4	6	6	6
Ditto	20 in.	"	4	6	6	0	7	6
Soup Tureens only	9 in.	"	1.	6	2	0	4	6
Ditto ditto	10 in.	"	2	0	2	6	5	0
Ditto ditto	11 in.	"	2	6	3	0	5	6
Ditto ditto	12 in.	"	3	6	4	0	6	0
Soup Tureens complete		"					10	0
Soup Tureen Stands		"	1	0	1	6	2	6
Soup Tureen Ladles		"	0	10	1	0	1	6
Sauce Tureens, complete	5 in.	"	0	10	1	3	2	6
Ditto ditto	6 in.	"	1	0	1	6	2	6
Sauce Tureen Stands		"	0	4	0	6	0	9
Sauce Tureen Ladles		"	0	4	0	6	0	9
Covered Dishes	8 in.	"	0	8	1	2	2	0
Ditto	9 in.	"	0	10	1	4	2	3
Ditto	10 in.	"	1	0	1	6	2	6
Ditto	11 in.	"	1	3	1	9	3	0
Ditto	12 in.	"	1	6	2	0	3	6
Covered Plates	10 in.	"					2	0
Covered Twiflers	8 in.	"					1	9
Covered Muffins	7 in.	"					1	6
Ditto	6 in.	"					1	3
Drainers to the above		each					0	6
Hot Water Plates	10 in.	"	0	10	1	0	1	9
Ditto ditto	8 in.		0	7	0	9	1	6
Beef Steak Dishes, in three parts		"					10	0
Hash Dishes, in two parts		"					8	0
Salad Dishes	7 in.	doz.	2	0	3	6		
Ditto	8 in.	"	2	6	4	0		
Ditto	9 in.	"	3	6	6	0		
Ditto	10 in.	"	4	6	8	0		
Ditto	11 in.	"	6	0	10	0		
Ditto	12 in.	"	8	0	12	0		
Square Salads, one size higher in price.								
Deep Salad Bowls and Dishes	7 in.	each	0	4	0	6		
Ditto ditto	8 in.	"	0	5	0	8		
Ditto ditto	9 in.	"	0	6	1	0		
Ditto ditto	10 in.	"	0	8	1	3	2	6
Ditto ditto	11 in.	"	0	10	1	6	3	0
Ditto ditto	12 in.	"	1	0	1	9	3	6
Root Dishes	10 in.	"	2	0	3	0	6	0
Ditto	11 in.	"	2	6	3	6	7	0
Ditto	12 in.	"	3	0	4	0	8	0
Compotiers	8 in.	doz.	3	0	4	0	18	0
Ditto	9 in.	"	4	0	6	0	18	0

TABLE WARE cont.

	Inches	doz.	Cream colored		Edged		Printed	
			s.	d.	s.	d.	s.	d.
Ditto	10 in.	"	6	0	8	0	18	0
Ditto	11 in.	"	8	0	10	0	18	0
Ditto	12 in.	"	10	0	12	0		
Cheese Stands		each	1	6	1	9	2	6
Thrown Custards, unhandled, 12's		doz.					2	6
Ditto handled, 12's		"					3	0
Ditto ditto, covered, 12's		"					4	6
Prest French Fluted Custards, unhandled, 12's		"					3	0
Ditto ditto handled, 12's							3	6
Ditto ditto ditto, covered, 12's							5	3
Custard Stand, single		each					3	6
Custard Stands complete, three stories		"					10	0
Sauce Boats, No. 1		doz.	3	0	4	0	6	0
Ditto No. 2		"	2	6	3	6	5	6
Ditto No. 3		"	2	0	3	0	5	0
Ditto No. 4		"	1	9	2	6	4	6
Ditto No. 5		"	1	6	2	0	4	0
Ditto Stands		"					3	0
Sauce Boat and Stand		each					0	9
Pap Boats		doz.	3	0	4	0	6	0
Pickles		"	3	0	4	0	6	0
Egg Cups, 12 to dozen			1	3	1	6	3	0
Mustards, 24 to dozen			3	0	4	0	7	6
Peppers, 12 to dozen			2	0	3	0	5	0
Salts, 36 to dozen			3	0	4	0	7	6
Knife Rests, 12 to dozen			2	6	3	0	3	6
Egg Stands, three holes		each					2	9
Ditto four holes		"					3	6
Ditto six holes		"					5	0
Dessert Plates		doz.					4	0
Cream Bowls and Stands		each					3	0
Centre Pieces		"					4	0
Baskets and Stands		"					4	0
Comports		"					1	6

TEA WARE, &c.

		Cream colored		Dipt.		Painted		Printed	
		s	d.	s.	d.	s.	d.	s.	d.
Norfolk sized Teas, handled	doz.							5	0
Ditto ditto unhandled	"							4	0
GrecianTeas, London, unhandled	"	1	10			2	3	4	6
Ditto ditto handled	"	2	10			3	3	5	6
Ditto Irish, unhandled	"	2	4			2	9	5	6
Ditto ditto handled	"	3	4			3	9	6	6
Ditto Bowls and Saucers, unhand	"	3	6			4	6	7	6
Ditto ditto handled	"	4	6			5	6	8	6
Ditto Bowls, all sizes	"	2	6	3	0	4	0	7	0
French Fluted shaped Teas, unhandled	"							5	0

TEA WARE, &c. cont.

		Cream colored		Dipt.		Painted		Printed	
	doz.	s	d.	s.	d.	s.	d.	s.	d.
Ditto ditto handled	"			6	0				
Ditto ditto Irish, unhand.	"							6	0
Ditto ditto ditto handled	"							7	0
Ditto Bowls & Saucers, unhand	"							8	0
Ditto ditto handled	"							9	0
Ditto Bowls all sizes	"							8	0

Canova shapes Teas and Bowls, 6d. per doz.
extra to Grecian shape in Cream Color
and Painted.

		Cream colored		Dipt.		Painted		Printed	
Oval Teapots, 18's and 24's	"					16	0	24	0
Oval Sugars, to 24's	"					16	0	24	0
Oval Creams, to 24's	"					8	0	12	0
Oval Teapots and Sugars, 30's to count 24's									
Oval Creams, 30's to count as 24's									
Rd. Cap. Teapots & Sugars, down to 24's	"	8	6			9	6	14	0
Ditto ditto down to 30's	"	9	6			10	6	16	0
Rd. Uncapt ditto down to 24's	"	7	6			8	6		
Rd. ditto ditto down to 30's	"	8	6			9	6		
Round Creams	"	4	0			5	0	7	0
Round Cream Ewers	"	5	0			6	0	9	0
Coffee-pots, French Fluted, 3's to 9's	"							18	0
Chocolates, 36's	"							10	6
B. and B. Plates	each							0	8
Flat Pail shape Butter Tubs, 24's & 30's	doz.							24	0
Ditto Stands	"							6	0
Ditto Drainers	each							0	6
Tall Hooped Butter Tubs and Fixed Stands, 24's and 30's doz.								30	0
Drainers to ditto	each							0	6
Tall Hooped Butter Tubs and no Stands, 24's and 30's	doz.							18	0
Drainers to ditto	each							0	6
Thrown common ButterTubs	doz.							14	0
Drainers to ditto	each							0	6
Toast Racks	"							2	0
Roll Trays	"							3	0
Toy Tea Set, handled, Grecian	"					1	6	3	0
Ditto unhandled	"					1	3	2	6
French Fluted ditto handled	"							3	6
Ditto ditto unhandled	"							3	0

Consisting of
9 Cups and 9 Saucers ⎫
1 Teapot ⎪
1 Sugar Box, ditto ⎬
1 Cream ditto ⎪
1 Slop ditto ⎭

		Cream colored		Dipt.		Painted (Common Shapes)		Printed (French Fluted Shapes)	
Grecian Toy Teas, unhandled	doz.					1	3	2	6
Ditto ditto handled	"					1	6	3	0
French Fluted Toy Teas, unhandled	"							3	0
Ditto ditto handled	"							3	6

273

TEA WARE, &c. cont.

		Cream colored		Dipt.		Painted		Printed	
		s	d.	s.	d.	s.	d.	s.	d.
Ditto Toy Teapots	each					0	3	0	6½
Ditto Toy Sugars	"					0	3	0	6½
Ditto Toy Creams	"					0	2	0	4½
Ditto Toy Slops	"					0	1½	0	2½

(Painted column marked *Common Shapes*; Printed column marked *French Fluted Shapes*)

Toy Dinner Set, consisting of
    12 Plates, flats   6 ditto Soups
    12 Twiflers   12 Muffins
    5 Dishes, five sizes
    1 Soup Tureen, complete
    1 Sauce Tureens, complete
    2 Covered Dishes
    2 Pie Dishes
    2 Sauce Boats   1 Salad
                        Printed 8 0

		Cream colored		Dipt.		Painted		Printed	
Oval Putting Pots	doz.	3	8					8	6
Round Potting Pots	"	3	0					7	6
Broth Bowls and Stands, 18's	each							1	6
Ditto ditto 24's	"							1	3
Ditto ditto 30's	"							1	0
Lipped Bowls	doz.	3	6						
Punch Bowls, 2's to 6's								8	6
Ditto 9's to 12's	"							10	0
Covered Bowls	"	7	0	9	0	12	0	18	0

Ditto with handles, 6d. per doz. extra

TOILET WARE, &c.

		Cream colored		Dipt.		Painted		Printed	
		s	d.	s.	d.	s.	d.	s.	d.
Pudding Bowls	doz.	2	9					7	0
Fancy Ewers and Basins 4's & 6's	"							8	6
Ditt ditto 9's								8	6
Mouth Ewer and Basin, the pair								2	0
Common Hand Basins	"	3	0						
Common Flanged Basins	"	3	6	5	0	5	0	8	6
Common Ewers, 4's and 6's	"	3	6	5	0	5	0		
Ditto, 9's	"	4	0	5	6	5	6		
Chambers, 4's and 6's	"	2	6	3	0	4	0	7	0
Ditto 9's	"	3	0	3	6	4	6	7	0
Ditto 18's & 24's, for Spitting Pots	"	4	6					9	0
Covered Chambers, price and half.									
Soaps and Trays, covered	each							1	6
Ditto uncovered	"							1	0
Round Soap Cups and Drainers	doz.	6	0					8	0
Round Soap Linings, 12's	"	2	6					4	6
Oval and Round Shaving Basins	each	2	0					3	0
Foot Baths, 14 in.	"	6	6					12	0
Ditto 16 in	"	7	6					14	0
Ditto 18 in	"	9	0					16	0
Slop Jars and Covers, No. 1	"	8	0					12	0
Ditto ditto No. 2	"	6	0					10	0
Ditto ditto No. 3	"	5	0					8	0

TOILET WARE, &c. cont.

	each	Cream colored		Dipt.		Painted		Printed	
		s	d.	s.	d.	s.	d.	s.	d.
Tab Jugs, No. 1	"	6	0					8	0
Ditto No. 2	"	5	0					7	0
Ditto No. 3		4	0					6	0
Sponge Box and Cover	"							3	6

JUGS & MUGS WARE.

	each	Cream colored		Dipt.		Painted		Printed	
Thrown Common Jugs, 4's and 6's	doz.	2	6	3	0	4	0		
Ditto ditto 12's	"	3	0	3	6	4	6		
Ditto ditto 24's	"	3	6	4	0	5	0		
Ditto ditto 30's and 36's	"	4	0	5	0	6	0		
Dutch Jugs, 4's and 6's	"	3	0	4	0	5	0	6	0
Ditto 12's	"	3	6	4	6	5	6	7	6
Ditto 24's	"	4	0	5	0	6	0	9	0
Ditto 30's and 36's	"	4	6	6	0	7	0	10	6
Prest Hexagon Jugs, 4's and 6's	"							6	0
Ditto ditto 12's	"							7	6
Ditto ditto 24's	"							9	0
Ditto ditto 30's and 36's	"							10	6
Porter Mugs, 6's and 12's	"	3	0	4	0	5	0	6	0
Ditto 24's, 30's, and 36's	"	3	6	4	6	5	6	7	6
Common Tankard Mugs, 6's to 24's	"	2	6	3	0	4	0		
Ditto 30's and 36's	"	3	0	3	6	4	6		
Fancy Cans, 36's, with names	"							4	6
Lipped Mugs and Covers	"	5	3	7	6	9	0	12	0
Covered Jugs and Mugs, price and half.									
Spitting Mugs, with Funnel & Covers	"	6	0					12	6
Ditto Pots, with loose top, spout, & handle	"	8	0					14	6
Spittoons, 6 in	each	1	0					1	6
Ditto 7 in.	"	1	3					1	9
Ditto 8 in.	"	1	6					2	3
Ditto 9 in.	"	1	9					3	0
Casserole, 7 in.	"							2	0
Ditto 8 in.	"							2	3
Ditto 9 in	"							2	6
Jelly Cans. all sizes	doz.	2	6						

MISCELLANEOUS

		each	Cream colored		Dipt.		Painted		Printed	
Oyster Pails, 12 in.		each	5	0					8	0
Ditto 14 in.		"	6	6					10	0
Ditto 16 in.		"	8	0					12	6
Ditto 18 in.		"	10	0					15	0
Round Turtle Pots,	8 in.	"	0	8					1	0
Ditto ditto	9 in.	"	1	0					1	6
Ditto ditto	10 in.	"	1	6					2	0
Bed Pans, No. 1		"	3	3						
Ditto No. 2		"	2	6						
Ditto No. 3		"	2	0						
Bidet Pans,	14 in.	each	1	9						

MISCELLANEOUS cont.

				Cream colored		Dipt.		Painted		Printed	
			each	s	d.	s.	d.	s.	d.	s.	d.
Ditto	15 in.		"	2	0						
Ditto	16 in.		"	2	3						
Ditto	17in.		"	2	6						
Ditto	18 in.		"	3	6						
Ditto	19 in.		"	4	0						
Ditto	20 in.		"	4	6						
Ditto	22 in.		"	6	0						
Coach Slippers,	No. 1		"	1	8						
Ditto	No. 2		"	1	2						
Blancmange Moulds,		4 in.	doz.	5	0						
Ditto		5 in.	"	7	0						
Ditto		6 in.	"	9	0						
Ditto		7 in.	"	10	0						
Ditto		8 in.	"	12	0						
Ditto		9 in.	"	14	0						
Ditto		10 in.	"	18	0						
Ditto		11 in.	"	21	0						
Ditto		12 in.	"	25	0						
Tall Candlesticks,	6in		each							1	3
Ditto	7in.		"							1	6
Ditto	8 in		"							2	0
Ditto	9 in.		"							2	6
Ditto	10 in.		"							3	0
Bed-room Candlesticks			"							1	8
Taper Candlesticks			"							0	9
Single Extinguisher Tray			"							1	0
Double ditto ditto			"							1	6
Cullenders, handled			doz.	3	8						
Ditto unhandled			"	3	0						
Wine labels			"	6	0						
Nursery Lamps			each	4	0					6	0
Sick Feeders			doz.	6	0						
Suckling Bottles			"	6	0						
Gally Pots, 1 to 4 oz.			"	0	6						
Covered Jars, flat tops,		3's to 12's	"	5	6						
Ditto ditto	24's to 36's		"	7	0						
Ditto Canopy or Dome Tops,											
		3's to 12's	"	8	3						
Ditto ditto ditto 24's to 36's			"	10	0						

Chair Pans—Cream Colored

5	6	7	8	9	10	11	12	Inches.
5d.	6d.	8d.	10d.	1s.	1.2d.	1s.4d.	1s.6d	each.

Oval Milk Dishes—Cream Colored

13	14	15	16	17	18	19	20	21	22	24	Inches.
1s.	1s.3d.	1s.6d.	2s.	3s.	4s.	5s.	5s.6d.	6s.6d.	7s.6d.	10s.	each.

Round Shape Milk Pans, one size higher in price.

EGYPTIAN BLACK

		PER DOZ.	
		s.	d.
Oval Teapots, any shape,	12's	21	0
Ditto	18's	24	0
Ditto	24's	26	0
(None to be counted more than 24 to a dozen.)			
Sugars and Creams the same price as Teapots			
Oval Coffee-pots		21	0
Round Thread fluted Teapots,	12's, 18's and 24's	12	0
Ditto	30's	14	0
(None to be counted more than 30 to a dozen.)			
Sugars, Creams, and Coffee pots		12	0
Round Satin-striped Teapots, lamp-spouts, 12's, 18's, and 24's		14	0
Ditto	30's	16	0
Sugars, Creams, and Coffee pots		14	0
Round Imaged, or Figured Teapots, 12's, 18's, and 24's		16	0
Ditto	30's	18	0
Sugars, Creams, and Coffee Pots		16	0
Bowls, Thread fluted, not figured		15	0
Bowls, figured		18	0
Round Milk Jugs and Covers, not figured		15	0
Ditto	figured	18	0
Oval Milk Jugs, and Covers		26	0

Should Cream Colored Ware be wanted in Octagon, Hexagon, Verona, or any similar Fancy Shapes, in Table, Tea, or Toilet Ware, Jugs and Mugs, the same to be charged as the Pearl White Granite, with five per cent. more discount than is allowed from the Pearl White Ware.

Common Painted, made in the above shapes, to be charged at Printed prices, with five per cent. more discount than is allowed from Printed Ware.

30's Prest Teapots and Sugars, to count 24 to the dozen, and charged same price as 24's.

30's Prest Creams, to count 24 to the dozen, and charged same price as 24's.

9's Jugs, of any description, to count 6 to the dozen, and charged as 6's.

18's Ditto   ditto   ditto   12 to the dozen, and charged as 12's.

BROUGHAM, PRINTER, BURSLEM.
[Entered at Stationer's Hall]

Appendix 9

FACTORY BACKSTAMPS FROM 1770-1970 AND PATTERN NUMBERS
WITH DATES FROM COPELAND & GARRETT TO SPODE

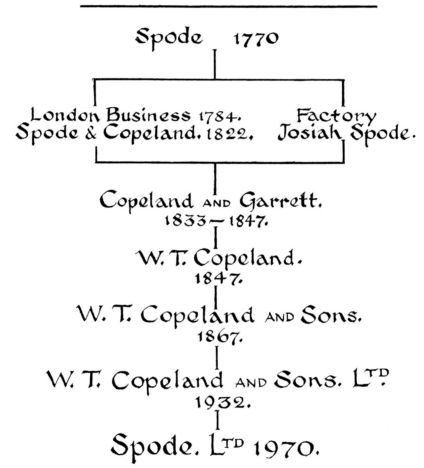

FACTORY PEDIGREE

Spode   1770

London Business 1784.
Spode & Copeland. 1822,

Factory
Josiah Spode.

Copeland AND Garrett.
1833 — 1847.

W. T. Copeland.
1847.

W. T. Copeland AND Sons.
1867.

W. T. Copeland AND Sons. L^{TD}
1932.

Spode. L^{TD} 1970.

The backstamps of the Spode works are many and various and in themselves are a history of the famous pottery. As the Spode works changed ownership, so did the backstamps vary. However, the art department and sales department also played their part in the changing style and name. When William Taylor Copeland and Thomas Garrett became partners many new and interesting designs were given to the backstamps on the ware. Again, when William Taylor became the sole owner of the Spode works the backstamps told the story. Collectors have always found these changes of name confusing, even more so when in the early twentieth century the name Spode once again appears on the ware.

The explanation, however, is quite simple. William Taylor Copeland was proud to put his own name solely on the ware and directed his art directors to produce new designs for them during the period from the Great Exhibition of 1851 through to the Paris exhibition of 1889. His son Richard Pirie Copeland continued this policy but when Ronald and Gresham Copeland became joint owners of the company the marketing of all pottery was to change. The demand for elaborately decorated ware was declining and by the 1930s, when the Art Deco fashion swept the country, many of the old Spode patterns were reintroduced under the direction of Thomas Hassall, re-establishing the firm in the marketplace as the company which produced hand-painted traditional table ware. The backstamps reflected this change and the name Spode appeared on them, trading as Spode Copeland's China, England.

Yet another facet was to affect the backstamps, that of customer demand. Customers were asking the company to add the words 'Bone China' and they also became part of the backstamp. When Ronald Copeland toured America, he and Sidney Thompson adopted the policy of trading as W.T. Copeland and Sons Ltd., the producers of fine Spode bone china, so the ware became known as Copelands producing Spode Bone china at the Spode Works. Under the Art Direction of Harold Holdway the customers found even this rather confusing, so first the 's' was dropped from Copeland's and the backstamp read Copeland-Spode Bone China England.

By the 1960s a new backstamp was designed. Spode was now shown in various scripts and on earthenware the name of the pattern was added. There is little doubt that from the beginning of the Copeland ownership this detailed attention to the backstamp became part of their marketing success, being constantly changed to the marketing needs of the time.

All back stamp references numbers are from Robert Copeland's book *Spode and Copeland Marks*.

Spode 1770–1833
Impressed marks

SPODE

2a

SPODE

b

SPODES
NEW STONE

7a

SPODES
NEW STONE

b

1822–1833

Spode

SPODE

Transfer-printed marks
1800–1820

Rare mark
1822–1833

1822

SPODE
Stone·China

1812–1833

SPODE
Stone China

1815–1833

SPODE'S
NEW FAYENCE

1826–1833

Copeland & Garrett
period 1833–1847
Impressed marks

COPELAND
& GARRETT

1833–1847

1839

COPELAND & GARRETT
LATE
SPODE

COPELAND & GARRETT
LATE
SPODE

1833–1847

1838–1847

COPELAND
AND
GARRETT
STOKE UPON TRENT
&
LONDON
VINTAGE of SORRENTO
CHINA GLAZE

1842

CONTINENTAL VIEWS

163 and 164 show
the Pattern Name

Copeland 1847–1970
Impressed marks

COPELAND

1847–1958

COPELAND

1860–1969

Embossed mark

COPELAND
30

1845

Transfer-printed marks

Copeland
Late Spode.

Copeland
Late Spode

1847–1890

SPODE
COPELAND CHINA
ENGLAND

1954–1956

SPODE
BONE CHINA
ENGLAND

1956–1960

Spode
BONE CHINA
ENGLAND

1960–1970

SPODE'S Royal Jade
ENGLAND

1932–1938

SPODE
COPELAND
ONYX
ENGLAND
1932

Spode's *Velamour*
ENGLAND
1932-1940
1953-1969

COPELAND'S
PORCELAIN STATUARY
1847-1848

COPELAND
1850-1890

COPELAND
1847-1890

COPELAND'S CHINA
1862-1891

SPODE
COPELAND'S CHINA
ENGLAND
1904-1954

Spode's
"Royal Jasmine"
England
1932-1939
1949-1962

Spode
Flemish Green
England
1949-1965

1492-1892
"COLUMBUS"
Made in England
by
W.T. Copeland & Sons
Stoke upon Trent
for
BURLEY & Co
CHICAGO
Rd No 195703
1892

SPECIALLY DESIGNED
BY LIONEL EDWARDS.
MANUFACTURED BY
W.T. COPELAND & SONS.
ENGLAND.
SOLELY FOR SOANE & SMITH LTD
OXFORD ST, LONDON, W.I.
Rd No. 691840.

No 7
"HOMEWARD"
BY
LIONEL EDWARDS
1922

SPODE
COPELAND
1883

1930-1980

SPODE
COPELAND
ENGLAND
1891-1910

MANUFACTURERS
SPODE
COPELAND
STOKE-UPON-TRENT
1880-1890

COPELAND
LATE
SPODE
ENGLAND
1906 & later

COPELAND
SPODE
ENGLAND
1920-1957

COPELAND LATE SPODE
1887-1894

T.GOODE & Co
LONDON
COPELAND'S CHINA
ENGLAND
1899

WIGMORE St
DANIELL
LONDON
COPELAND'S CHINA
1889

COPELAND
SPODE'S
ITALIAN
ENGLAND
5
1891-1970

LOUIS QUATORZE
COPELAND
IV
C
Rd 2
3
1847

COPELAND
SPODE'S TOWER
ENGLAND
1891-1970

Spode's
"Camilla"
Copeland
ENGLAND.
1891-1970

Spode's
"Royal Jasmine"
England
Autumn
by
Ronald Copeland
Rd No 798464
1934

Spode
ENGLAND
BONE CHINA
502
c.1970

Pattern numbers with dates

Spode period to March 1833

1801 up to 150	1812 up to 1800	1823 up to 3750
1802 up to 300	1813 up to 1950	1824 up to 4000
1803 up to 450	1814 up to 2100	1825 up to 4150
1804 up to 600	1815 up to 2200	1826 up to 4300
1805 up to 750	1816 up to 2300	1827 up to 4450
1806 up to 900	1817 up to 2600	1828 up to 4500
1807 up to 1050	1818 up to 2700	1829 up to 4600
1808 up to 1200	1819 up to 2800	1830 up to 4700
1809 up to 1350	1820 up to 3000	1831 up to 5050
1810 up to 1500	1821 up to 3250	1832 up to 5200
1811 up to 1650	1822 up to 3500	1833 up to 5350

Spode period B patterns

1823 up to B40	1827 up to B185	1831 up to B330
1824 up to B70	1828 up to B220	1832 up to B365
1825 up to B110	1829 up to B265	1833 up to B388
1826 up to B150	1830 up to B300	

Copeland & Garrett period and Copeland B patterns

1833 up to B388	1839 up to B600 L	1845 up to BB830
1834 up to B420	1840 up to B654 L	1846 up to B906
1835 up to B430	1841 up to B711 L	1847 up to B930
1836 up to B445	1842 up to B748 L	1848 up to B959
1837 up to B459	1843 up to B770 L	
1838 up to B576	1844 up to B800	

Copeland & Garrett period 1 March 1833 to 30 June 1847

1833 up to 5350	1838 up to 6138	1843 up to 6991
1834 up to 5466	1839 up to 6367	1844 up to 7128
1835 up to 5662	1840 up to 6508	1845 up to 7342
1836 up to 5738	1841 up to 6700	1846 up to 7547
1837 up to 5841	1842 up to 6819	1847 up to 7747

W.T. Copeland period 1847 to 1867

1847 up to 7747	1851 up to 8734	1855 up to 9700
1848 up to 7983	1852 up to 9033	1856 up to 9880
1849 up to 8301	1853 up to 9250	1857 up to 9999
1850 up to 8521	1854 up to 9475	

D patterns

1852 up to D90	1860 up to D2091	1868 up to D5600
1853 up to D180	1861 up to D2500	1869 up to D6930
1854 up to D290	1862 up to D3016	1870 up to D7690
1855 up to D400	1863 up to D3466	1871 up to D8475
1856 up to D521	1864 up to D4018	1872 up to D8973
1857 up to D655	1865 up to D4430	1873 up to D9523
1858 up to D967	1866 up to D4810	1874 up to D9999
1859 up to D1412	1867 up to D5200	

W.T. Copeland & Sons period 1867 to 1932

1/China numbers

1874 up to 1/104	1883 up to 1/3500	1892 up to 1/6491
1875 up to 1/154	1884 up to 1/3975	1893 up to 1/7859
1876 up to 1/863	1885 up to 1/4366	1894 up to 1/8199
1877 up to 1/1230	1886 up to 1/4891	1895 up to 1/8457
1878 up to 1/1425	1887 up to 1/5268	1896 up to 1/8802
1879 up to 1/1847	1888 up to 1/5610	1897 up to 1/9186
1880 up to 1/2193	1889 up to 1/6120	1898 up to 1/9540
1881 up to 1/2708	1890 up to 1/6536	1899 up to 1/9930
1882 up to 1/3041	1891 up to 1/7105	1900 up to 1/9999

R China numbers

1901 up to R750	1910 up to R4188	1919 up to R7023
1902 up to R1205	1911 up to R4503	1920 up to R7257
1903 up to R1595	1912 up to R4815	1921 up to R7506
1904 up to R2127	1913 up to R5106	1922 up to R7710
1905 up to R2167	1914 up to R5409	1923 up to R7908
1906 up to R3003	1915 up to R5682	1924 up to R8478
1907 up to R3279	1916 up to R5959	1925 up to R9170
1908 up to R3552	1917 up to R6378	1926 up to R9778
1909 up to R3834	1918 up to R6584	1927 up to R9999

2/Earthenware numbers

1874 up to 2/56	1894 up to 2/4049	1914 up to 2/6721
1875 up to 2/349	1895 up to 2/4172	1915 up to 2/6808
1876 up to 2/472	1896 up to 2/4341	1916 up to 2/6966
1877 up to 2/748	1897 up to 2/44-51	1917 up to 2/7107
1878 up to 2/1047	1898 up to 2/4564	1918 up to 2/7194
1879 up to 2/1473	1899 up to 2/4704	1919 up to 2/7346
1880 up to 2/1613	1900 up to 2/4807	1920 up to 2/7433
1881 up to 2/1884	1901 up to 2/4932	1921 up to 2/7562
1882 up to 2/2117	1902 up to 2/5121	1922 up to 2/7658
1883 up to 2/2323	1903 up to 2/5248	1923 up to 2/7790
1884 up to 2/2501	1904 up to 2/5417	1924 up to 2/7955
1885 up to 2/2675	1905 up to 2/5569	1925 up to 2/8039
1886 up to 2/2856	1906 up to 2/5820	1926 up to 2/8218
1887 up to 2/2967	1907 up to 2/5923	1927 up to 2/8320
1888 up to 2/3096	1908 up to 1/6057	1928 up to 2/8498
1889 up to 2/3258	1909 up to 2/6173	1929 up to 2/8816
1890 up to 2/3472	1910 up to 2/6287	1930 up to 2/9204
1891 up to 2/3632	1911 up to 2/6368	1931 up to 2/9401
1892 up to 2/3787	1912 up to 2/6502	1932 up to 2/9721
1893 up to 2/3946	1913 up to 2/6613	1933 up to 2/9999

Y China numbers

1927 111 to 1125	1941 up to Y6597	1956 up to Y7688
Y26 to Y398	1942 up to Y6681	1957 up to Y7772
1928 up to Y1222	1943 up to Y6737	1958 up to Y7930
1929 up to Y2030	1944 up to Y6775	1959 up to Y7985
1930 up to Y2484	1945 up to Y6813	1960 up to Y8001
1931 up to Y2807	1946 up to Y6881	1961 up to Y8006
1932 up to Y3069	1947 up to Y7004	1962 up to Y8026
1933 up to Y3525	1948 up to Y7067	1963 up to Y8070
1934 up to Y3948	1949 up to Y7126	1964 up to Y8084

1935 up to Y4414	1950 up to Y7193	1965 up to Y8105
1936 up to Y4884	1951 up to Y7229	1966 up to Y8112
1937 up to Y5336	1952 up to Y7299	1967 up to Y8122
1938 up to Y5881	1953 up to Y7361	1968 up to Y8138
1939 up to Y6253	1954 up to Y7480	1969 up to Y8155
1940 up to Y6439	1955 up to Y7607	

From 1927-1932 – W.T. Copeland & Sons

From 1932-1970 – W.T. Copeland & Sons Ltd.

Thomas Goode & Co., Mayfair, London – Special numbers with prefix C

1880 to 1885	C200 to C540	1920 to 1925	to C1980
1885 to 1890	to C850	1925 to 1930	to C2020
1890 to 1895	to C1000	1930 to 1935	to C2070
1895 to 1900	to C1225	1935 to 1940	to C2115
1900 to 1905	to C1540	1940 to 1945	to C2150
1905 to 1910	to C1650	1945 to 1950	to C2195
1910 to 1915	to C1760	1950 to 1956	to C2240
1915 to 1920	to C1880		

The series ended with pattern C2240 in January 1956

Fancy Patterns and Items – F numbers

June	1937 to F209	Nov	1965 to F1224
Mar	1941 to F420	Dec	1966 to F1226
Sept	1954 to F706	Dec	1967 to F1249
May	1957 to F945	Oct	1968 to F1253
Dec	1962 to F1152	Sept	1969 to F1256
Dec	1963 to F1180	Dec	1964 to F1212
		Nov	1970 to F1285

F numbers found on ornamental items, vases, etc.

Appendix 10

THE FAMILIES OF SPODE AND COPELAND

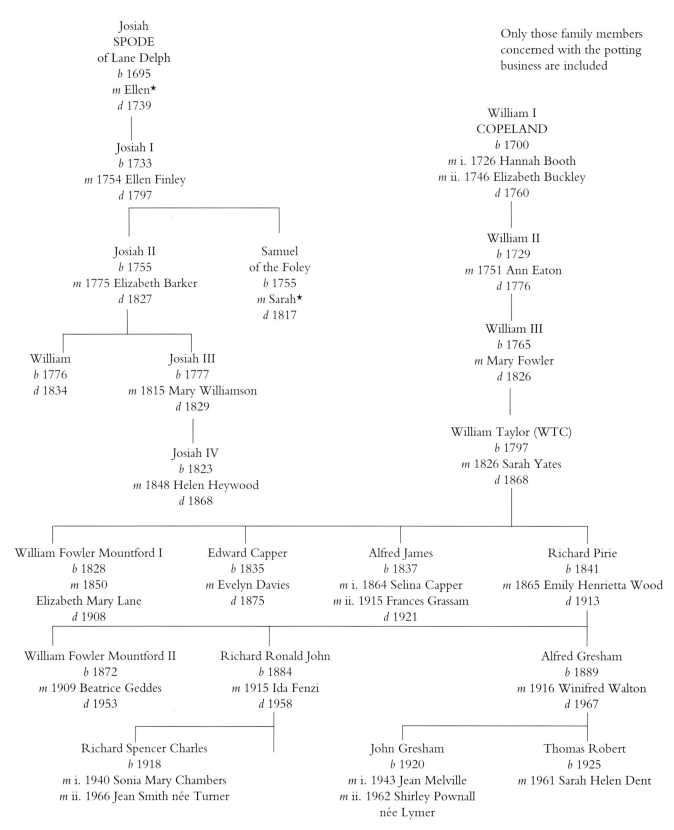

Josiah
SPODE
of Lane Delph
b 1695
m Ellen★
d 1739

Only those family members
concerned with the potting
business are included

William I
COPELAND
b 1700
m i. 1726 Hannah Booth
m ii. 1746 Elizabeth Buckley
d 1760

Josiah I
b 1733
m 1754 Ellen Finley
d 1797

William II
b 1729
m 1751 Ann Eaton
d 1776

Josiah II
b 1755
m 1775 Elizabeth Barker
d 1827

Samuel
of the Foley
b 1755
m Sarah★
d 1817

William III
b 1765
m Mary Fowler
d 1826

William
b 1776
d 1834

Josiah III
b 1777
m 1815 Mary Williamson
d 1829

William Taylor (WTC)
b 1797
m 1826 Sarah Yates
d 1868

Josiah IV
b 1823
m 1848 Helen Heywood
d 1868

William Fowler Mountford I
b 1828
m 1850
Elizabeth Mary Lane
d 1908

Edward Capper
b 1835
m Evelyn Davies
d 1875

Alfred James
b 1837
m i. 1864 Selina Capper
m ii. 1915 Frances Grassam
d 1921

Richard Pirie
b 1841
m 1865 Emily Henrietta Wood
d 1913

William Fowler Mountford II
b 1872
m 1909 Beatrice Geddes
d 1953

Richard Ronald John
b 1884
m 1915 Ida Fenzi
d 1958

Alfred Gresham
b 1889
m 1916 Winifred Walton
d 1967

Richard Spencer Charles
b 1918
m i. 1940 Sonia Mary Chambers
m ii. 1966 Jean Smith née Turner

John Gresham
b 1920
m i. 1943 Jean Melville
m ii. 1962 Shirley Pownall
née Lymer

Thomas Robert
b 1925
m 1961 Sarah Helen Dent

★Entries of these marriages remain undiscovered.

Josiah Spode I

Josiah Spode II

William Copeland

William Taylor
Copeland and (right)
his sons.

William F.M.

Edward C.

Alfred J.

Richard Pirie

Richard Ronald John Copeland

Arthur Gresham Copeland

Richard Spencer Charles Copeland

Thomas Robert Copeland

Appendix 11

SOME OF THE MOST POPULAR PATTERNS OF THE 1920s–1960s

Name of Pattern	Pattern number	Year introduced	Name of Pattern	Pattern number	Year introduced
Aster	2/8130	1926	Gainsborough	S.245	1933
Billingsley Rose	2/8867	1930	Herring Hunting		
Blue Bird	S.3274	1958	(Green)	2/9265	1932
Blue Camilla	C.1829		India Tree	2/959	1876
Blue Flowers	S.3369	1962	Luneville	2/6770	1915
Blue Italian	1815		Madeira	S.3187	1956
Blue Tower	1815		Mayflower	2/8772	1931
British Flowers	S.3366	1962	Olympus	S.2933	1955
Buttercup	2/7873	1924	Polka Dot	2/9695	1932
Byron	S.518	1935	Reynolds	S.2188	1938
Chelsea Bird	2/6837	1916	Rock Bird	S.2658	1951
Cherry Picker	S.2579	1942	Romney	S.228	1934
Chinese Rose	2/9253	1931	Rosalie	S.1878	1937
Cowslip	S.713	1935	Rose Briar	2/7896	1925
Eden	8.2655	1951	Rosebud Chintz	2/8401	1928
Fairy Dell	2/8093	1925	Springtime	S.1573	1937
Field Sports	2/8584	1929	Tittensor Flowers	S.2863	1954
Florence	2/8411	1928	Valencia	S.1248	1935
Frascati	S.3355	1961	Vienna Rose	S.3375	1963
French Flowers	S.3309	1959	Wicker Dale	2/4088	1894

Appendix 12

SOME SPODE AND COPELAND SHAPE NAMES AND THEIR ORIGIN

CHELSEA
Examples date from 1809 on teawares and it is thought they were adapted from the original model of the Chelsea factory. The shape was used for both bone china and earthenware The shape for dinner ware and holloware was patented on 15 November 1879. One of the most popular patterns on this shape is India Tree. Chelsea Wicker shape, an adaptation of the original Chelsea shape, incorporating a basket weave, was used with great effect with Buttercup and Wicker Dale patterns

GADROON
The earliest pattern number recorded is 3934. This shape was used by Spode for bone china and felspar porcelain and is thought to have been copied from the silverware of the time It continued in popularity into the twentieth century. Patterns Tower and Romney.

HAMBURG
Possibly first introduced at the end of the nineteenth century,

it became very popular in the 1930s for both bone china and earthenware with patterns of Rhododendron, Audubon birds and Shanghai.

MARLBOROUGH
Copied in 1915 from French faience made by the Luneville factory, but originally dates from the eighteenth century when silver and pewter of this shape were popular. Used for patterns Polka Dot and Reynolds.

REGIMENTAL
Dating from 1880, this shape was chosen by many regimental officers' and sergeants' messes from that time into the twentieth century. The most popular pattern on this shape is Byron.

STAFFORD
Based on the silver shape and first used c.1850. Shown to great effect with the pattern Crimson Lancaster.

Appendix 13

THE INDENTURE FOR ROBERT JOHN WALLACE, DATED 1864

Keele University, Spode Archives No. 222/2332

This Indenture made the *27* day of *January* in the year of our Lord one thousand eight hundred and *Sixty four* BETWEEN *Robert John Wallace* of *Hanley* *and four months* in the Parish of *Stoke upon Trent* in the County of Stafford an Infant of the age of *Fourteen* years (hereinafter called the said Apprentice) of the first part *James Wallace* of *Hanley* aforesaid Father of the said *Robert John Wallace* of the second part and *William Taylor Copeland* of *Stoke upon Trent* in the said County of Stafford Potter (hereinafter called the said Master) of the third part WITNESSETH that the said *Robert John Wallace* of his own free will and with the consent of his said *James Wallace* Doth by these Presents put place and bind himself Apprentice unto the said *William Taylor Copeland* to learn that branch of a Potter's art or business called *Gilding* and them to serve after the manner of an Apprentice from the *Twenty seventh* day of *January* for the term of *Five* years *and eleven months being the completion of the term of Seven years* (the usual holidays excepted) from thence next ensuing and fully to be complete and ended during all which term the said *commenced verbally the 20 Dec 1862* Apprentice shall and will faithfully honestly and diligently serve and obey his said Master as a good and faithful Apprentice ought to do And the said Master *to himself his* do hereby covenant for *themselves their* executors and administrators to and with the said *James Wallace* his executors and administrators that *they* the said Master shall and will teach and instruct the said Apprentice or cause him to be taught and instructed in the said branch of the Potter's art or business called *Gilding* in the best manner *they* can during the said term And also shall and will find the said Apprentice fair and reasonable work during the said term And also shall and will pay the said Apprentice for his work and services during the said term (the usual holidays excepted) such wages as are hereinafter mentioned that is to say *For the first year of the said term after the rate of two shillings per week For the second year of the said term after the rate of two shillings and sixpence per week For the third year of the said term after the rate of three shillings per week In the fourth year of the said term after the rate of three shillings and sixpence per week And for the remainder of the said term for all work executed by the said apprentice one half the amount paid for the time being by the said master to journeymen for work of the like description* And the said *Robert John Wallace* and *James Wallace* do hereby severally covenant and agree with and to the said Master *their his* executors and administrators that the said Apprentice shall during the said term honestly and faithfully serve his said Master and well and truly perform the Conditions and Agreements herein contained on the part of the said Apprentice to be done and performed And that the said Apprentice shall not nor will during the said term become or be a party to or concerned or concurring in any Agreement or proceeding commonly called or resembling a Turn-out by or between any journeymen or other workmen And in case there shall be any Turn-out and the said Apprentice shall be concerned in or shall encourage the same or otherwise not obey the reasonable commands of his said Master then the said Master shall be at liberty to put an end to and determine this Indenture and to cease to teach or instruct the said Apprentice during all or any part of the then residue of the said term And further that the said Master shall not be liable or called upon to pay any wages to the said Apprentice so long as *his* business shall or may be interrupted or impeded by or in consequence of any Turn-out And the said Apprentice is hereby expressly authorised and allowed during any such Turn-out to employ himself in any other manner or with any other person for his own benefit And the said *James Wallace* doth hereby further agree with the said Master that he the said *James Wallace* shall and will find and provide the said Apprentice with sufficient meat drink washing lodging clothes and all other necessaries at all times during the said term In witness whereof the said parties have hereunto set their hands and seals the day and year first above written

Signed Sealed and delivered by the above named *Robert John Wallace*

Robert John Wallace ●

James Wallace and *William Lambert*
for William Taylor Copeland in the presence
Edward Copeland

James Wallace ●

William Lambert
for William Taylor Copeland ●

Bibliography

Anon. *Copeland's (late Spode) China established 1770* (Hanley: Wood Mitchell, n.d., c.1902)

Art Journal (title varies)

Atterbury, P. (ed.) *The Parian Phenomenon: A Survey of Parian Porcelain Statuary and Busts* (Shepton Beauchamp, Somerset: Richard Dennis, 1989)

Baker, D. *Potworks: The Industrial Architecture of the Staffordshire Potteries* (London Royal Commission on the Historical Monuments of England, 1991)

Burton, W. *The use of Lead Compounds in Pottery, from the Potter's Point of View* (London: Simkin, Marshall, Hamilton, Kent, 1899)

Cole, W. (ed.) *The Spode Society Recorder and Review*

Copeland, R. *Spode* (Princes Risborough: Shire, 1994)

Copeland, R. *Spode and Copeland Marks and other relevant intelligence* (London: Studio Vista, 1993)

Copeland, R. *Spode's Willow Pattern and other designs after the Chinese* (London: Studio Vista, 1990)

Drakard, D. and Holdway, P. *Spode Printed Ware* (London: Longman, 1983)

Goss Hawk (December 2001, No.366) 'The Persian Dessert Service' by Vega Wilkinson and Nigel Griffin.

Gunnis, R. Dictionary of British Sculptors 1660-1851 new revised edition (London: Abbey Library, n.d., post-1951)

Haggar, R. *A Century of Art Education in the Potteries* (Centenary Exhibition Catalogue 1853-1953, 1956)

Hayden, A. *Spode and His Successors: a History of the Pottery Stoke on Trent from 1765-1865* (London: Cassell, 1925)

Jewitt, L. *The Ceramic Art of Great Britain* new edition, revised (New York, Worthington, 1883, rep. New Orchard Editions, 1985)

Johnson, J. (comp.) *The Royal Society of British Artists 1824-1893 and The New English Art Club 1888-1917* (Woodbridge: Antique Collectors' Club, 1975)

King, L.S. *The Industrialisation of Taste: Victorian England and the Art Union of London* (Ann Arbor, Michigan: U M I Research Press, 1985)

Pottery Gazette and Glass Trade Review (title varies)

Raynor, P. *Thomas Goode of London* (published to celebrate the 150th Anniversary of the Company, 1977)

Redgrave, R. and S. *A Century of British Painters* revised edition (Oxford: Phaidon, 1981)

Roden, P.F.C. 'Josiah Spode (1733-1797): his formative influences and the various Potworks associated with him' in *Journal of the Northern Ceramic Society* Volume 14, 1997, 1-43

Roden, P.F.C. 'The Spode London Warehouse in Portugal Street' in *The Spode Society Recorder* Volume 1, 27

Savage, G. and Newman, H. *An Illustrated Dictionary of Ceramics* (London: Thames and Hudson, 1986)

Shaw, S. *History of the Staffordshire Potteries* (Hanley: privately, 1829, rep. Newton Abbot: David & Charles, 1970)

Spode Factory Archives, Spode Works, Stoke-on-Trent

Spode Papers, Keele University Library

Spours, J. *Art Deco Tableware: British Domestic Ceramics 1925-1939* (London: Ward Lock, 1988)

Staffordshire Advertiser, The

Stuart, D. (ed.). *People of the Potteries: a Dictionary of Local Biography Volume I* (Keele; Department of Adult Education, 1985)

Sussman, L. *Spode Copeland Transfer-printed Patterns found at 20 Hudson's Bay Company Sites* (Hull, Quebec: Parks of Canada, 1979)

Trelissick Archives, Trelissick Mansion, Cornwall

Warburton W.H. *The History of Trade Union Organisation in the North Staffordshire Potteries* (London: Allen & Unwin, 1931)

Ward, J. *The Borough of Stoke-upon-Trent* (London: Lewis, 1843, rep. Hanley: Webberley, 1984)

Warnecke, Auguste. *Kultur in Glas und Porzellan* (printed in Germany 1965)

Whiter, L. *Spode: A History of the Family, Factory and Wares from 1733 to 1833*, 1985 edition (London: Barrie & Jenkins, 1970)

Wilkinson, V., *Copeland* (Princes Risborough: Shire, 1994)

Wilkinson, V. *The Copeland China Collection at Trelissick Mansion, Cornwall* (Trelissick: Copeland, 1989)

Wilkinson, V. 'The Medal Controversy 1851' in *The Spode Society Recorder*, Volume 1, 23

Williams, S.B. *Antique Blue and White Spode* (London: Batsford, 1943, 1949, rep. 1987)

Willis-Fear, M.J.W. 'The History of the Pottery Firm of W.H. Goss of Stoke-on-Trent', Volume I, Number 4, 1965, *Proceedings of the University of Newcastle on Tyne Philosophical Society*

Wood, C. *The Dictionary of Victorian Painters* second edition (Woodbridge: Antique Collectors' Club, 1978)

Glossary

AEROGRAPHY – A method of projecting powdered colour or slip (often coloured) on to the surface of the ware by the use of compressed air. The modern aerograph invented by C.L. Burdick is used largely for *ground laying* and shading.

BAITING – Fuelling the oven and kilns with small quantities of fuel to ensure even firing, usually every four hours.

BANDING – Putting rings or bands on the ceramic surface of all types of ware. It can be done by hand or machine.

BAT-PRINTING – A method of printing in which a bat (sheet of gelatin or soft glue) is printed with oil from an engraved copper plate, then dusted with colour. The process is thought to have originated c.1792. See *Spode Printed Ware* by D. Drakard and P. Holdway.

BISCUIT KILN – The oven in which the finished clay articles were fired. The temperature was between 1100°C and 1250°C depending on the type of clay body being fired. This cemented the clay into very hard 'biscuit'.

BISCUIT WARE – Unglazed, undecorated ceramic articles which have been fired in the oven or kiln once. They are then taken to the biscuit warehouse where they are brushed, sorted and carefully checked for faults.

BLUNGER – A large, quite often round tank for the mixing by a high speed paddle of clay etc. to form a slip.

BODY – The particular form of mixture which was used in china, earthenware and a coloured basic china, earthenware or stoneware.

BONE ASH – Produced by boiling ox bones, drying them and calcining them. The white ash that remains is ground into a powder.

BONE CHINA – A translucent porcelain made from approximately

        25% Cornish china clay
        25% Cornish stone (granitc)
        50% *bone ash*

and fired at a high temperature until it becomes vitreous and translucent.

BUNGS – Formed by placing *saggars* one on top of the other in the oven or kiln called **BUNGING-UP**. Filling the oven or kiln was a very specialised art as the successful firing of the ware depended upon it.

BURNISHING – Polishing overglaze gold by various bloodstone or agate hand tools.

CASTING – Thought to have been invented in Staffordshire c.1720. The clay body is mixed with water to form casting slip which is poured into a plaster mould. The plaster absorbs the water and when the correct thickness of clay has been deposited in the mould the surplus slip is poured off. It is left to dry until the article can be lifted from the mould.

CHINA CLAY – In England found only in Cornwall. First experimented with by William Cookworthy in 1755. By 1768 he had patented its use for the making of porcelain. Also used to whiten the earthenware body.

CHROMO-LITHOGRAPHY – A process of colour printing to create a colour transfer.

CLOCK FOR KILNS – A mechanical device which rings a bell every fifteen minutes to alert the kiln fireman, either at the works or at home, that the fires need attention.

COLOURS – Used in the form of a fine powder. At the Spode works the important colours, such as the blue for the underglaze blue prints, were mixed and ground on the site until the late 1950s. The main constituents for the colours were:

White	Tin Oxide (tin ash)
Red	Salts of Iron, Chromium, Copper and Gold
Yellow	Salts of Iron, Antimony, Lead, Uranium, Titanium, Chromium
Green	Salts of Copper or Chromium
Blue	Salts of Cobalt or Copper
Violet	Manganese
Brown	Salts of Manganese, Nickel, Iron, Chromium
Grey	Platinum, Iridium, Nickel, Manganese and Cobalt

DECORATING KILN – A kiln or oven used to fire decorated ware at a temperature of 600°C to 900°C to melt the colour into the glaze.

DICING (engine turning) – A form of decoration using a lathe.

DIPPING – Dipping the ware in a mixture of water and ground glaze which is then fired.

DRYING – An important part of the process of making earthenware and porcelain The ware is dried after nearly every process by being placed on drying-racks. A great deal of factory floor space is needed for drying.

ENAMEL COLOURS – The name given to colours used in on-glaze decoration.

ENAMEL KILN – A kiln used for firing the colours into the glaze at temperatures between 600°C to 900°C, but it could be as high as 1000°C.

FELDSPAR – A mineral found in granite rock.

FELSPAR PORCELAIN – A variety of bone china first introduced by Josiah Spode using *feldspar* instead of Cornish stone.

FETTLING – Part of the finishing process in clay, insuring that the surface of the ware is fine and smooth, no seams showing or imperfections on the body of the ware. A skilled craft.

FILTER PRESS – A mechanical device for removing water from clay slip and converting the slip into a paste by pumping it into linen cloths retained in wooden trays. The filter press was first introduced by Needham and Kite in 1856. Those suitable for fine earthenware and porcelain were made of wood – either oak, deal or pine – by William Boulton Ltd., Burslem in the late 1880s. The Boulton filter press at the Spode works (dated 1932 and made of metal) is still working perfectly. W.T. Copeland & Sons are thought to have been the first pottery to introduce the filter press to the industry and were one of the first firms to use nylon cloths instead of linen; linen cloths went mouldy and had to be replaced often.

FINISHING – A term used in the pottery industry to indicate further improvement of the ware.

FLATWARE – Plates, saucers, dishes and other flat articles.

FRIT – The original ingredients used in the glaze were soluble in water. To prevent this they were melted together in a frit kiln to form a glass or frit which was then ground to a fine powder and suspended in water ready for the *dipping* process. Originally the frit kilns were fired with coal. Once gas-fired ovens had been invented they were always used as they were much cleaner.

GILDERS – Artists who decorated the ware with gold. They were highly paid and capable of creating fine artistic patterns on all types of ware. In the early twentieth century they were allowed to initial their work.

GILDING – Decorating by using metallic gold. Before the gold could be applied to the ware it was mixed with mercury and ground in oil. After firing the gold had to be sanded to obtain a shiny finish. By adding other ingredients with the mercury a cheaper form of gold finish was obtained known as brown gold or liquid gold.

GLAZE – A mixture of materials which, when fired, melted to form a glass giving a pleasing shiny look to the surface of the ware. The glaze slip was composed of a high percentage of lead and prepared just as clay slip. In former days symptoms of lead poisoning were evident amongst the dippers and eventually in the mid-twentieth century glazes had to be made from insoluble lead compounds.

GLOST KILN – Used to melt the prepared glaze into the ware. The ware was supported on *stilts*, thimbles and spurs to ensure the articles did not touch one another in the kiln as the glaze melted. The kiln firemen were experts in the art of placing the ware in the kiln to get the best result and firing the kiln to the correct temperature.

GLOST WARE – Articles which had been glazed.

GOLD FLUX – Sometimes mixed with the gold used for gilding so that it would adhere to the ware. A typical recipe would be:

Red Lead	three parts
Borax	two parts
Flint	three parts

GREEN HOUSE – A large room where 'Green' ware was stored. Green ware was the finished clay article which had to be dried before it could be fired. The *placers* selected the correct pieces of ware which they need to fill the biscuit oven.

GROUND LAYING – The handcraft process by which the powdered colour is applied as a 'ground' colour to the ware. First the piece of ware is brushed to remove any loose particles, then coated with the ground laying oil (the recipe for which differs from factory to factory). It is 'dappled' with a silk covered pad which produces an even coat of oil. The ceramic colour is dusted on and smoothed with cotton wool so that it 'sticks' to the oily surface. The article is then plunged into cold water which removes all excess colour, dried and sent to the kiln to be fired. The skill of the ground layer is in ensuring the ground colour applied is perfectly evenly distributed over the ware. This art is slowly dying out; very few pieces are now ground laid and instead the colour is applied by *Aerographing*.

HANDLEING – The process of attaching handles to jugs, cups etc. and also applying teapot spouts.

HARDENING-ON – Powdered colours have to be mixed with oil to enable them to be painted or printed on to the ware. Underglaze colours are melted into the biscuit ware and all the oil has to be removed before the ware can be glazed by being placed into the hardening-on kiln where it is fired to a temperature of 850°C.

HOLLOWWARE – Covered dishes, vases, bowls, cups etc.

HOVEL KILN – A kiln or oven surrounded by a bottle-shaped structure known as the hovel which ensures an even draught to the fire. Often called bottle ovens.

INTERMITTENT KILN – A kiln which, being a single chamber, is filled, heated, cooled and emptied before the cycle starts again.

JEWELLED WARE – Jewels simulated on china ware by raised paste which is then coloured white, red or turquoise, to represent pearls, rubies, etc.

JIGGER – A machine used to make flatware.

JOLLEY – A machine used to make hollowware.
KILN – Used to fire ware.
MILL – Used in the pottery to grind materials to a fine powder.
MIXING ARK – A tank, usually below floor level, in which the various clays and other materials are mixed by rotating paddles.
MODELLING – A highly skilled craft. Before the article can be made in quantity, it is handmade in clay by the modeller. Then, for multiple production, moulds are made from the clay original.
MOULD – In the pottery industry moulds are made from plaster of Paris. Hollowware is made by pouring slip clay into the mould to produce a cast of the original model.
MOULD MAKER'S SIZE – When making a duplicate plaster of Paris mould from a block mould, a thin paste of various recipes is applied to the mould so that the cast taken from it can be easily removed.
'OSS, THE BIG and LITTLE 'OSS – Terms used by the placers to describe the ladders used in the ovens. They loaded the kiln with *saggars* full of ware, climbing the ladders to place the saggars on the top of the oven.
OVEN – See Biscuit, Glost, Decorating and Enamel Kilns.
OVERGLAZE DECORATION – The decoration of ware over the glaze, sometimes called enamelling, by applying enamel colours or gold, i.e. gilding, by hand painting, printing, ground laying or aerographing.
PLACING by a **PLACER** – The pieces of ware are placed in *saggars* which are placed in the oven, or they can be placed in specially constructed kiln furniture on tunnel oven trucks. The skill of the placer is essential to ensure correct firing and to prevent the twisting or warping of the ware.
PRINTING – A form of decoration which can be either underglaze or on glaze.
PUG MILL – The clay taken from the filter press is put into the pug mill for de-airing and giving the clay a perfect plastic consistency. When finished the clay is extruded in the form of a long sausage which is cut into workable lengths and taken to the making shops.
SAGGARS – Usually circular or oval containers into which the ware is carefully packed ready to be fired in the oven. Made of fireclay and grog, they are arranged in columns (known as *bungs*) which are placed in rings around the oven. In later years rectangular saggars were made which increased loading space in the continuous firing tunnel ovens.
SCOURING – After biscuit firing all extra particles of aluminium and sand (used to keep the ware from distorting in the fire) must be removed to create a smooth surface. The scourer may achieve this by using a small grindstone, or by rubbing the article with hard sand or emery paper or by using tools made for the purpose.

SPIT OUT – Small blobs on the surface of the ware caused by bubbles of gas from the biscuit ware raising through the glaze during the decorating fire.
STILT – A small support made of clay used in the *glost* fire to separate articles so they do not stick together as the glaze melts.
STRING WHEEL – A potter's wheel. The assistant turned a wheel of a certain size which was connected to a different size potter's wheel by a rope (string), thus creating a gearing effect. The turner would direct his assistant to go faster or slower as he created his piece of ware.
SUN PAN – A tank or pit in the open air full of clay slip drying.
THROWING – The shaping by hand of an article on a potter's wheel.
TRANSFER PRINTING – A copper plate which has been engraved with a decoration is placed on a warm stove where it is coated with a specially prepared printer's colour (there are many recipes for this). The colour and oil is rubbed well into the copper plate's surface, then the excess colour is carefully removed with a knife, followed by cleaning the surface with a dabber. The special transfer paper, which has been treated with soft soap size so that after printing it can easily be removed, is laid on the copper plate. The colour is transferred to the paper by pressing the copper plate between the flannel covered rollers of the printing press. The paper with the printed image is then removed and passed to the transferers' team who apply it to the ware.
TURNING – Finishing the ware by turning it on a lathe against a shaped tool, e.g. cups.
TUNNEL KILN – A kiln or oven in which the ware is placed on cars or wagons which then travel along rails or tracks slowly through a heated tunnel usually fired by electricity or gas.
UNDERGLAZE DECORATION – This is applied directly to the biscuit ware and can be painted or transfer printed.
WEATHERING – Used solely in the pottery industry. The various types of clay are left to weather in the open air. The action of rain, snow, sun and frost is beneficial as chemical changes take place which facilitates the working of the various clays.

This Glossary has been compiled from the following sources:
An Encyclopedia of the Ceramic Industries by Alfred Searle, published by Ernest Benn Limited, London, Bouverie House E.C.4 1929. Many of the illustrations used in this three volume work were taken at W.T. Copeland and Sons.
Mr. R. Spencer C. Copeland
Mr. H. Holdway

Index

Page numbers in bold type refer to illustrations and captions
Page numbers in italic type refer to the Appendices